# London's Monuments

*by Andrew Kershman*

London's Monuments
Written by Andrew Kershman
Photography by Andrew Kershman & Susi Koch
Edited by Miranda Moore
Fact checking by Tony Whyte
Design by Susi Koch & Lesley Gilmour
Maps by Lesley Gilmour
Cover Design by The Partners

Published 2007 by
Metro Publications Ltd
PO Box 6336
London
N1 6PY


Printed and bound in India
© Metro Publications Ltd 2007

British Library Cataloguing in Publication Data.
A catalogue record for this book is available from the
British Library.

ISBN 1 902910 25 7

*In Memory of Meinrad A. Koch*
*(1930–2006)*

# Acknowledgements

This book has involved the help of a great many people, most especially my colleagues, Susi and Lesley, at Metro who have worked hard to make this book as good as it can be. Thanks also go to my editor, Miranda Moore, who went to such lengths to ensure my writing was fit for publication. Tony Whyte has been a learned, enthusiastic and painstaking fact checker, drawing my attention to numerous mistakes and misunderstandings and placing these pages on a much sounder footing. Tim Mackintosh-Smith deserves my thanks for providing an accurate translation at a moment's notice, and my friend Brynmor Lloyd-Evans was kind enough to read through my book and offer advice and most importantly encouragement.

I have required permission to gain access to both Westminster Abbey and the Guildhall and the press officers at both institutions have been very helpful. Likewise the press office at the Bank of England was kind enough to provide me with information and photographs of their monument of William III which I would not have been able to find elsewhere. Other institutions which merit thanks include the Corporation of London, Tower Hamlets Council, the National Archive at Kew and the London Metropolitan Archives.

Metro Publications would like to thank Trish, Jack, Bob and all those at The Partners that have contributed to the design of our new covers and logo.

# Contents

'You are those who have gone before us,
and we shall come after you'
**Egyptian memento mori**

'Monuments are for the living, not the dead'
**Frank Wedekind**

# Introduction

This book has taken over two years to research and write and has cost the author a considerable amount of blood, sweat and tears. The blood was shed after falling on wet paving while walking around the monument to the Duke of Bedford in Russell Square. Perspiration should not be elaborated on too much, but I have walked many miles to find a monument in Hyde Park that, despite assurances, has never existed, and put as much effort into tracing the statue of Pochontas in Red Lion Square which has since disappeared into a private collection. There have been a few tears, but these have largely been shed over the lives of those immortalised on London's streets, whether the tragic betrayal of General Sikorski and the Polish people or the generosity of Quintin Hogg, who disregarded his father's wealth to dedicate his life to teaching street children.

The people commemorated in London are not all worthy of our admiration or our tears. George IV has one of the most prominent monuments in Trafalgar Square and yet history has judged him to be a profligate and foolish monarch. He squandered the money raised for a monument to his daughter, Princess Charlotte, but expended considerable time and money on his own memorial. Likewise, standing on a 123ft column is George IV's brother, the Duke of York, whose monument is as prominent as were his debts and the scandal which surrounded his corrupt sale of army commissions to pacify his creditors. The tablet to W.T. Stead on the Embankment makes him sound like a great and principled journalist, but in reality he was the first tabloid hack who led a campaign to send General Gordon to Khartoum which resulted in the soldier's death and the fall of Gladstone's government. Stead later spent time in prison for perjury having fabricated a salacious story about the white slave trade.

One man's hero is often another man's villain and there are quite a few people commemorated in the capital that are figures of controversy. Lord Palmerston was the Victorian prime minister who led the country into a disastrous war in the Crimea and suffered several sex scandals and yet, through skill and charm, kept his job. It is also worth remembering that when Nelson Mandela's monument was erected by the soon-to-be-abolished Greater London Council, the Conservative government of Margaret Thatcher still regarded the man as a terrorist. The monuments of London demonstrate that Britain has a culture that manages to swallow controversy and argument with barely a murmur of indigestion. Oliver Cromwell has a place, as does the king he dethroned and decapitated. James II is not forgotten but nor are the treacherous son-in-law and daughter who took his throne, and the arch enemies William Pitt and Charles Fox are also commemorated – although kept at a distance.

The idle and the feckless, the corrupt and the incompetent, all manner of persons can find themselves immortalised on the streets of London through luck or privilege, but there are many who have gained their place by virtue of their genius and achievements. Many of the great names from the arts and sciences feature, including Shakespeare and Dickens, Virginia Woolf and Oscar Wilde, Sir Henry Irving and Charlie Chaplin, Isaac Newton and Isambard Kingdom Brunel, Reynolds and Hogarth. Explorers are also well represented with great names like Captain James Cook, Scott and Shackleton all receiving their due. Giants of British industry and commerce, such as Julius Reuter and George Peabody, are also recognised – despite many being migrants from other shores.

In the course of my travels I have often been struck by the invisibility of many of London's monuments. One parks police-woman assured me that the monument of Dr Jenner was not on her patch and yet within five minutes I was standing by the seated figure of the great man. Likewise, the café staff close to the monument to Brunel on the Embankment did not know of its existence. I do not think this ignorance is an indication of indifference for I was often asked questions by curious passers-by as I took photographs of a monument. I hope this book stimulates further interest by animating these lifeless effigies and bringing their fascinating and surprising stories to life.

# Trafalgar Square

1)  King George III
2)  The Fourth Plinth
3)  King James II
4)  George Washington
5)  Oscar Wilde
6)  Edith Cavell
7)  King George IV
8)  Admiral Viscount Cunningham
9)  John Rushworth, Earl Jellicoe
10) Admiral Earl David Beatty
11) Sir Henry Havelock
12) Lord Horatio Nelson, Duke of Bronte
13  King Charles I
14) General Sir Charles Napier

# Trafalgar Square

The area occupied by Trafalgar Square was cleared of its old stable buildings in 1830 by John Nash (see page 263), but it was not until 1840 that the paved public square we recognise today was created by Sir Charles Barry. A year later the square was named after Nelson's great naval victory at Trafalgar and in 1843 the great man was placed upon his vast 170ft column from where he has continued to look down upon the city. Trafalgar Square has for centuries been considered the capital's centre and all measurements of distance from London are taken from Charles I's monument on the south side. Since its creation Trafalgar Square has been a place of political protest and national celebration from the Chartist protests of the 1840s, to VE Day celebrations of May 1945 to the more recent anti-war marches of 2003.

Over the years Nelson has been joined in the square by the great naval and military men of later generations. Sir Henry Havelock and Sir Charles Napier defended the interests of Britain's 19th century empire and stand either side of Nelson. Behind the fountains are busts of admirals Beatty and Jellicoe from the First World War and the great Admiral Cunningham from the Second World War. A less worthy occupant of the square is the vain and profligate George IV whose large equestrian monument was placed here as a temporary measure but has remained to this day. The mayor of London, Ken Livingstone, has suggested that Napier and Havelock should be replaced by statues 'ordinary Londoners would know'; part of the democratisation of the square has seen the use of the empty fourth plinth for the display of public art since 1999. Just outside the National Gallery stand the figures of James II and George Washington with monuments to George III, Charles I, Oscar Wilde and Edith Cavell within easy walking distance.

# 1. King George III (1738-1820)
*Location: Junction of Cockspur Street and Pall Mall East, SW1*
*Sculptor: Matthew Cotes Wyatt*
*Material: Bronze*
*Date: 1836*

This equestrian statue commemorates Britain's longest serving king, his 59-year reign straddling the latter half of one century and the first two decades of the next. Though the third of our Hanoverian monarchs, this George was the first to call himself an Englishman, his predecessors all having been very much German in character and loyalties. His reign, during a time of factional politics, endured considerable difficulties, not least those engendered by colonial restiveness in America. George disliked the nature of British politics and with the instability of many Whig governments was often in conflict with them as he tried to assert the crown's authority. He is widely thought to have mismanaged Britain's American colonies and precipitated their loss, though much blame also lies with his politicians.

Catastrophic though losing the American War of Independence in 1783 was to Britain's esteem and influence, the latter part of George's reign proved more stable and less fraught with difficulties as stronger and more effective governments were formed. Pitt the Younger's administration, in particular, helped lessen the crown's responsibilities. The French Revolution boosted the constitutional role of the British monarchy by contrasting it to the disorder and tyrannous terror that reigned over the channel. But the King's worsening mental health – now recognised as the symptoms of porphyria – also helped evolve a constitutional monarchy and inadvertently increased the popularity of the crown. If he was not the dominant political figure he aspired to be, George III had at least become that rare being, a popular king. Lampooned as 'Farmer George' in the popular press for his preference for the simple country life, this only heightened the affection his people had for him. His last years were spent in the virtual seclusion of mental illness and in 1811 the Regency Act gave royal responsibility to the Prince Regent who as George IV did so much to undermine the respectability of the British monarchy (see page 14).

## 2. The Fourth Plinth

*Current sculpture: Alison Lapper Pregnant*
*Location: Trafalgar Square, SW1*
*Sculptor: Marc Quinn*
*Material: Marble*
*Date: September 2005*

The fourth plinth of Trafalgar Square has remained largely empty for the last 166 years. On the 15th September 2005 this situation changed with the unveiling of Marc Quinn's spectacular 3.55 metre-high statue of the artist Alison Lapper who is both disabled and, at the time the sculpture was made, heavily pregnant. The response to this new arrival has been very positive and few would argue that a woman who has overcome disability to create art and make a success of her life merits a monument as much as the royal and military figures with whom she shares the square. Marc Quinn's work will stay in Trafalgar Square until April 2007 to be replaced by Thomas Schütte's *Hotel for the Birds*. It is planned that the occupancy of the fourth plinth will change every 18 months.

7

## 3. James II (1633-1701)
*Location: Trafalgar Square, SW1*
*Sculptor: Grinling Gibbons*
*Material: Bronze*
*Date: 1686*

This is a companion piece to the monument of Charles II which stands in the Royal Hospital, Chelsea (see page 317) and was commissioned by the same man, Tobias Rustate to depict both monarchs in Roman costume. James II was the second son of Charles I and spent many of his formative years, in exile, fighting in French and Spanish armies. He gained a great deal of military experience but as a result acquired a stubborn and impatient approach to political matters. The failure of his brother to provide an heir, combined with James's conversion to the Catholic faith triggered the Exclusion Crisis, a campaign to prevent him being crowned. James kept his place as the successor to the crown and at 51 became king on the death of his brother in 1685. James's religious zeal and wilful nature were soon to turn even loyal supporters against him as he attempted to force the political and religious establishment to abolish anti-Catholic laws and place Catholics in prominent positions formerly withheld from them.

The birth of a son in June 1688 brought about the prospect of a Catholic dynasty and proved the trigger for James's removal from power by his son-in-law William of Orange and his daughter Mary. James soon realised he was unlikely to win against William's forces and he fled in December 1688 to Ireland, where he had more support. His reforms had naturally proved popular among the majority Catholic population, but even here his forces were crushed and he was forced into exile. He spent the last few years of his life in

8

France in a state of religious mania, praying constantly and seeing his downfall as a punishment from God for his many affairs. The overthrow of James II has been termed the Glorious Revolution and this monument has, not surprisingly, been treated with a similar lack of respect, having been moved many times since it was first placed in St James's Park. James now enjoys a position of some prominence outside the National Gallery, looking towards his father on the other side of Trafalgar Square.

## 4. George Washington (1732-1799)

*Location: Trafalgar Square, SW1*
*Sculptor: Jean Antoine Houdon*
*Material: Bronze*
*Date: 1785*

The marble original of this statue stands in Richmond, Virginia. This bronze copy was a gift from the Commonwealth of Virginia in 1921, to commemorate the first President of the United States. George Washington was born in 1732 into a planter's family and received the education of an 18th century Virginia gentleman. He trained as a surveyor before taking command of the Virginia militia and fighting on the side of the British during the French and Indian War. From 1759 to the outbreak of the American Revolution in 1775, Washington managed his lands and served in the Virginia House of Burgesses.

Washington was not initially in favour of independence but the bad administration of the British and the writings of Thomas Paine helped to persuade him. From May 1775 Washington fought for six gruelling years against the well-trained British troops with his own poorly equipped militia forces. Finally, in 1781, with the aid of French allies the Continental Army forced the surrender of Cornwallis at Yorktown. Washington could easily have assumed power at the head of his army, but instead retired from the military and set about establishing a constitution enshrining the rights of the citizen and placing limits upon government. It was as a civilian that Washington was elected America's first president in 1789. He served two terms of office but retired in 1797 and died only two years later from a throat infection.

## 5. Oscar Wilde (1854-1900)
*Location: Adelaide Street, SW1*
*Sculptor: Maggie Hamblin*
*Material: Bronze*
*Date: 1998*

Oscar Wilde, among the best playwrights, essayists and short story writers of his generation, was also a noted wit and public figure whose ascent was as rapid as his downfall. He was born and brought up in Dublin in a talented family, his father being a surgeon and his mother a writer. Wilde was a brilliant scholar who first studied classics at Trinity College, Dublin before winning a scholarship to Magdalen College, Oxford, where he joined the aesthetic and decadent movements which promoted the importance of art and pleasure in life. He left Oxford in 1878 with a double first in classics, a sharpened wit and the manners of a dandy, soon coming to the public's attention as a spokesman for the Aesthetic movement by giving lectures both in England and the United States. He was engaged to Florence Balcombe, a noted Irish beauty but she broke off the engagement to marry the writer Bram Stoker. Wilde was already aware of his homosexuality when he married Constance Lloyd in 1884, and had two children with her while leading a second life as a promiscuous gay man.

While leading this complicated private life Wilde began to achieve success and recognition as a writer. His book of fairy tales (1888) was well received and his only novel, *The Picture of Dorian Gray* (1891) was an instant success. It was Wilde's comic plays that were to prove his greatest triumph with *Lady Windermere's Fan* (1892), *A Woman of No Importance* (1893) and *The Importance of Being Earnest* (1895) establishing his reputation and fortune.

11

It was at the height of his success that Wilde became embroiled in a scandal that was to destroy his reputation and his life. He had begun a passionate affair with Lord Alfred Douglas which brought him into conflict with Douglas's father, the Marquess of Queensbury, who confronted Wilde in several public scenes. Wilde was disastrously persuaded to take legal action against Queensbury which failed and only brought on subsequent counter prosecutions which led to his imprisonment for acts of 'gross indecency'. The scandal and two years incarceration, combined with the death of his wife in 1898, were to take a terrible toll on Wilde. He died in poverty and isolation in Paris in November 1900, his reputation and stature only fully recognised once homosexuality was decriminalised in the 1960s. Wilde's own words are inscribed on this contemporary monument, 'We are all in the gutter, but some of us are looking at the stars.'

# 6. Edith Cavell (1865-1915)

*Location: St Martin's Place, WC2*
*Sculptor: George Frampton*
*Material: Marble*
*Date: 1920*

The execution by German firing squad of the English Red Cross nurse Edith Cavell, for spying, quickly became a *cause célèbre* when it became know in 1915. The propaganda posters depicting her death, together with that of her Belgian accomplice, Phillipe Baucq, with the exhortation 'remember the murder of Edith Cavell', did much to stir up anti-German feeling in Britain. The notoriety of her martyrdom belied a life of hard work and dedication to the care of others which began as the daughter of a Norfolk rector. Her aptitude for languages gained her a position as a governess in Belgium but she returned to England to nurse her dying father and afterwards took up nursing as a profession.

After completing her training, Edith worked on the Continent, becoming the first matron of the Berkendael Medical Institute in Brussels. During the First World War Cavell worked in occupied Belgium for the Red Cross, treating soldiers from both sides. It was here that she became involved in the smuggling of wounded Allied troops to neutral Netherlands from where they could return home. After the plot was discovered Edith admitted to her role in the escape of over 200 troops and was executed despite a campaign for mercy. Edith Cavell's last written testament contained the words 'patriotism is not enough, I must have no hatred or bitterness towards anyone'. These words are inscribed on this vast monument that was erected in 1920, just one year after her body was returned for burial in the grounds of Norwich Cathedral.

## 7. George IV (1762-1830)
*Location: Trafalgar Square, SW1*
*Sculptor: Sir Francis Legatt Chantrey*
*Material: Bronze*
*Date: 1843*

This massive equestrian statue was commissioned by George IV in 1829 and was intended for the top of Marble Arch then located in front of the newly built Buckingham Palace. The king died in 1830 before the statue was completed and it was placed in Trafalgar Square as a temporary measure, one which has now become very much permanent.

The future George IV had the misfortune of having to wait until the age of 58 before becoming monarch, and in many years of inactivity failed to acquire any of the skills of statecraft but instead accumulated vast debts, a taste for opium and alcohol and a reputation for scandal. George was a dashing and fashionable young man, but by the time of his coronation in 1821 he was forced to wear elaborate corsets to hide his enormous girth. He resorted to similar measures for this statue which represents him in Roman dress and on horseback even though he was by then too large to ride. Although George IV was extravagant when it came to immortalising himself, he spent the funds allocated for a memorial to his daughter and heir, Princess Charlotte, when she died in childbirth in 1817. There were insufficient funds to pay Sir Francis Legatt Chantrey for this statue and it was left to his estate to pursue payment from the state after his death. When the King died in June 1830 national apathy was summed up by the comment in The Times 'There never was an individual less regretted by his fellow-creatures than this deceased king. What eye has wept for him?'

14

# 8. Admiral Viscount Cunningham (1883-1963)

*Location: Trafalgar Square, SW1*
*Sculptor: Franta Belsky*
*Material: Bronze*
*Date: 1967*

Andrew B. Cunningham was known, unsurprisingly, as 'ABC' in the navy. His distinguished naval career led to his becoming Commander-in-Chief of the Mediterranean Fleet in 1939. His seamanship and Nelsonian instinct to attack the enemy at every opportunity were to have considerable success against the Italian fleet. In March 1941 at the Battle of Cape Matapan his fleet sank three heavy cruisers without any British casualties. However, during the evacuation of Crete in the spring of 1941, his fleet suffered heavy casualties, including three cruisers and six destroyers, but succeeded in evacuating over  two thirds of the Allied Troops. Cunningham later directed the invasion of North Africa in mid-1942 and as the Axis forces tried to flee Africa from mid-1943 he ordered that none should be allowed to escape. In October, having gained control of the Mediterranean, he became First Sea Lord and was present at the Yalta and Potsdam conferences. Cunningham retired from the navy in 1946 and despite his distinguished war record, played no further part in public life.

## 9. John Rushworth, Earl Jellicoe (1859-1935)
*Location: Trafalgar Square, SW1*
*Sculptor: William Macmillan*
*Material: Bronze*
*Date: 1948*

Born the son of a merchant seaman, Jellicoe joined the Royal Navy in 1872 and quickly rose within its ranks to be appointed to the Admiralty in 1888. He was involved in the relief of Peking during the Boxer Rebellion of 1900 where he was shot – the bullet remaining in his lung for the rest of his life. Jellicoe was promoted to Commander-in-Chief of the Grand Fleet on the eve of the First World War. The most prominent event in his career was the inconclusive Battle of Jutland in 1916 for which Jellicoe received some criticism – one of his major critics being a young Winston Churchill. He became First Sea Lord in 1916, being replaced by David Beatty as Commander-in-Chief. Jellicoe was by this stage exhausted and unable to deal with the threat of the new German submarines. He was sacked by Lloyd George and the convoy system successfully introduced against his advice. Jellicoe retired in 1917 and was raised to the peerage the following year. He became Governor-General of New Zealand between 1920-24 and was made an Earl in 1925. Jellicoe was popular, hard working and intelligent, but there seem few major successes in his career to merit his position next to Cunningham and facing the great Nelson.

## 10. Admiral Earl David Beatty (1871-1936)

*Location: Trafalgar Square, SW1*
*Sculptor: Sir Charles Wheeler*
*Material: Bronze*
*Date: 1948*

This monument elegantly captures the handsome features of David Beatty who became the youngest British admiral since Nelson. Beatty came to the Admiralty's attention when forced to take command of HMS Alexandra during Kitchener's invasion of Sudan in the late 1890s. It was while in North Africa that he became friends with Winston Churchill, a friendship that was to help him in later life. Beatty was promoted to Commander in 1898 and was wounded in 1900 during the Boxer Rebellion, as was his contemporary Jellicoe. Unlike the hard-working but rather dull Jellicoe, Beatty was a glamorous and charismatic figure who married an American heiress in 1901 and so became financially independent of the navy and a member of high society. In 1910 he was promoted to Rear-Admiral but fell out with the Admiralty over his next posting and was only found a post when Churchill became First Lord of the Admiralty.

During the First World War Beatty had a number of successes commanding the Battle Cruiser Squadron. It was Jellicoe's indifferent performance at Jutland that enabled Beatty to replace him as Commander-in-Chief and issue new instructions allowing more initiative to be used in battle. His finest hour came when he accepted the surrender of the High Seas Fleet on 21 November 1918. He went on to become Admiral of the Fleet in 1919 and spent the interwar years arguing for greater expenditure on the navy. He died in 1936 and lies buried in St Paul's, close to Nelson's crypt.

17

# 11. Sir Henry Havelock, Major General (1795–1857)

*Location: Trafalgar Square, SW1*
*Sculptor: William Behnes*
*Material: Bronze*
*Date: 1861*

General Sir Henry Havelock joined the army in 1815 and saw action in the Burma War (1824-26), the first Afghan War (1839) and the Sikh Wars (1843-49), eventually rising to the rank of General. His greatest military achievement was during the Indian Mutiny, when he fought a number of battles across India, recapturing Cawnpore from mutinous forces in July 1857 but too late to prevent a massacre. Havelock fought on and gained public attention when he relieved Lucknow from siege in September 1857. Unfortunately, Havelock's forces were too small to liberate the city and a new siege began which only ended in November when further reinforcements arrived. Havelock died of dysentery within a few days of the relief of the city and so assured himself a place as one of Britain's military heroes, his death causing widespread public grief.

Havelock had become a committed evangelical Christian and his heroic exploits did much to gain acceptance of non-conformists within the British army. This monument was erected soon after his death and was the first to be based on a photograph. The legacy of Britain's empire is now a matter of political debate and Havelock has become another Victorian with huge sideburns whose exploits have largely been forgotten by the British public. In 2000 Mayor Ken Livingstone suggested that both Havelock and Napier be removed from Trafalgar Square and replaced with more recognisable figures.

## 12. Horatio Nelson, 1st Viscount Nelson (1758-1805)

*Location: Trafalgar Square, SW1*
*Sculptor: E.H. Baily (Statue), W. Railton (Column), E. Landseer (Lions)*
*Material: Bronze*
*Date: 1843*

The design and construction of Trafalgar Square was begun 25 years after the eponymous battle and death of Britain's greatest naval hero, Lord Horatio Nelson. Sir Charles Barry designed the square 'fit for a hero', while the towering column and statue of Nelson are (like the Albert Memorial) the work of a great number of artists and cost the then remarkable sum of £50,000. The 17 foot statue of Nelson was erected upon the column in 1843, once the square was completed. The reliefs illustrating Nelson's life are made from captured French cannon from his four greatest victories (St Vincent, the Nile, Copenhagen and Trafalgar). Sir Edwin Landseer's four enormous lions were added in 1867 and are now rarely seen without a vast number of gleeful tourists sitting upon them posing for a photo. Unlike Wellington, Nelson was a down-to-earth man who would probably have enjoyed the irony of French school children climbing upon this symbol of British maritime glory.

Horatio Nelson was a sickly and slender child. His mother died when he was only nine years old and in 1771 at the age of only 12, with the help of his seafaring uncle, he joined the navy. Nelson was not an obvious choice for a maritime hero. He stood only 5'4" and suffered from sea sickness throughout his life. Despite these disadvantages by the age of 20 Nelson had seen service in the West Indies, the Baltic and Canada and risen to the rank of captain. It was at this stage in his life, after several affairs, that he met and married a young widow by the name of Fanny Nisbet.

Britain entered the French Revolutionary Wars in 1793 and Nelson served in the Mediterranean helping to capture Corsica, losing an eye at Calvi and achieving his first great victory at the Battle of St Vincent. Within a year of losing his arm at the Battle of Santa Cruz de Tenerife (1797) Nelson captained H. M. S. Vanguard and destroyed the French fleet at the Battle of the Nile in 1798.

It was while in port at Naples after his victory that he met and fell in love with Emma, Lady Hamilton, embarking on a very public affair which effectively ended his marriage, though Lady Hamilton's marriage continued with the indulgence and understanding of her elderly husband. It was partly because of his personal life that Nelson was sent to the Baltic under Sir Hyde Parker. The Battle of Copenhagen was to prove one of Nelson's greatest victories when he ignored Parker's command to retreat and decisively defeated the Danish fleet. He was made a Viscount for this victory and soon after allowed to retire. His retirement lasted for a brief two years, spent in domestic harmony with the Hamiltons despite – or perhaps because of – fathering a child, Horatia, with Emma. All too soon he was back at sea on HMS Victory in the Mediterranean, a two-year stint with only one brief shore leave before his last and infamous Battle at Cape Trafalgar in 1805. Struck by a bullet on the first day of battle he died a few hours later to the grief of both navy and nation. While the Battle of the Nile was Nelson's most notable victory, effectively annihilating Napoleon's navy and with it his dreams of an empire to the east, it is Trafalgar that is forever associated with his name and which captures the popular imagination. Unless you're a pigeon, it is impossible to see any of the detail of his statue, being over 170 feet up, but there is a very fine bust in the grounds of the National Maritime Museum at Greenwich (see page 340).

## 13. King Charles I (1600-1649)

*Location: Trafalgar Square, SW1*
*Sculptor: Hubert le Sueur*
*Material: Bronze*
*Date: 1633*

This equestrian statue of Charles I was originally commissioned by the High Treasurer Lord Weston just before the English Civil War. The defeat of the royal armies made this statue an embarrassment to the Commonwealth government and it was given to brazier John Rivett to be destroyed. Rivett instead buried it in his garden and sold trinkets claiming they were made from the same metal. After the restoration of the monarchy the statue came into the hands of Charles II who had it erected here in 1665. The location is particularly ironic as Charles I looks down towards Parliament, the disagreements with which helped bring about the civil war. It is also the site where the last remaining signatories to the King's death warrant were executed after the monarchy's restoration, and within walking distance of the Banqueting Hall where the king was executed on the 30th January 1649. The Royal Stuart Society lays a wreath here each year on the anniversary of the king's death. It is thought that the pedestal is the work of Grinling Gibbons from a Wren design, but over the centuries much of the detail has been lost due to erosion. For more details about the Civil War and its aftermath see the statue of his nemesis Cromwell (page 78).

# 14. General Sir Charles Napier (1782-1853)

*Location: Trafalgar Square, SW1*
*Sculptor: George Cannon Adams*
*Material: Bronze*
*Date: 1855*

Born into an illustrious military family – his father was a colonel and his brother also a distinguished soldier – Charles Napier first saw action in the Irish rebellion in 1798. He went on to fight in the Danish campaign in 1807 and was a prominent figure in the famous retreat of Corunna of 1808. Despite being wounded several times Napier continued to play a leading role in the Napoleonic wars and was then put in charge of a regiment fighting against the United States forces between 1812-13. One of his greatest achievements was his governorship of Cephalonia from 1822-30.

He became an eloquent advocate of Greek independence and a friend of Lord Byron (see page 278). Napier left Greece after a fierce quarrel with the high commissioner and spent time writing and bringing up his children after the death of his wife. He became commanding officer in the north of England during the height of the Chartist troubles and showed considerable restraint in preserving law and order.

Napier went to India in 1842 to command the region of Sind. He decided that the ruling emirs were the obstacle to effective British rule and adopted a brutal policy to defeat them. His actions in India were the most controversial aspect of his career and ran counter to the wise council of General Outram (see page 145). Napier left India in 1847 and received public acclaim for his military success. He is credited with anticipating the uprising in India in 1857, but died in Portsmouth before his warning came true.

# Leicester Square

1) Sir Henry Irving
2) Sir Isaac Newton
3) William Shakespeare
4) John Hunter
5) William Hogarth
6) Charlie Chaplin
7) Sir Joshua Reynolds
8) Eros - 7th Earl of Shaftesbury
9) King George II
10) Sir Joshua Reynolds (RA)

# Leicester Square

Leicester Square was laid out in the 1670s as a fashionable residential area and in the 17th and 18th centuries it was the home to several aristocratic families as well as famous artists and scientists. Hogarth and later Reynolds both lived in the square, Reynolds' house serving as a meeting place for notable characters such as Burke, Goldsmith and Johnson. In 1748 Burchard's statue of George I was bought by the wealthy residents of the square as a monument to George II and erected where Shakespeare's statue stands today.

During the 19th century Leicester Square was abandoned by its wealthy residents and became a place of entertainment with grand hotels, Turkish baths and theatres. The imposing equestrian figure at the square's centre fell to ruin along with the square itself, and after the tatty statue was painted to look like a cow by a prankster the monument was removed and destroyed. By the late 19th century the public square was a squalid and dilapidated place. It was rescued by the flamboyant MP and successful businessman Albert Grant who bought the land in 1874 and commissioned James Knowles to design the gardens complete with all the statues found here today with the exception of Chaplin's, which was added in 1981.

The square is now largely known for the many film premieres that are held here and as one of the most central meeting places in London is always thronging with tourists. Included in this chapter are three monuments which are a few minutes walk from the square but still worth visiting.

# 1. Sir Henry Irving (1838-1905)

*Location: Charing Cross Road, WC2*
*Sculptor: Thomas Brock*
*Material: Bronze*
*Date: 1910*

Henry Irving was born John Brodribb in Somerset to a Methodist mother who disapproved of the theatre, yet became the most successful actor of his generation and the first to receive a knighthood. As a young man he attempted to follow his mother's advice and took up a career as a clerk, but the lure of the stage proved too strong and in 1856 he first stepped on stage under the name of Henry Irving. For the next ten years Irving played over 600 parts in provincial stock companies and gradually acquired the mannerisms, timing and presence that were to make him famous. In 1866 he moved to London, but it was not until 1871 that he finally gained public recognition as the lead in *The Bells* at the Lyceum Theatre. For the next 30 years Irving was to dominate the English stage as actor-manager of the Lyceum playing all the classical roles – most notably his 200 performances of Hamlet in 1874 – usually accompanied by his leading lady Ellen Terry. In the last 20 years of his career Irving toured North America eight times to great public acclaim and as a manager introduced the convention of lowering the curtain to denote a scene change and pioneered gas lighting in the theatre. Irving's acting was equally innovative with his emphasis on realism rather than showmanship, but his choice of material was conservative, ignoring the contemporary works of Wilde, Ibsen and Shaw. Irving died not long after leaving the stage in October 1905 during his farewell tour. He is buried in Westminster Abbey.

# 2. Sir Isaac Newton (1643-1727)

*Location: Leicester Square, WC2*
*Sculptor: William Calder Marshall*
*Material: Stone*
*Date: 1874*

This small bust of Isaac Newton commemorates probably the greatest scientist and mathematician this country has produced. The bright lights of Leicester Square make it hard to imagine that Newton kept an observatory near this site. Newton's early life showed little sign of his genius and it was only his failure to manage his country estate that persuaded his mother to send him to Cambridge. It was in 1666 when Cambridge shut its doors during the plague that Newton returned to his country estate and began his ground-breaking work on calculus and later, optics, mechanics and celestial dynamics. Within three years he was made Lucasian Professor and came to the attention of the Royal Society through his invention of the refracting telescope. The publication of *Mathematical Principles of Natural Philosophy* in 1687 unified his ideas of gravity and motion and were to remain unchallenged until Einstein's *Theory of Relativity* over two centuries later. In 1787 Newton abandoned his studies and moved to London to become Master of the Mint and president of the Royal Society. He spent the next 40 years defending his achievements against his critics and amassing a considerable fortune. There is a darker side to the character of Newton who suffered from severe bouts of depression, mental breakdown and many bitter disputes with his rivals. After his death in 1727 Newton's assistant, Whiston, wrote that 'Newton was of the most fearful, cautious and suspicious temper that I ever knew'.

27

## 3. William Shakespeare (1564-1616)

*Location: Leicester Square, WC2*
*Sculptor: Giovanni Fontana*
*Material: Marble*
*Date: 1874*

William Shakespeare left a huge body of plays and sonnets to posterity and yet very little is known of the man and there remains considerable controversy about his identity, sexuality and the authorship of some of his plays. Even the famous Chandos Portrait in the National Portrait Gallery is of dubious authenticity. It is certain that William Shakespeare was born and brought-up in Stratford-upon-Avon, Warwickshire, that his family were prosperous gentry and that he did not go to university. His marriage to Anne Hathaway in 1582 is recorded, as are the births of his children, but little else is known of his personal life. His professional life is better documented and it is certain that he came to London during the 1580s to become an actor and playwright and that he was a leading figure in a theatrical company known as The Lord Chamberlain's Men, which later, under the patronage of James I, became The King's Men. English theatre underwent a revolution during this time as the traditional academic and morality plays were replaced with a form of secular theatre that could be both entertaining and profound. Shakespeare was in the vanguard of this revolution and by the age of 30 had become a great success as a playwright, actor, theatre-owner and manager. His reputation in life has been far exceeded by his pre-eminence in the centuries that followed his death in 1616. It is perhaps fitting that a man who could write so profoundly of the human condition should have become such an enigma. This monument is a copy of an original by Scheemakers which stands in Westminster Abbey (see page 84).

28

# 4. John Hunter (1728-1793)

*Location: Leicester Square, WC2*
*Sculptor: Thomas Woolner*
*Material: Stone*
*Date: 1874*

John Hunter was one of the founding fathers of modern surgery whose skill with a knife was matched by a rigorous scientific approach to the study of nature. Hunter's Scottish childhood in East Kilbride showed little promise and he left school at the age of 13 to spend his time exploring the countryside and studying wildlife. His life changed when he came down to London to join his brother William who was a successful anatomist. The young John soon showed his promise as a medical student and he quickly rose to became Master of Anatomy at Surgeons Hall in 1753 at the age of only 25. Due to poor health Hunter joined the surgical staff of the army in 1760. He served in France and Portugal during the Seven Years War and managed to make significant advancements in the treatment of gunshot wounds during this period. On his return from war he set up his own anatomy school in London in 1764 and started in private surgical practice; three years later he was elected to the Royal Society. In 1783 he moved to a house on Leicester Square where he was able to arrange his vast collection of anatomical preparations of over 500 species of plants and animals. It is this collection that formed the basis of the Hunterian Museum after his death in 1793. John Hunter made advancements in the study of teeth, inflammation, venereal disease and the digestive system. He was known to be an irascible man, but with a good nature, who would often offer his services to the poor free of charge and who cared little for money and status.

29

# 5. William Hogarth (1697-1764)

*Location: Leicester Square, WC2*
*Sculptor: Joseph Durham*
*Material: Stone*
*Date: 1875*

Born in Smithfield in 1697 in the reign of William III (see page 108), from whom he took his name. His father was an unsuccessful businessman and after the failure of a coffee shop was sent to debtors' prison in 1707. Young William began his career as an engraver, under the instruction of Sir James Thornhill, whose daughter he later married. By his early 20s Hogarth was a portrait painter and engraver and started to produce the political satires that were to bring him fame and fortune. Hogarth was living in a time of unparalleled corruption as Whig politicians enriched themselves through political intrigue. Hogarth's satire of prime minister Robert Walpole – *The Punishments of Lemuel Gulliver* – was an instant success in 1726 and he followed it with *The Harlot's Progress* (1732) and *The Rake's Progress* (1733-35). Hogarth was to be instrumental in the passing of the Engravers' Copyright Act to prevent the widespread illegal sale of his work and with his new-found wealth established a school for young artists. Hogarth made a fortune painting conventional portraits of the aristocracy, but it is the works of satire such as *Gin Lane* (1751), *The Election* (1754) and *The Times* (1762) that have brought him lasting fame. The later work is an anti-war satire that is still relevant today. William Hogarth died in October 1764 having lived for some time in the square in which his statue now stands. The National Gallery and Sir John Soane's Museum both have fine examples of his work. A further monument to Hogarth and his dog, Trump, was unveiled in Chiswick in 2001.

# 6. Charlie Chaplin ( 1889-1977)
*Location: Leicester Square, WC2*
*Sculptor: John Doubleday*
*Material: Bronze*
*Date: 1981 (unveiled by Sir Ralph Richardson)*

Charlie Chaplin's was born to theatrical parents, he made his entrance in 1889 in Walworth, London and appeared in music hall as a child. His family life was unstable and they were forced into the workhouse when their father abandoned them. Chaplin was always a natural comic and as a teenager found acting work which eventually took him to America. It was while touring the States in 1913 that Chaplin was spotted by the movie producer Mack Sennett and started appearing in comic silent movies. Chaplin was intelligent and ambitious and within a year he had begun writing and directing his own films – slowing the pace and developing characters. During this period Chaplin made *The Tramp* (1915), *Easy Street* (1917) and *A Dog's Life* (1918) and became the first movie star to sign a million–dollar contract in 1918. Chaplin's success was only matched by his ambition and within a year he had established a film studio with other film stars of the day – United Artists. Directing and producing his own films, Chaplin was one of the few actors to make a successful transition to talking pictures. Despite having very little formal education he formed friendships with some of the leading intellectuals of his day including H. G. Wells, Harold Laski and Albert Einstein. Chaplin was a socialist with strong sympathies for Soviet Russia and made some of the most overtly political films of the period with *Modern Times* (1936) and the *Great Dictator* (1938). During the war he devoted his energies to Soviet war relief and the campaign for the opening of a second front in Europe. With the rise of anti-communism and the start of the Cold War, Chaplin fell under suspicion by J. Edgar Hoover's FBI and in 1952 Chaplin's right to enter the United States was revoked and he became an exile in Europe. Chaplin made several films in Europe – none of which were distributed in the US – and was only allowed back into the country in 1972 to receive an award. He died in Switzerland on Christmas Day 1977 having become one of the most successful and controversial figures of the 20th century. This monument has avoided any political controversy, representing Chaplin in his early days as a loveable tramp with the inscription 'The comic genius who gave pleasure to so many'.

## 7. Sir Joshua Reynolds (1723-1792)
*Location: Leicester Square, WC2*
*Sculptor: Henry Weekes*
*Material: Stone*
*Date: 1874*

Joshua Reynolds lived at 47 Leicester Square which is now demolished. For more details about Reynolds see the review of his statue at the Royal Academy p.36.

# 8. Eros 7th Earl of Shaftesbury (1801-1885))

*Location: Piccadilly Circus, W1*
*Sculptor: Alfred Gilbert*
*Material: Aluminium (fountain)*
*Date: 1893*

Few people who sit at the foot of Eros in Piccadilly realise that this London landmark was erected in memory of the 7th Earl of Shaftesbury – one of the great Victorian reformers. Anthony Ashley Cooper was an aristocrat, educated at Harrow and Oxford and destined to inherit his father's title. Despite his privileged background, Ashley spent most of his adult life fighting for the rights of the poor and downtrodden, inspired by his Christian Evangelical faith. Lord Ashley entered parliament in 1826 having assumed the seat through his family's control of the rotten borough of Woodstock. The young MP did not seek power but reform and was soon involved in a committee concerning the treatment of lunatics. This achieved little in terms of legislation at the time, but Ashley kept a keen interest in the subject and was later involved in the passing of the Lunatic Act of 1845 which helped improve their treatment. Lord Ashley joined the movement to limit child labour in factories and although his bill was rejected the government passed the limited Factory Act in 1833. He continued to press for further reforms to improve the conditions of working-class children and in 1840 helped establish the Employment Commission to investigate such issues. Ashley was instrumental in some of the key reforms of the day including the Coal Mines Act (1842), the Ten Hours Act (1847) and the Lodging House Act (1851) which attempted to improve the living conditions of the working poor. He became 7th Earl of Shaftesbury in 1851, but continued his reforming

33

work in the House of Lords and as chairman of the Ragged Schools Union which established elementary schooling for the poor. During the Crimean War (see page 106) Lord Shaftesbury was able to give considerable assistance to his friend and ally Florence Nightingale (see page 104) and so improve the treatment of wounded soldiers in the conflict. Shaftesbury's evangelical zeal was popular with those who benefited from his efforts and he played a key role in calming the mood for revolt on the streets of London in 1848 – when revolutions were widespread on the Continent – through his work with the City Mission. The Earl was a popular figure in public life and his 80th birthday was celebrated in grand style at the Guildhall. This famous monument depicts a Christian angel of charity upon a fountain which states the virtues and efforts of the Earl of Shaftesbury. The Christian nature of the monument and the man it commemorates have been forgotten by most people and it is now commonly known as Eros.

## 9. George II (1683-1760)

*Location: Golden Square, W1*
*Sculptor: John Van Nost*
*Material: Portland stone*
*Date: 1753*

The origins of this monument are not certain but it is believed to have come from the
Duke of Chandos's country estate and to have
been purchased by an anonymous bidder at
auction there in 1848 and presented to the
public. The statue has been in residence in
this fine square since it was built in 1753 and
is briefly mentioned by Dickens in *Nicholas
Nickleby*. For a biography of George II see
the review of his monument in Greenwich
(see page 332).

# 10. Sir Joshua Reynolds (1723-1792)

*Location: The Royal Academy, Burlington House, W1*
*Sculptor: Alfred Drury*
*Date: 1931*
*Material: Bronze*

Joshua Reynolds was a schoolmaster's son from Devon who rose to become the outstanding portrait artist of the 18th century. In 1740 he was apprenticed to Thomas Hudson, with whom he studied for two years before embarking on his own career. Reynolds continued to develop his own style, greatly influenced by his travels in Italy between 1749 and 1752, where he was inspired by the works of Roman antiquity and the artists of the Venetian renaissance. Reynolds returned to England determined to establish the 'Grand Style' of Continental painters on home soil and set up house and studios in London's fashionable Leicester Square. Reynolds was an instant success, painting portraits of the country's leading aristocratic families – even being commissioned to paint several allegorical works for Catherine the Great of Russia. Despite having lost his hearing while in Rome, Reynolds had a considerable talent for friendship and was close to many of the leading figures of his day including Dr Johnson, Oliver Goldsmith and Edmund Burke. Reynolds founded the Royal Academy with Gainsborough in 1768 and in the same year was knighted by George III. He was a man of considerable intellect and gave a series of 16 discourses on the classical ideal which are still referred to today. Reynolds's health was beginning to fail by the 1780s but his studio, with its team of apprentice artists, continued to be remarkably productive – exhibiting 244 paintings at the Academy until 1790. Reynolds died in February 1792 and was buried with great pomp in St Paul's Cathedral.

# Whitehall

THE WOMEN OF WORLD WAR II

London's Monuments • Whitehall

1) Field Marshal HRH George, 2nd Duke of Cambridge
2) Spencer Compton Cavendish
3) The Gurkha Soldier
4) King Charles I
5) Field Marshal Earl Douglas Haig
6) Field Marshal the Viscount Slim
7) Field Marshal Viscount Alanbrooke
8) Field Marshal Viscount Montgomery of Alamein
9) Women of World War II
10) Cenotaph
11) Charles Dickens
12) Robert Clive, 1st Baron of Bengal
13) Bali Memorial
14) Lord Mountbatten
15) Horatio Herbert Field, 1st Earl Kitchener
16) Cadiz Memorial
17) Frederick Sleigh, Field Marshal Earl Roberts
18) Garnet Joseph, 1st Viscount Wolseley

38

# Whitehall

Whitehall has been the administrative centre of British government since before the eponymous Palace of Whitehall was destroyed by fire in 1698. Most of the grand buildings that line the wide thoroughfare of Whitehall and Parliament Street are Victorian and 20th-century creations, but Banqueting House is an original Inigo Jones building dating from 1622. Charles I was beheaded outside this building in 1649 and a small bust now commemorates this infamous regicide.

The unfortunate king is one of the few political figures to be commemorated in Whitehall along with the domineering full-length figure of the Liberal politician Spencer Compton Cavendish which stands at the entrance to Horse Guards Avenue. The Department of Health is located in Whitehall but there are no monuments to famous nurses or doctors. HM Treasury also has fine offices here but there are no influential economists immortalised in the area. It is the Ministry of Defence which seems to exert a dominant influence over the choice of monuments that surround its modern concrete offices complete with wired fences, security cameras and armed guards. In this area can be found no less than five field marshals, three commander-in-chiefs of the British army, one admiral, five war or army memorials as well as a vast monument to the military adventurer and capitalist Robert Clive, who with guile, cunning and brutality founded British rule in India. Those who agree with the late foreign secretary Robin Cook's argument that British government is dominated by the interests of the military would find their opinion reinforced by a walk around Whitehall. The small bust of perhaps this country's greatest novelist, Charles Dickens, on the second floor of a public house on Parliament Street, does little to weaken the strength of such an argument.

## 1. Field Marshal HRH George, 2nd Duke of Cambridge (1819-1904)

*Location: Whitehall, SW1*
*Sculptor: Adrian Jones ◆ Material: Bronze*
*Date: 1907*

The Duke of Cambridge was Queen Victoria's cousin and a career soldier who saw action in the Crimea (see page 106). In 1856 the Duke was promoted to Commander-in-Chief of the British Army and spent the next 39 years preventing any kind of military reform. Under his command the army stagnated while European rivals made major advances. The Duke also promoted officers on the basis of their class rather than merit and so filled the higher ranks of the army with men of little talent. He once said 'There is a time for everything, and the time for change is when you can no longer help it.'

The victory of Prussia in the Franco-Prussian War (1870-71) demonstrated the need for reform and Gladstone's government passed the War Office Act (1881) which attempted to remove powers from the Commander-in-Chief and pass them to the Secretary of State. This reform was resisted by the Duke and the senior officers that owed their positions to him. It was only after a royal commission (led by the 8th Duke of Devonshire, see page 41) published a critical report in 1890, that reforms were finally made. It took a further five years before the Duke of Cambridge was finally forced to resign. The only imagination or divergence from precedent the Duke demonstrated was his marriage to actress Sarah Louisa Fairbrother (in contravention of the 1772 Royal Marriages Act). It is a surprise to anyone with knowledge of the Duke's career that a grand monument should stand in his honour.

# 2. Spencer Compton Cavendish, 8th Duke of Devonshire (1833-1908)

*Location: Horseguards Avenue, Whitehall, SW1*
*Sculptor: H. Hampton* ◆ *Material: Bronze*
*Date: 1910*

Spencer Compton Cavendish was a Liberal politician who served in several of William Gladstone's reforming administrations. Cavendish declined the opportunity to form a government after the fall of Disraeli and preferred to step aside to allow Gladstone to resume as Prime Minister. As Secretary of State for War (1882-1885) he was widely criticised for his policy in Sudan which left General Gordon under siege in Khartoum and eventually to his death (see page 148). In 1886 Cavendish broke with Gladstone over Irish Home Rule and ended his career as a minister within Lord Salisbury's Conservative government. Cavendish is now relegated to the margins of British history but he was one of the most important and most recognisable parliamentary figures of his day.

41

## 3. The Gurkha Soldier

*Location: Horse Guards Avenue, SW1*
*Sculptor: Philip Jackson*
*(after work in India by Richard Goulden circa 1924)* ◆ *Material: Bronze*
*Date: 1997*

The Gurkha regiments have their origin in Britain's colonisation of India under the auspices of the East India Company. To the north of the British-controlled regions of India was the northern city-state of Gurkha in a region that was later to become Nepal. Disputes arose between the Nepalese and British which eventually led to war in 1814. The Gurkha army managed to hold the British at bay for two years and a peace treaty was signed in 1816. The British were so impressed with the ability of these hardy mountain men that provision was made for the Gurkha soldiers to volunteer for service in the East India Company's army. It is from this 19th-century treaty that the regiments of the Gurkha Brigade were formed which have served in the British army to the present day. The Gurkhas played a major role in the Second World War in Burma (see Viscount Slim page 45) and the 4th battalion of the 10th Gurkha Rifles formed the core of the Chindits (see page 153). This bronze statue of a Gurkha Soldier commemorates the bravery and skill of the Gurkha regiments. The plaques below the statue detail Gurkha regiments and campaigns and outline their service during the First and Second World Wars. A simple plate at the front of the monument reads 'Bravest of the brave'.

## 4. King Charles I (1600-1649)
*Location: Banqueting House, SW1*
*Sculptor: Unknown*
*Material: Lead*
*Date: About 1800, placed here 1950*

This small lead bust of Charles I stands just above the entrance to Banqueting House at the corner of Horse Guards Avenue. A plaque below the bust explains that it is situated close to the spot where the King was executed on 30th January 1649. On each anniversary a service of dedication and wreath-laying is carried out here. A much larger equestrian statue stands at the top of Whitehall (see page 21).

## 5. Field Marshal Earl Douglas Haig (1861-1928)

*Location: Whitehall, SW1*
*Sculptor: Alfred Hardiman*
*Material: Bronze*
*Date: 1937*

As a young officer, Haig fought in the Sudan, the Boer War and held administrative posts in India. He joined the War Office in 1906 and was responsible for establishing the British Expeditionary Force. The high point of his career was as Commander-in-Chief of British Armies in France between 1915-18. It was in this post that Haig expressed his strategy for fighting the war as 'Kill more Germans'. This blunt and unthinking approach to warfare was to lead to the terrible casualties of the Somne and Passchendaele between 1916-17 in which hundreds of thousands of British and French soldiers were sacrificed for the gain of very little territory. Haig planned his strategy in the comfort of his staff offices and knew nothing of the conditions under which his soldiers were fighting. Despite these failures and the opposition of Lloyd George, Haig remained in his post and had greater success towards the end of the war once the Americans had joined the conflict. After the Allied victory there was little mood for recrimination and Haig was made an Earl and given a tax free sum of £100,000. This statue won the Royal Society of British Sculptors award in 1939, despite the horse upon which Haig sits being in a posture for urination.

# 6. Field Marshal Viscount Slim (1891-1970)

*Location: Raleigh Green, Whitehall, SW1*
*Sculptor: Ivor Roberts-Jones*
*Material: Bronze*
*Date: 1990*

William Slim led the 14th Army in Burma from 1943-45 – one of the most important and least recognised fields of battle of the Second World War. As a young soldier he had fought in Gallipoli and Iraq during the First World War. In the early years of the Second World War he was to command British forces in Sudan, Iran and Iraq, but it was in the jungle conditions of Burma that Slim was to prove his qualities as a military leader. In 1942 Slim took charge of British and Indian troops as they were driven back by the Japanese over 1000 miles to the borders of India. Slim and his troops held their position and when reinforcements arrived fought the Japanese back to Mandalay and Rangoon between 1943-45. The conditions of the Burma campaign were the toughest faced by British troops but the 14th Army and the Indians that fought along side them have never been given the credit they deserve. Earl Mountbatten was probably right when he described Slim as 'the finest general World War II produced'. After the war Slim served as chief of the Imperial General Staff from 1948 to 1952 and was made field marshal in 1953. He served as governor-general of Australia from 1953 to 1960 and was created a viscount in 1959.

# 7. Field Marshal Viscount Alanbrooke (1883-1963)

*Location: Raleigh Green, Whitehall, SW1*
*Sculptor: Ivor Roberts-Jones*
*Material: Bronze*
*Date: 1993*

Alan Brooke had a distinguished military career which included active service in Ireland, India and on the Western Front during the First World War. At the start of World War II Brooke was head of Southern Command and went to France as a member of the British Expeditionary Force. In June 1940 he played a leading role in the evacuation of British troops at Dunkirk. Brooke was a forceful character and had several disagreements with Churchill before he was surprisingly appointed, by the Prime Minister, Chairman of the Chiefs of Staff in December 1941. Brooke continued in the role until the end of the war, acting as a vital brake upon the wilder plans of Churchill. He was promoted to Field Marshal in January 1944 and finally received both the GCB and GCVO in 1953.

# 8. Field Marshal Viscount Montgomery of Alamein (1887-1976)

*Location: Raleigh Green, Whitehall, SW1*
*Sculptor: Oscar Nemon* ◆ *Material: Bronze*
*Date: 1980*

Bernard Law Montgomery was known as 'Monty' to his troops and the British public. As a young soldier he served in India and was seriously injured in the First World War. He became the most famous soldier in the British army during the Second World War when as commander of the British Eighth Army he defeated Rommel's Afrika Korps at El Alamein (Egypt) in October-November 1942. Winston Churchill said of the victory 'Before Alamein we never had a victory, after Alamein we never had a defeat', although this probably had more to do with the US joining the war than the victory in North Africa.

Montgomery went on to command British forces in Sicily, France, the Netherlands and Germany between 1943-45. The last few years of war saw him in conflict with the Americans as he sought a more prominent role in the invasion of Europe. His plan to concentrate on the North was not universally supported by Allied Command and failed in its main objective of taking Arnhem. Despite this failure and his increased marginalisation within Allied Command, Montgomery was made Field Marshal in 1944 and Viscount in 1946.

This statue was unveiled by the Queen Mother in 1980 just four years after his death and shows him sporting his famous beret. Montgomery's reputation has been tarnished in recent years with the publication of previously secret papers from 1947-1948 which show him to be against African independence and in favour of a 'racist master plan' for postwar Africa.

47

# 9. The Women of World War II

*Location: Parliament Street, SW1*
*Sculptor: John W. Mills*
*Material: Bronze*
*Date: July 2005*

When the war started in 1939 men left their work to enlist in the forces and this created a vast labour shortage which women helped to fill. The Women's Land Army (WLA) recruited women to work on the land and provided much needed food during Germany's U-Boat blockade. Women also worked in Britain's factories to provide the munitions and armaments needed to wage war. When times are hard Britain reaches for the kettle and many women too old to work on the land or in factories joined the Women's Voluntary Service (WVS) to provide tea and refreshments to firemen and those sheltering from German bombing. Women also served in the various non-combat roles within the military, with a select few joining the Special Operations Executive, working as spies behind enemy lines. By the end of the war in May 1945 there were 460,000 women serving in the military and 6.5 million in civilian work. Many women were forced back to the kitchen when the men returned from the war, but progress had been made towards greater equality and a recognition of the skills and abilities of women. This large bronze memorial was unveiled by the Queen just over 60 years after the end of the Second World War and is a much-needed reminder of women's contribution to the Allied victory.

## 10. The Cenotaph

*Location: Parliament Street, SW1*
*Sculptor: Sir Edward Lutyens*
*Material: Portland Stone*
*Date: 1919*

The Cenotaph was initially built as a temporary structure as part of the Allied Victory Parade of 1919 to commemorate the fallen of the First World War. A Peace Celebrations Committee had been formed with Lord Curzon (see page 49) as chairman, but the real impetus for the Cenotaph came from Lloyd George. He had attended the French victory celebrations in July 1919 and was impressed by their temporary monument commemorating the dead. On his return, the architect Edward Lutyens was commissioned to design a similar temporary structure. The simple Lutyens design was initially made in plaster but after it was favourably received a permanent Portland Stone version was constructed in 1920. Since 1945 the Cenotaph has been the national monument for the fallen of both world wars and is the site of the ceremony of remembrance held every November. The word Cenotaph comes from the Greek words *kenos* which means empty and *taphos* meaning tomb.

## 11. Charles Dickens (1812-1870)

*Location: Red Lion (2nd Floor),*
*Parliament Street, SW1*
*Material: Terracotta*
*Date: 1900*

No writer of any period is so strongly associated with London as Charles Dickens; people even use the term 'Dickens' London' to refer to his fictional vision of the city. One of the great qualities of Dickens' work are the characters which populate his novels and the diversity of life he was able to convey. Dickens was able to write about such a broad section of London's society because he had managed to transcend an impoverished childhood in Camden Town to attain a position of wealth and fame. The Dickens family experienced great deprivation, after moving to London in 1822. They were eventually sent to debtor's prison, while Charles was forced to work in a shoe blacking factory at the age of 12. They were eventually saved from penury by a small inheritance and Charles was able to receive a basic education which he completed at the age of 15 without distinction.

Dickens began work in a solicitor''s office. He disliked the work and decided that he wanted to be a writer, teaching himself shorthand and becoming a court and later parliamentary reporter. He had a good deal of success as a journalist and campaigned in his writing for parliamentary and social reform. It was at the age of 21 that Dickens first came to the public's' attention as a writer of fiction under the pen-name 'Boz'. The publication of *The Pickwick Papers* (1836-7) was the first work of fiction under his own name and marked the start of the most productive period in his life which saw the publication of *Oliver Twist* (1837), *Nicholas Nickleby* (1838-39), *The Old*

*Curiosity Shop* (1840-1), *Barnaby Rudge* (1841), *Martin Chuzzlewit* (1843-4) and *A Christmas Carol* (1843). Dickens was a famous figure in his own lifetime partly because all his works were published in popular periodicals rather than in book form. Each instalment of his stories was eagerly anticipated by the increasingly literate public. The serialisation of *The Old Curiosity Shop* engrossed the country in the fate of little Nell, with Dickens receiving hundreds of letters asking for her to be spared her fate. The country went into mourning when the tale of her death was published. Never has an author cast such a spell over his readership.

Dickens enjoyed the publics attention and embarked on readings of his works to packed theatres both in Britain and also during a tour of America in 1842 and later in 1867-8. He was thought by many to be the best actor of his generation, but such talent and energy took its toll on his health. Like his contemporary Isambard Kingdom Brunel (see page 127), Dickens worked himself to a state of exhaustion and died prematurely at the age of 58. There are several small memorials to Dickens, but it is a great shame that such a prominent literary figure and one so associated with London should not have a major statue in his honour.

## 12. Robert Clive, 1st Baron Clive (1725-1774)

*Location: King Charles Street (on the steps at the St James's Park end)*
*Sculptor: John Tweed*
*Material: Bronze*
*Date: 1912*

In the latter part of the 18th century Britain lost its American colonies while gaining dominance over the vast domain of India. One of the key reasons for Britain's success in India was the role played by Robert Clive. Through military conquest and political intrigue Clive rapidly brought India under the control of Britain's East India Company. The bronze reliefs on the plinth of this monument illustrate the beginning and end of this process; the siege of Arcot (1751) and Clive receiving the grant of Bengal, Behar and Orissa at Allahabad (1765).

Clive went to India as a young man after a difficult childhood in which he exhibited a troubled and sometimes violent nature which led to his expulsion from Charterhouse School. When Clive first arrived in India at the age of 18 in 1743 he was employed as an administrator, but the capture of Madras (now Chennai) by the French forced him to flee the city and later enlist in the East India Company army. Clive came to national prominence in 1751 when he occupied the city of Arcot and held it under siege against a much larger French and Indian army. This was to be the beginning of a long series of campaigns which first secured southern India and later established the supremacy of the East India Company in the north with the defeat of Siraj-ud-daulah, the Nawab of Bengal, at the Battle of Plassey in June 1757. The aspirant to the Nawab's throne, Mir Jafar, was induced to throw in his lot with Clive and the war was won in a matter of hours, illustrating Clive's skill as a politician as well as a soldier. The Treaty of Paris in 1763 confirmed the gains Clive had made and recognised the British rule of Muhammad Ali in the north.

Clive returned from India for the final time in 1767, but a life of extravagant expenditure (he made and lost more than one fortune), battling in harsh conditions and years of opium addiction had taken their toll on his mental and physical health. An attempt was made to impeach him for financial wrong-doing which although unsuccessful was enough to drive him into a depression to which he was always prone, and in November 1774 he killed himself. It is the manner of his death amid scandal that perhaps explains the passage of nearly a century and a half before this monument was erected.

## 13. Bali Memorial
*Location: Horse Guards Road*
*Sculptor: Gerry Breeze and Martin Cook*
*Material: Marble*
*Date: October 2006*

This memorial was unveiled by Prince Charles on the fourth anniversary of the Bali terrorist bombing which it commemorates. The attack was carried out by an Indonesian Islamist group with links to Al-Qaida on the holiday resort of Kuta on 12th October 2002. The ensuing carnage claimed the lives of 202 innocent people, making the Bali attack the most deadly Al-Qaida related terrorist incident since the attack on the World Trade Centre on September 11th 2001. The monument consists of a 5ft-high marble globe to symbolise the international nature of the atrocity and has 202 doves carved upon it to represent each victim. On a curved wall behind the globe are inscribed the names of all those who died – 28 of which were British.

## 14. Lord Mountbatten (1900-1979)
*Location: Foreign Office Green, Horse Guards Parade, SW1*
*Sculptor: Franta Belsky*
*Material: Bronze*
*Date: 1983*

Louis Mountbatten, who was the grandson of Queen Victoria, spent the interwar years as a naval captain and glamorous socialite, marrying the heiress Edwina Ashley and forming a close friendship with Edward, Prince of Wales. He played a major role in the Second World War firstly as Chief of Combined Operations (1941-3) and later as Supreme Allied Commander in South East Asia (1943-6). Mountbatten was a popular leader but his only major military initiative was the disastrous Dieppe Raid of August 1942. While in South East Asia he was constrained in his actions by more experienced American planning staff. After the war Mountbatten's socialist sympathies won him favour in Attlee's Labour government and he was appointed the last Viceroy of India in 1947. He was a significant figure in the events leading to India's independence and the formation of Pakistan but has been criticised for his handling of the situation which contributed to the bloodshed. Despite such criticism, Mountbatten was made an Earl in 1947 and later became the First Sea Lord in 1955. His marriage to Edwina was troubled, suffering infidelities on both sides – most famously her affair with Nehru (see page 171). In 1960 Edwina died and Mountbatten spent his latter years as a mentor to the young Prince Charles and fending off newspaper stories regarding his personal life. He was assassinated by an IRA bomb while on holiday in Ireland in August 1979. This monument stands behind the Foreign Office and shows Mountbatten in naval uniform.

## 15. Horatio Herbert Field, 1st Earl Kitchener (1850-1916)

*Location: Horse Guards Parade, SW1*
*Sculptor: John Tweed ◆ Material: Bronze*
*Date: 1926*

Kitchener joined the Royal Engineers in 1871 and served in Palestine (1874–78) and Cyprus (1878–82). The young Kitchener came to the nation's attention through the successful campaign in Sudan (1883–85) and after his victory at Omdurman he was knighted. During the Boer War (1899–1902) Kitchener was chief of Staff to Earl Roberts (see page 57) and developed the strategy of burning Boer farms and placing civilians in concentration camps. The policy was effective but criticised for its brutality by politicians such as Lloyd George.

Kitchener was made Minister for War at the start of the First World War. His face was used on the famous 'Your Country Needs You' recruiting poster which helped to enlist three million young men to the army. Many of these recruits were killed during the Somme and Dardanelles Campaigns, partly because of the leadership of Earl Haig (see page 44) and partly because of the old-fashioned views of Kitchener who supplied unsuitable munitions and refused to use tanks. Following these disasters and the further catastrophe of Gallipoli (1916) Kitchener offered to resign, but was kept on by Prime Minister Asquith. Later that year Kitchener was killed when HMS Hampshire struck a German mine. Sir Arthur Conan Doyle was probably right when he wrote 'Kitchener grew very arrogant. He had flashes of genius but was usually stupid.'

## 16. Cadiz Memorial

*Location: Horse Guards Parade, SW1*
*Sculptor: Not known*
*Material: Cast-iron*
*Date: 1816*

The Cadiz Memorial consists of a French mortar mounted on a cast-iron Chinese dragon. It was a gift of the Spanish government to the Prince Regent in memory of the lifting of the siege of Cadiz following the defeat of French forces near Salamanca in July 1812 by the Duke of Wellington's army. The battle was a decisive one in the Peninsular War and helped establish Wellington's reputation as a great battlefield strategist. Despite the serious intention behind the memorial the general public and caricaturists were tired of war and its commemoration immediately following the end of hostilities with Napoleon. The memorial became satirically known as the 'Regent's Bomb' and, given the Prince's many mistresses, cartoons made lewd references to the size and angle of the cannon. One such satirical drawing is entitled 'A representation of the Regent's tremendous thing erected in the park'. For a more serious assessment of the future George IV and the Duke of Wellington see pages 14 and 208.

## 17. Frederick Sleigh,
## Field Marshal Earl Roberts (1832-1914)

*Location: Horse Guards Parade, SW1*
*Sculptor: Harry Bates  ◆  Material: Bronze*
*Date: 1923*

Frederick Sleigh Roberts was born in India to a military family and joined the Bengal Artillery in 1851. He fought with distinction during the Indian Mutiny (1857–58) and was awarded the Victoria Cross. He came to the public's attention for the relief of Kandahar during the Second Afghan War (1878–80) and was recognised as a military hero in the same way that Sir Henry Havelock had been for the relief of Lucknow (see page 18). Roberts was rapidly promoted after the relief of Kandahar and became field marshal in 1895. In 1899 when the British army encountered set backs during the Boer War Roberts was appointed to take charge. With the aid of Kitchener (see page 55), Roberts set about reforming the army in South Africa and reversed the course of the war in Britain's favour. On his return to Britain in 1900, he became the last Commander-in-Chief of the British army but soon found himself in conflict with the government and resigned in 1904. He died of pneumonia in France in 1914 while visiting Indian troops fighting in the First World War. Roberts was such a popular soldier that he was one of only two non-royals in the 20th century whose body lay in state in Westminster Hall, the other being Winston Churchill. He is buried in St Paul's Cathedral.

## 18. Garnet Joseph, 1st Viscount Wolseley (1833-1913)

*Location: Horse Guards Parade, SW1*
*Sculptor: Sir William Goscombe John ◆ Material: Bronze*
*Date: 1920*

Garnet Joseph Wolseley followed his father into the military at the age of 19 serving with distinction in the Second Burmese War (1852–53). Despite being injured in battle, he soon returned to service in the Crimea (1854-56), India (1857-58) and China (1860). It was in India that Wolseley made his name serving under Sir Colin Campbell (see page 102) in the relief of Lucknow and defending Alambagh under the command of General Outram (see page 145). In 1862 Wolseley spent some time as an observer during the American Civil War and served in Canada where he established Canadian sovereignty over the Northwest Terrritories. On his return home Wolseley received the Order of the Bath (CB), and began work in the War Office to institue the Cardwell Scheme of reform against the wishes of the Duke of Cambridge (see page 40). Wolseley became the most prominent advocate for reform while also successfully commanding forces in Ashanti, South Africa and taking a seat on the Council of India in 1876. His most brilliant campaign was to defend the Suez Canal against a rebellion in 1882 for which he was promoted to the rank of General and awarded a peerage. It was Wolseley who attempted the rescue of General Gordon (see page 148) from Khartoum in 1885. He briefly became Commander-in-Chief in 1895, a position he held until 1901. By the time of his death in 1913 Wolseley had established his reputation as the most capable soldier of his generation. He wrote numerous books on soldiering and history and was a close friend of the author Henry James.

Parliament Square

GREAT GEORGE ST

PARLIAMENT

BRIDGE ST

SQUARE

BROAD ST

ST. MARGARET'S STREET

Houses of Parliament

River Thames

Westminster Abbey

Victoria Tower Gardens

## Parliament Square

1) Queen Anne
2) George Canning
3) Abraham Lincoln
4) Sir Robert Peel
5) Benjamin Disraeli, Earl of Beaconsfield
6) Edward Stanley, 14th Earl of Derby
7) Viscount Palmerston
8) Field Marshal Jan Christian Smuts
9) Sir Winston Churchill
10) Oliver Cromwell
11) Richard I (Coeur de Lion)
12) George V
13) Emmeline & Christabel Pankhurst
14) Burghers of Calais

# Parliament Square SW1

This area of Whitehall is dominated by Sir Charles Barry's Palace of Westminster, built in 1858, and Parliament Square which was laid out ten years later to complement the neo-gothic edifice. Parliament was heavily bombed during the Second World War and the site was partially re-developed by George Grey Warnum in the late 1940s without changing the nature of the place. The greatest intrusion upon the Victorian and Edwardian uniformity is Westminster Abbey which dates from medieval times (see page 82) and the post-modern structure of Portcullis House which was completed in 2001. The area has been the focus of British parliamentary democracy for over 400 years and many leading British politicians and royalty are commemorated here as well as a few important politicians from abroad, such as South African Jan Smuts and president Abraham Lincoln.

It would be comforting to suppose that the characters commemorated in stone and bronze outside the Houses of Parliament were more dignified in their conduct than our political contemporaries, but history is never comforting and there are just as many tales of power, ambition and scandal among the statuary. Disraeli hated Robert Peel after being turned down for a cabinet place as a young man and exacted revenge by bringing down the Peel administration over the Repeal of the Corn Laws. The two now stand mute alongside each other on Parliament Square. A seated George Canning looks passively towards one of the great Victorian politicians, Lord Palmerston, who was his assistant and prodigy at the Foreign Office. Palmerston was adventurist in his foreign policy, but a reactionary at home and always distrusted the democratic spirit of the United States. He was not a supporter of the Union during the American Civil War, much to the annoyance of Lincoln who sits alongside Canning looking towards Parliament.  Oliver Cromwell stands apart from the fray behind concrete barriers within the grounds of a fortified parliament which he did much to establish after victory in this country's own 17th century Civil War.

The suffragette Emmeline Pankhurst is the only radical political figure to be found here and she is consigned to a corner of Victoria Embankment Gardens along with the much put upon Burghers of Calais.  Radicalism still thrives in Parliament Square, but it is represented in the living form of Brian Haw who has been camped outside parliament since June 2001 in protest at the government's policy towards Iraq. His lone vigil has upset many politicians behind the security gates of parliament and the Serious Organised Crime and Police Act of 2005 was in part designed to make his protest illegal – which it has yet to achieve. Visitors should be aware that any form of unauthorized political protest in this area is now an offence due to this act.

# 1. Queen Anne (1665-1714)
*Location: Queen Anne's Gate, SW1*
*Sculptor: Not known, perhaps Francis Bird*
*Material: Stone*
*Date: 1708*

For more details about Queen Anne see the review of her statue outside St Paul's Cathedral (p. 222)

# 2. George Canning (1770-1827)
*Location: Parliament Square*
*Sculptor: Richard Westmacott*
*Material: Bronze*
*Date: Palace Yard 1832, moved to present site in 1867*

George Canning's statue in Parliament Square shows him as a toga-clad Roman senator which is fitting as his eloquence and reason had earned him the title "The Cicero of the British Senate". He came from a modest Irish family, but the patronage of a wealthy uncle allowed him to acquire a gentleman's education and an introduction into the Whig party. Canning was soon to change allegiances due to his antipathy towards the French Revolution (which many Whigs supported) and his admiration for and friendship with Pitt the Younger. Under Pitt's war administration, Canning was to prove an effective minister

63

and in 1808 devised the seizure of the Danish fleet preventing it falling into the hands of Napoleon. It was at this time that Canning fell out with the aristocratic war minister, Castlereagh. The feud became so bitter that the two fought a duel in September 1809, in which Canning was injured. Both men were obliged to resign following the incident.

Canning held a few minor positions in government after his resignation, but only achieved a position of prominence after the suicide of Castlereagh in 1822. Canning took over the position of foreign secretary and adopted a more populist approach to Britain's foreign policy than any before him. Canning pursued a more liberal stance in response to the reactionary states of France, Austria and Russia who dominated Europe after 1815. He was unable to prevent the suppression of independence in Spain by the French, but he used Britain's naval power to successfully promote independence for the Spanish colonies of South America and the liberation of Greece from Ottoman rule. Canning's populist style was much disliked by more reactionary Tories such as Wellington and Eldon, both of whom refused to serve in his brief administration which was formed after the death of Lord Liverpool in 1827. Canning was only to serve as prime minister for 100 days. He died in office from a lung infection brought on by a cold caught at the funeral of the Duke of York. He was a progressive foreign minister, but a conservative when it came to domestic policy, a style of politics that was to be adopted by his young pupil Palmerston. Disraeli was later to credit Canning with being one of the originators of progressive Conservatism. Canning's own account of his philosophy is worth quoting:

'I consider it to be the duty of a British statesman in internal as well as external affairs, to hold a middle course between extremes; avoiding alike extravagancies of despotism or the licentiousness of unbridled freedom'

## 3. Abraham Lincoln (1809-65)
*Location: Parliament Square*
*Sculptor: Augustus Saint-Gaudens*
*Material: Bronze*
*Date: 1920*

The 16th president of the United States and one of the most controversial. Lincoln came from a humble second generation family of frontiersmen. He was born in a Kentucky log cabin and as a youth worked as a farm hand. The young Abraham was an avid reader and would often get into trouble with his father for showing too much interest in learning. Lincoln struggled to make a living and did all kinds of jobs as he made his way in the world. In 1831, while a store clerk in New Salem, Illinois, Lincoln fought a famous wrestling match with Jack Armstrong, the leader of a rowdy gang of youths. Lincoln stood 6'4" tall and although slight of build was renowned for his physical strength. It is said that Lincoln had the better of the fight but the two protagonists shook hands and became life-long friends. Lincoln later successfully defended Armstrong's son against a murder charge and charged no fee for his work. Had Lincoln become president during less troubled times he may have achieved a great deal; however his presidency was to be overshadowed by the bloody civil war which was already imminent when Lincoln took office. When the southern confederates overran Fort Sumter in 1861, Lincoln had little choice but to raise an army to maintain the Union and so the Civil War began. After four long and bloody years of war the Confederate General, Robert E. Lee, surrendered on April 9, 1865. Two days later Lincoln gave a speech outside the White House which so infuriated a southern-sympathising actor by the name of John Wilkes Booth, that he determined to assassinate the president. On April 14th Booth shot Lincoln while he was attending the theatre. As Lincoln was set upon reconciliation and a just peace, this act did little to help Booth's cause.

There is a very fine bust of Lincoln at the Royal Exchange in the City (see page 210). This statue is a copy of the one that stands in Chicago. These statues and Britain's history as a pioneer in abolishing slavery lead most people to assume that Britain supported the Northern cause during the civil war. In fact the British political establishment was divided over the issue and prominent figures such as Gladstone, Palmerston and Russell were supporters of the South. After the Northern victory and Lincoln's assassination, fulsome speeches were made in the House of Commons in praise of the fallen president and the establishment's southern sympathies quickly forgotten.

# 4. Sir Robert Peel (1788-1850)

*Location: Parliament Square*
*Sculptor: Matthew Noble*
*Material: Bronze*
*Date: 1851*

Born in Lancashire, the son of a wealthy cotton mill owner, Robert Peel was a man of considerable intellect and the most important figure in Parliament between 1820 and his death in 1850. His political importance is all the more remarkable for a man who was said by contemporaries to be rather cold and haughty in his manner, and to suffer bouts of mad temper which did not make him many friends in parliament.

Peel entered the Commons in April 1809. When Lord Liverpool became prime minister he took up the position of chief secretary for Ireland in which capacity he became renowned for his opposition to Catholic Emancipation. Peel nearly fought a duel with the Irish nationalist Daniel O'Connell in 1815. O'Connell had called him 'orange Peel' for his support of the Protestant cause. As with O'Connell's later attempted duel with Disraeli, the authorities intervened to prevent any blood shed.

Peel soon resigned his post in Ireland, exhausted by the constant travel involved. He was to return to ministerial office as home secretary for both Lord Liverpool and Wellington. It was as home secretary under Wellington that Peel performed one of his first major changes of mind. Having opposed Catholic Emancipation for many years, Peel was persuaded that change was necessary to avoid crisis and so in March 1829 he introduced the Emancipation Act. It was also at this time that Peel created the Metropolitan Police Force for which he is most famous. The term 'peelers' or 'bobbies' for policemen derives from Peel's name. As Tory leader through most of the 1830s, Peel also had to make an accommodation with the 1832 Parliamentary Reform Act which he had formerly opposed. It was Peel's attempt to accommodate such change which was to mark the beginning of the transformation of the Tory party into the modern-day Conservative party.

Peel was to head several Tory ministries making major reforms such as the introduction of income tax and several laws to lessen the problems in Ireland. In 1843 there was an attempt made on Peel's life by a mentally deranged Scottish woodsman named Daniel M'Naghten. Peel was unscathed, but his personal secretary was killed by mistake. The subsequent trial established the rules on insanity pleading in law that are still used to this day and bare the mad woodsman's name. Peel's final change of mind came when he repealed the Corn Laws in 1846, after years of opposition to the proposal. The Corn Laws kept corn prices high for farmers, but in so doing impoverished the weakest in society. The Tory party was split on the issue and the repeal brought an end to Peel's ministry and let the Whigs into power for many years. Peel remained active in politics after the end of his government. He fell from his horse on 28th June 1850 and died from his injuries several days later.

# 5. Benjamin Disraeli, Earl of Beaconsfield (1804-1881)

*Location: Parliament Square*
*Sculptor: Mario Raggi*
*Material: Bronze*
*Date: 1883*

Benjamin Disraeli was probably the most interesting and certainly the most exotic politician of his day. He was a dandy, a wit and a successful novelist whose character can be contrasted with the rather worthy seriousness of his contemporary Gladstone. Disraeli was also the first and last Prime Minister of Jewish decent, although he was christened after his father converted to Christianity.

As a young man Disraeli travelled through Europe, had several affairs, contracted venereal disease and began his career as a novelist and politician. Before entering parliament Disraeli became embroiled in a long-running dispute with the Irish nationalist Daniel O'Connell. The two were to have fought a duel in 1835, but the police intervened to prevent it.

After several attempts he was finally elected as a Tory MP for Maidstone in 1837. When the party won the 1841 general election, Disraeli presented himself to prime minister Robert Peel as a suitable candidate for ministerial office. Peel did not share Disraeli's high opinion of his talents and declined the offer. Disraeli became a leading figure of the 'Young England' group who criticized the government from the back benches. It was during this period that Disraeli developed his idea of a popular 'one nation' Tory party which intended to reduce the divide between rich and poor. Despite the Thatcherite 1980s, this idea is still alive today within the modern Conservative party.

After the fall of Peel's ministry (see page 67) Disraeli was to return as chancellor of the exchequer under Lord Derby's premiership in the Conservative governments of 1852, 1858-59 and 1866-68. His greatest achievement during this period was the passing of the 1867 Reform Act which gave a further two million citizens the vote. Disraeli became prime minister in 1868 and declared in the Commons 'I have climbed to the top of the greasy pole'. His triumph was short.lived with the elections of the same year bringing Gladstone and the Liberals into office. It was not until 1874 that Disraeli finally became PM with sufficient power to put into practice some of his reforming ideas, by which time he was 70 years old. He continued the trend to social reform, begun by Gladstone, with important laws such as the Public Health Act (1875) and the Education Act (1876), radically changing the role of the state. His progressive domestic policy was contrasted with an aggressive foreign policy which included the annexation of the Fiji islands (1874) and the Transvaal (1877), the war against the Afghans (1878–79), and the Zulu War of 1879. Disraeli's imperial ambitions were finally realised with Queen Victoria assuming the title of Empress of India in 1876. The Liberals defeated the Conservatives in the 1880 general election and Disraeli decided to retire from politics. He died on 19th April 1881. His favourite primrose flowers are placed at his monument on the anniversary of his death.

# 6. Edward Stanley, 14th Earl of Derby (1799-1868)

*Location: Parliament Square*
*Sculptor: Matthew Noble*
*Material: Bronze*
*Date: 1874*

This bronze figure of three times prime minister Edward Stanley wearing the Garter is interesting for the bronze reliefs which depict him publicly speaking at various stages in his long career. One of the reliefs shows St Stephen's Chapel, which was the meeting place of the Commons before the present parliament was built. Stanley entered parliament as a Whig in 1820 and soon acquired a reputation as an orator; Lord Lytton described him as "the Rupert of Debate", no doubt after Prince Rupert the head of the Cavaliers in the Civil War. Like many politicians of his day, Stanley changed parties and formed cross-party alliances when necessary. He served in Canning's government of 1827 and after a period out of office was made Secretary of State for War and the Colonies in 1837 in Peel's second ministry. In this position he took over the responsibility for the conduct and conclusion of the Opium Wars with China and concluded the Treaty of Nanking in August 1842. Although a fairly progressive young man, Edward Stanley became increasingly conservative with age and resigned from Robert Peel's government over the repeal of the Corn Laws. His three periods as prime minister were not particularly eventful and his greatest single achievement, the 1867 Reform Act, was not his work but that of Benjamin Disraeli, who succeeded him as prime minister just before his death in 1868. There is a stone bust of the Earl of Derby in Great Windmill Street, W1

# 7. Henry Temple, 3rd Viscount Palmerston (1784-1865)

*Location: Parliament Square*
*Sculptor: Thomas Woolner*
*Material: Bronze*
*Date: 1876*

Palmerston was one of the giants of the late Victorian political scene, but his name is not as well known as that of his contemporaries Gladstone or Disraeli. The reason for this may well be that Harry Temple (later Lord Palmerston) was old fashioned for his time; he was over 50 when Victoria was crowned and was 70 when he became Prime Minister for the first time in 1855. In truth Palmerston was a creature of the Regency period and disliked the Victorian spirit of parliamentary and domestic reform, doing all he could to prevent such changes and preserve the rights and privileges of the aristocracy of which he was a member.

Despite being a reactionary in his domestic policy, Palmerston was a very popular political figure largely because of his foreign policy and in this he followed the aggressive populism of his mentor Canning (see page 72). A good example of this is the bombing of Canton by the British navy on the instruction of the governor of Hong Kong, Sir John Bowring, following the Chinese seizure of a pirate boat registered under the British flag. Palmerston supported Bowring despite his actions being clearly excessive and the Chinese having a legal case for seizing the boat. Palmerston lost the vote in parliament and was forced to call an election. He fought the election on jingoistic lines and won a landslide victory.

Palmerston was also popular with the general public for his jaunty and energetic character and gained the nickname 'Lord Cupid' for his many affairs. His reputation did not endear him to Queen Victoria. On one occasion he attempted to seduce one of the queen's ladies-in-waiting, entering her bedroom while staying as Victoria's guest at Windsor Castle. It was only due to the intervention of Lord Melbourne (whose sister Palmerston married) that

Palmerston remained in office. Even at the age of 78 Palmerston was cited as co-respondent in a divorce case, which only increased his popularity with the British public. Lady Palmerston was a witty and fun-loving woman who tolerated her wayward husband. Her London parties were renowned for their grandeur as well as being occasions for political intrigue. Palmerston fell ill in October 1865, and it is said his last words were "Die, my dear doctor? That is the last thing I shall do!"

73

# 8. Field Marshal Jan Christiaan Smuts (1870-1950)

*Location: Parliament Square*
*Sculptor: Jacob Epstein*
*Material: Bronze*
*Date: 1956*

Jan Smuts was a South African politician and soldier of exceptional talent who received an English education, but fought against the British on his return to South Africa during the Boer War (1899-1902). There can be few monuments in London to those that fought a guerilla war against the British, but Jan Smuts was to prove a loyal ally to Britain once the Vereeniging Peace Treaty (1902), which he helped to draft, was signed. During the First World War, Smuts fought an effective campaign against the Germans in East Africa, before joining the Imperial War Cabinet in 1917. Smuts participated in the Treaty of Versailles before returning to South Africa to play a key role in his country's politics, including many years as prime minister. Jan Smuts was again to prove a key ally to the British during the Second World War and was promoted to field marshal in the British army in 1941. Smuts participated in the Paris Peace Treaty at the end of the war, making him the only politician to be involved in the conclusion of both world wars. He was a major figure in the forming of the United Nations after the war, but his anglophile position proved unpopular amongst the Afrikaners and he was to lose the 1948 election to a pro-apartheid party. Jan Smuts coined the term 'holism' and 'holistic' from his academic studies. He died in 1950 at the age of 80.

# 9. Sir Winston Churchill (1874-1965)

*Location: Parliament Square*
*Sculptor: Ivor Roberts-Jones*
*Material: Bronze*
*Date: 1973*

There are five monuments to Winston Churchill to be found in London, but this is by far the largest and most prominent. Churchill will forever be associated with the travails of the Second World War and what he termed 'our finest hour'. British culture has remained in some way deeply attached to this image of itself as a bastion of freedom against Nazi oppression and Churchillian rhetoric is used in all kinds of circumstances including our dealings with Europe.

Churchill was half American, his mother being a New York heiress, but his father was a full-blooded English aristocrat descended from the Duke of Marlborough. Churchill received the education of a young English gentleman at Harrow and then, due to his poor academic performance, was sent to Sandhurst before joining the army and seeing action in India and the Sudan. Winston had a way with words and sent dispatches to the papers recounting his exploits. When he left the army in 1899 he became a war reporter and was taken prisoner during the Boer War. His escape made the headlines and he wrote a book of his adventure on his return home. In 1900 he was elected as Conservative MP for Oldham, but the young Churchill soon changed sides to the Liberal party. It was as a Liberal that Churchill first entered the cabinet in 1908 under Herbert Asquith. Promoted to home secretary after the 1910 election, Churchill passed many liberal reforms of the prison service before losing the job because of his mishandling of the miners' strike. He was moved to the Admiralty where he helped develop the Royal Naval Air Force. At the outbreak of World War One Churchill joined the War Council, but his Gallipoli campaign of 1915 led to heavy casualties. Most politicians would make excuses for such failing, but Churchill joined the army and saw action at the Western Front. He was brought back into the cabinet by David Lloyd George, but again he made some radical and wrong decisions. In Iraq, Churchill believed that British rule could be maintained with a very small number of troops through the use of the Royal Air Force. The policy was a disaster and in 1920 there was an uprising of Kurdish and Arab tribes that continued for many years and led to heavy casualties. It is interesting to note that Churchill favoured the use of chemical weapons in Iraq against "recalcitrant Arabs".

Churchill was returned as a Conservative MP in the 1924 election. As Chancellor he returned Britain to the Gold Standard (which proved a disaster) and took a hard line against the General Strike (which proved unpopular). The Conservatives were defeated in 1929, and the 1930s were to be Churchill's years of political isolation – a lone voice on the back benches warning against Hitler and condemning the policy of appeasement. The start of the Second World War marked the end of Neville Chamberlain's policy and career and in May 1940 Churchill was appointed prime minister. The war did not initially go well for Churchill and he even faced a vote of no confidence in the house but he played a vital role in inspiring the country and involving both the Soviet Union and the United States in the war against Hitler. After victory over Germany in 1945 Churchill lost the 1945 election to Clement Attlee's Labour party but was again to win power in 1951. Old and unwell he retired from politics in 1955 and died in 1965 having lived his early life under the reign of Queen Victoria and died while the Beatles were at their height. Like all great men Churchill was a mixture of the very good and the very bad. Those that see him as one or the other are usually engaged in some form of propaganda.

# 10. Oliver Cromwell (1599-1658)

*Location: Westminster Hall, Parliament Square*
*Sculptor: Sir William Hamo Thornycroft*
*Material: Bronze*
*Date: 1899*

In 1640 Oliver Cromwell was an obscure MP for Cambridgeshire and modest country squire. Cromwell was also a devout Puritan and in 1634 had even attempted to emigrate with his family to America to avoid the widespread persecution of Puritans by archbishop Laud with the support of the crown. It was this religious and political conflict between parliament and Charles I and the bloody civil war that followed that were to prove Oliver Cromwell's making. When the war began in the summer of 1642 Cromwell joined the parliamentary army and was a key contributor to the parliamentary victory at Marston Moor in 1644. By the battle of Naseby in the summer of 1645 Cromwell had risen to second-in-command of parliament's New Model Army. He proved as effective a politician as he was a soldier and was the dominant figure during the trial of Charles I in the winter of 1648, leading to his execution in January 1649. Within two years of the regicide Cromwell had subjugated both Ireland and Scotland in bloody conflict, succeeding where Charles I had singularly failed. The redistribution of land from Irish Catholics to Protestant settlers under Cromwell was to lead to centuries of bitterness. By the winter of 1653 Cromwell's domination of parliament was publicly acknowledged with his appointment as Lord Protector. The five years of Cromwell's reign were to see the establishment of religious tolerance and parliamentary civilian government in Britain.

On Cromwell's death in 1658, the republic soon fell apart and the monarchy was restored to the throne. The surviving signatories to the king's execution were themselves executed at Charing Cross (see Charles I statue page 21) and Cromwell's body was exhumed from Westminster Abbey and hung at Traitors' Gate. Despite these public displays of vengeance, Cromwell had changed the nature of British politics and the ultimate authority of parliament was never again questioned by the crown.

Cromwell remains a controversial figure in Britain's history. It took over two centuries for a statue to be erected in London to commemorate him and this was fiercely objected to by Irish Nationalist members of parliament for his brutality towards Ireland in 1649-50. It was eventually left to Lord Rosebery to personally pay for the erection of this statue, which shows Cromwell with the two great influences in his life in each hand, the sword and the bible.

# 11. Richard I (Coeur de Lion) (1157-1199)

*Location: Old Palace Yard*
*Sculptor: Cast of original by Carlo Marochetti*
*Material: Bronze*
*Date: 1851*

Richard 'the Lion Heart' is a symbol of Britain's heroic past and this bronze statue shows him in full military dress, to reinforce the national image. The monument was erected during the Great Exhibition to represent Britain to the world, but the real Richard I was very different from this myth.

Richard was more French than English having been brought up by his French mother. His first language was French and he cared far more for his continental possessions spending only six months of his ten-year reign in England. Power and good family relations are seldom compatible and Richard fought his brothers and father on several occasions before finally making an alliance with Philip II of France to overthrow his father.

After assuming the throne Richard joined the unsuccessful third Crusade to liberate the Holy Land in 1190. On the journey home Richard was captured and imprisoned for several years by Holy Roman Emperor Henry VI and in his absence Philip II formed an alliance with his brother John. On his release in 1194 Richard defeated his brother and recaptured the land taken by Philip II, defeating Philip near Gisors in 1198. In the spring of the following year he was killed in a minor skirmish. As Richard lay dying he asked to see the archer who had fired the fatal arrow, ordering that the man be pardoned and given a sum of money, but on Richard's death his killer was flayed alive and then hanged. Richard failed to produce an heir and his crown was passed to his brother John.

## 12. George V (1865-1936)

*Location: Old Palace Yard, SW1*
*Sculptor: Sir William Rein Dick, plinth by Sir Gills Gilbert Scott*
*Material: Stone*
*Date: 1947*

George V was born the second son of Edward VII in 1865. He was not expected to become king and began his adult life in the Royal Navy. It was only when his older brother died in 1892 that George became the heir to the throne. Despite the sudden change of circumstances George's character remained that of a middle-ranking naval officer, obsessed with punctuality, discipline and duty.

In 1910 Edward VII died in the middle of a constitutional crisis, the newly crowned George V kept his father's promise and supported the 1911 Parliament Act. The First World War was to present problems for a British Royal Family bearing the surname Saxe-Coburg-Gotha (See King William III statue p. 108). George V took the dramatic step of changing the family name to Windsor. and towards the end of the war refused refuge to his cousin, Tsar Nicholas II, fearing any such links would damage the popularity of the British royal family.

In 1924 the King recognised Ramsay MacDonald as the first Labour prime minister, and later helped lessen the severity with which the Conservative government dealt with the general strike of 1926. The formation of a coalition government in 1931 with MacDonald as prime minister owed a good deal to the political skills of the king. George V may have been a dull man, but he showed himself to be a rather wise statesman and his ordinariness endeared him to the British people who showed their affection for him during his silver jubilee of 1935. His death of influenza the following year was the cause of considerable national mourning.

# Westminster Abbey
*Broad Sanctuary, SW1*
*Open: Monday-Friday 9.30am-3.45pm, Saturday 9.30am-1.45pm*
*www.westminster-abbey.org*

Westminster Abbey was built around 1045–1050 by Edward the Confessor who became the first monarch to be buried on the site. Henry III (1207-1272) later continued Edward's work by rebuilding the Abbey in the Gothic style and was buried in the Confessor's Chapel in 1272 – beginning a tradition of royal burial that lasted until the internment of George II in 1760. It was during the reign of Richard II (1367-1400) that the first notable commoners were buried in the Abbey, and over the centuries hundreds of influential people have been commemorated here – many of them now forgotten.

There is a charge for visiting the Abbey, but the history of the building and the number of monuments and tombs make it well worth the expense. There are over 600 people commemorated in some way in the Abbey and below is a brief list of some of the more prominent figures still recognised by visitors today:

## The Nave

Anthony Ashley-Cooper, 7th Earl of Shaftesbury – reformer (see page 33)

Charles James Fox – politician (see page 239)

William Pitt the Younger – politician (see page 259)

Franklin D. Roosevelt – US President (see page 257)

Henry Fawcett – statesman (see page 135)

Lord Mountbatten – statesman (see page 54)

Robert Baden-Powell – founder of scouts (see page 311)

General Sir James Outram – soldier (see page 145)

Baron John L. Mair Lawrence – soldier (see page 98)

Major John André – soldier

George Peabody – Philanthropist (see page 212)

Robert Stephenson – engineer (see page 349)

Field Marshal Colin Campbell – soldier (see page 349)

Neville Chamberlain – politician

Michael Faraday – scientist (see page 131)

Sir Isaac Newton – scientist (see page 27) (see photograph)

James Stanhope – soldier and politician (see photograph)

Major General Charles George Gordon – soldier (see page 148)

Clement Attlee – politician (see page 356)

Ernest Bevin – politician (see page 360)

John Hunter – surgeon (see page 29)

## North and South Choir

Charles Darwin – scientist

Joseph Lister – surgeon (see page 269)

Benjamin Britten – composer

Henry Purcell – composer

William Wilberforce – reformer

Sir Thomas Foxwell Buxton – philanthropist

Baron Robert Clive – colonialist (see page 52)

Sir Noel Coward – actor and playwright

John Wesley – theologian (see page 221)

William Tyndale – theologian (see page 147)

## North Transept

Richard Cobden - politician (see page 350)
Robert Stewart, Viscount Castlereagh – politician
Henry John Temple, Viscount Palmerston – politician (see page 72)
William Pitt the Elder - politician (see page 216)
John Holles, Duke of Newcastle - politician
George Canning - politician (see page 63)
Benjamin Disraeli, Earl of Beaconsfield – politician (see page 69)
William Gladstone – politician (see page 173)
Sir Robert Peel - politician (see page 67)

## South Transept (Poets' Corner)

Geoffrey Chaucer - poet
W.H. Auden - poet
Robert Browning - poet
George Eliot - novelist
Dylan Thomas - poet
Henry James - novelist
George Gordon Byron - poet (see page 278)
Lewis Carroll - writer
Ben Jonson - dramatist and poet
John Milton - poet
Samuel Taylor Coleridge - poet
William Wordsworth - poet
Dr Samuel Johnson - writer and critic (see page 176)
Jane Austen - novelist
John Keats - poet
Percy Bysshe Shelley - poet
William Shakespeare - playwright and poet (see page 28)
Robert Burns - poet (see page 140)
Sir Henry Irving - actor (see page 26)
William Makepeace Thackeray - novelist
Charles Dickens - novelist (see page 50)
Thomas Hardy - novelist and poet

Sir Isaac Newton

Charles James Fox

Poet's Corner

Robert Peel

Stringer Lawrence

William Wilberforce

James Stanhope

# 13. Emmeline Pankhurst (1858-1928)

*Location: Victoria Tower Gardens*
*Sculptor: A.G. Walker*
*Material: Bronze*
*Date: 1930*

Emmeline Pankhurst was active in politics as a supporter of her radical husband Richard Pankhurst who campaigned among other things for votes for women. After the death of her husband Emmeline established the Women's Social and Political Union (WSPU) in 1903 with her eldest daughter Christabel to fight for women's right to vote.

The WSPU adopted the rallying cry 'deeds not words' and its members were increasingly prepared to damage property and obstruct the police for their cause with many suffragettes being imprisoned for their actions. The split in the suffragette movement came when Emmeline decided to support the government during the First World War. The WSPU slogan became "We have buried the hatchet, but we know where to find it." They even went so far as to hand out white feathers to civilian men not enlisted. The hatchet was never needed because immediately after the war the vote was given to women over 30 and in 1928 women were given the same voting rights as men.

Emmeline had moved to Canada after the war and only returned in 1926 when she attempted to get elected to parliament as a member of the Conservative party. When she died in 1928 the political establishment were keen to give her credit for her actions and this monument was unveiled next to parliament by Stanley Baldwin. Her daughter Christabel has a tablet next to her mother. There is currently a campaign to commemorate the more radical Sylvia Pankhurst who became estranged from her family.

# 14. The Burghers of Calais
*Location: Victoria Tower Gardens*
*Sculptor: Auguste Rodin*
*Material: Bronze*
*Date: 1915 (replica of an original of 1895)*

This is one of several copies of Rodin's famous sculpture – the original stands outside the town hall of Calais. The monument commemorates the terrible siege of Calais which lasted for over a year and ended in 1340 when the king of France abandoned the town with his army, leaving it to the mercy of the English king, Edward III. Edward was determined upon revenge having lost many men in the siege and demanded the complete subjugation of the town. Sir Walter Manny advised the king to show mercy and it was eventually agreed that six of the town's most important burghers should surrender themselves to the king with the keys to the city. Once the burghers presented themselves to the king he immediately ordered their execution, despite many of his own knights pleading for mercy. It was the queen that persuaded Edward to show leniency. The six were fed, clothed and returned safely to the town on her instruction.

## 15. Sir Thomas Fowell Buxton (1786-1845)

*Location: Victoria Tower Gardens*
*Sculptor: S.S. Teulon*
*Material: Stone (memorial fountain)*
*Date: 1865*

Thomas Buxton was the MP for Weymouth from 1818 and spent his energies attempting to reform the cruelty of that time. He was first a prison reformer, writing an influential book based on his investigations in Newgate Prison. He then attempted to abolish the death penalty and succeeded in restricting its use to only the most severe crimes. In 1825 Buxton took over the Society for the Mitigation and Gradual Abolition of Slavery after the retirement of William Wilberforce. His efforts were rewarded with the Slavery Abolition Act of 1833, but he continued to campaign for the improved implementation of the act until his death in February 1845. This memorial fountain was erected thanks to the efforts of his son Charles Buxton MP.

# The Mall

1) Royal Marines Memorial
2) Captain James Cook
3) The Police Memorial
4) South Africa Monument
5) Duke of York
6) Sir John Fox Burgoyne
7) John Laird Mair
8) Edward VII
9) Sir John Franklin
10) Sir Colin Campbell
11) Captain Robert Falcon Scott
12) Florence Nightingale
13) Sidney Herbert
14) The Guards Monument
15) King William III
16) George Nathaniel
17) General Charles André DeGaulle
18) George VI
19) Queen Alexandra
20) Queen Mary
21) Queen Victoria
22) Field Marshal Earl Alexander of Tunis

90

# The Mall

The Mall and Pall Mall were laid out in the 1660s during the Restoration as an area for London's rich and fashionable. The French croquet-like game of 'paille maille' was played here – after which both avenues are named. Until the game fell from favour The Mall was a place for courtship and flirtation. Jonathan Swift recorded in his diary of 1711, 'When I pass the Mall in the evening it is prodigious to see the number of ladies walking there':

When Lord Palmerston (see page 72) became prime minister in 1855 he would walk through this area on his way to Parliament passing only two monuments, to William III (1800) and the Duke of York (1833). Palmerston's leadership during the Crimean War contributed to the arrival of the Guards Monument of 1859 which commemorates that terrible conflagration. Between the death of Palmerston in 1865 and that of his successor, Disraeli, in 1881; Franklin, Campbell and Burgoyne were all to be commemorated on Waterloo Place. Baron Lawrence's monument was the last to be erected during Victoria's reign in 1882.

The Mall was redeveloped in 1903 and a new wave of memorials to the Royal Marines, the South African War, Queen Victoria and Captain Cook all found a place on the Mall. Pall Mall saw the arrival of Captain Scott and Florence Nightingale took her place next to the Guards Monument. An equestrian monument to Edward VII claimed a prime location on Waterloo Place in 1922 to be followed by an art deco fountain in memory of Queen Alexandra on Marlborough Road. The politician Lord Curzon was the last to find a place before the Second World War and since then a host of notables have joined him, culminating in the Police Memorial erected in 2005.

# 1. Royal Marines Memorial

*Location: The Mall (near Admiralty Arch), SW1*
*Sculptor: Adrian Jones, Sir Thomas Graham Jackson (ornamental panels)*
*Material: Bronze*
*Date: 1903*

This memorial commemorates the marines who fell in China during the Boxer Rebellion and in the South African Boer War. The main statue by Adrian Jones shows a defiant marine defending his injured comrade while the bronze reliefs by Sir Thomas Jackson illustrate battle scenes from the two wars. Both the Chinese Boxer Rebellion and The Boer War had recently been concluded when Admiralty Arch was being constructed and this helps explain the monument's subject matter at a time when the country was seeking assurance after the death of Queen Victoria. This monument to the courage of the marines remains long after the rights and wrongs of both imperial wars have become open to historical debate. It is worth noting that Field Marshal Smuts was an enemy during the Boer War, but later become a key ally during the Second World War. His monument stands in Parliament Square (see page 74).

## 2. Captain James Cook (1728-1779)
*Location: The Mall (near Admiralty Arch), SW1*
*Sculptor: Sir Thomas Brock*
*Material: Bronze*
*Date: 1914*

James Cook came from humble origins in
Yorkshire. As a young man he was fascinated by
the sea and took up work transporting coal in
large ships – called colliers – along the English
coast. Having received little formal education
Cook taught himself navigation, astronomy
and mathematics which were to make him
such a fine seaman and explorer. In 1755, on
the eve of the Seven Years War, he transferred
from the Merchant to the Royal Navy.

During the Seven Years War Cook's skills
as a draftsman were put to good use making maps of the coast of North America and
Canada. It was Cook who made the detailed
maps used by General Wolfe in his attack on the Plains of Abraham
(see page 342) in 1755. During the 1760's Captain Cook continued
to map Newfoundland and the Antarctic Circle, his maps being of
such accuracy that many were used until the 20th century. In 1768
he embarked on his first major voyage to the South Pacific on behalf
of the Royal Society. In just three years he became only the second
European to set foot in New Zealand, mapped the coastline and
became the first European to discover the east coast of Australia. In
June 1770 Cook's ship ran aground on the Great Barrier Reef where
the delay allowed the botanist Joseph Banks to collect a vast array of
the region's fauna and flora. During this voyage Cook prevented the
spread of scurvy by forcing his crew to take malt and was instrumental in the eradication of the disease.

Cook soon embarked on his second voyage between 1772-3 on which he disproved the existence of the mythical Terra Australis, discovered South Georgia and the South Sandwich Islands and circumnavigated the globe at a high southern latitude. Cook's voyage also successfully tested John Harrison's timekeeping instruments, which at last facilitated accurate measurement of longitude. Cook was offered retirement but instead embarked on his third and last voyage in 1776. He explored and mapped the coast from California all the way to the Bering Strait, on the way discovering what came to be known as Cook Inlet in Alaska. In 1779 Cook returned to Hawaii. Ill with a stomach upset and behaving erratically, Cook mishandled a dispute with the locals and was killed in the altercation that followed. This statue was erected next to Admiralty Arch, which was constructed at about the same time, and shows Cook in nautical attire. The inscription on this monument reads 'Circumnavigator of the globe, explorer of the Pacific Ocean, he laid the foundations of the British Empire in Australia and New Zealand...'

## 3. The Police Memorial
*Location: Corner of The Mall and
Horse Guards Parade, SW1
Sculptor: Sir Norman Foster and Per Arnoldi
Material: Marble and glass ◆ Date: 2005*

Unveiled in 2005 by the Queen, this monument commemorates British police who have died in the course of their duties. The monument is an uncompromisingly modern design consisting of a glass obelisk at the centre of a fountain alongside a black marble square structure which displays a book containing the names of 1,600 fallen officers. The memorial was conceived by the director Michael Winner, best known for his *Death Wish* films starring Charles Bronson.

# 4. South Africa Monument

*Location: The Mall, SW1*
*Sculptor: Robert Colton*
*Material: Bronze and stone*
*Date: 1910*

This monument is the only one specifically to the Boer War to be found in London. The South African War (or Second Boer War) was fought between the British Empire and the two independent republics of the Orange Free State and the Transvaal Republic. The war was fought over access to the gold discovered in these territories and the rights of the British prospectors who had flooded into the area seeking their fortune. The British were confident of victory and the Cape Colony governor, Sir Alfred Milner, held the ambition of securing a Cape-to-Cairo British Colony.

The Boers were far more resilient than expected under the leadership of Louis Botha and Jan Smuts (see page 74) and although there were only 88,000 of them they initially made considerable headway against British forces in the first months of the war, besieging the British garrisons at Ladysmith, Mafeking and Kimberley. Reinforcements arrived in 1900 and made advances against the Boers, capturing Pretoria by June 1900. The Boers reverted to guerilla tactics and the British, under the command of Lord Kitchener (see page 55), responded with brutality, burning Boer farms and placing Boer women and children in concentration camps. The British response was widely criticised and in May 1902 the Treaty of Vereeniging was signed which ultimately led to self-government for the two republics in 1907. Several key figures of the 20th century were involved in the Second Boer War, among them Mahatma Gandhi, Robert Baden-Powell and Winston Churchill (see pages 247, 311 and 75).

## 5. Frederick Augustus, Duke of York and Albany (1763-1827)

*Location: Carlton Gardens, SW1*
*Sculptor: Sir Richard Westmacott* ◆ *Material: Bronze on stone column*
*Date: 1833*

George III's second and favourite son was created a duke by the age of 21 having already been promoted to high rank within the army. Frederick was involved in the Napoleonic Wars, commanding at the Flanders Campaigns (1793-98) and the invasion of Holland (1799), both of which were considered disasters. The campaign in Holland inspired the nursery rhyme 'The Grand Old Duke of York' which ridiculed his indecisiveness. Frederick's position was never questioned and despite his many failings he became Commander-in-Chief of the army in 1795. As a strategist and reformer the Duke proved a success, but in 1809 he was to lose this position because of a scandal. Frederick had an expensive mistress named Mary Anne Clarke but because of his debts was often not able to pay her allowance. In 1809 it was discovered that his mistress had received money from soldiers and civil servants in return for promotion by the Duke. Frederick renounced his mistress, but she threatened to publish his letters and in return received a generous pension. Clarke spent the rest of her life in France; her great-granddaughter was the author Daphne du Maurier who wrote her life story. Frederick briefly resigned while the scandal raged but was reinstated as Commander-in-Chief in 1811 and served in that position until his death in 1827. The grandeur of this monument can be explained by Frederick's close relationship with his equally profligate older brother, George IV (see page 14) – it was funded by stopping one day's wages from every soldier in the British army.

# 6. Field Marshal Sir John Fox Burgoyne (1782-1871)

*Location: Waterloo Place, SW1*
*Sculptor: Sir Joseph Edgar Boehm*
*Material: Bronze*
*Date: 1877*

John Fox Burgoyne was the illegitimate son of the famous soldier and playwright General John Burgoyne and the opera singer Susan Caulfield. He joined the army in 1798 as second lieutenant and fought alongside Wellington in the Pyrenees, later being posted to San Sebastian where he participated in the siege of Rosetta. In the final phase of the Napoleonic War in 1812 he fought under General Pakenham and took part in the Battle of New Orleans. Burgoyne was responsible for providing relief to the starving during the Irish Potato Famine. He later played a key part in the Crimean War, assisting Turkish fortification and participating in the siege of Sevastopol. He retired as field marshal in 1868. Sir John led an exemplary but rather dull life in comparison to his dashing father - one of the few publications to bare his name was entitled *Treatise on the Blasting and Quarrying of Stone*.

# 7. John Laird Mair, 1st Baron Lawrence (1811-1879)

*Location: Waterloo Place, SW1*
*Sculptor: Sir Joseph Edgar Boehm*
*Material: Bronze*
*Date: 1882*

Lawrence spent his early years in Northern Ireland before travelling to India in 1829 with his older brother, Sir Henry Montgomery Lawrence, to serve as a colonial administrator. During the First Sikh War he organised the supply of British troops in the Punjab and later served under his brother as commissioner in the Jullundur district. In 1849, after the Second Sikh War, Lawrence worked as a member of the Punjab Board of Administration which carried through many significant reforms and helped limit the spread of mutiny in the region while it raged in other parts of India. As chief commissioner to the province, Lawrence became famous for his command of an army which recaptured Delhi after its fall to insurgents. For his actions he earned the subriquet 'Saviour of India'. After a brief return to England, Lawrence was sent back to India to serve as Viceroy between 1863 and 1869 where he acquired a reputation as a cautious administrator willing to make reform but determined to avoid involvement in the problems of neighbouring Afghanistan and Persia. He returned to England in 1869 and was raised to the peerage for his services. This statue is a replacement for a more bellicose original which depicted the administrator with a pen in one hand and a sword in the other bearing the inscription 'Will you be governed by the pen or the sword?'. After much criticism, Boehm replaced it with the more neutral work which stands in Waterloo Place today.

## 8. Edward VII (1841-1910)

*Location: Waterloo Place, SW1*
*Sculptor: Sir Bertram Mackennal*
*Material: Bronze*
*Date: 1922*

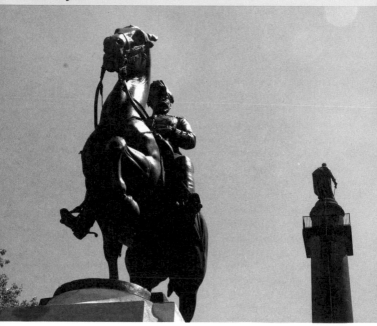

Edward was to have a difficult relationship with his parents whose seriousness and sense of propriety he did not share. Like George IV before him, Edward was to spend most of his adult life waiting to inherit the throne and like George he used this time to indulge in all manner of hedonistic activities. Edward's affair with an Irish actress became a public scandal just before Prince Albert fell ill and his mother unreasonably considered this to be one of the reasons for his premature death. Edward married the beautiful Alexandra, eldest daughter of King Kristian IX of Denmark, in 1863 and they moved to Marlborough House, just a little further along Pall Mall (see page 113). Edward's happy marriage did not calm his appetites and he was involved in several public scandals, being subpoenaed in the Mordant divorce case of 1870 and the Tranby Croft case of 1891, which concerned a close friend of Edward's being accused of cheating at cards.

The British public enjoyed reading about the antics of the Prince of Wales and these scandals seemed to increase Edward's popularity. He certainly had a more deft touch with public relations than his mother and appreciated the need for the monarchy to use ceremony and pageant. He made friends with numerous business people and so blurred the distinctions in class and helped the social rise of many wealthy Jewish families. Against his mother's wishes he cultivated a friendship with Gladstone that was to bolster the royal family's popularity – both Edward and his son George (see page 81) were pall bearers at Gladstone's funeral.

Generally of a conservative disposition, his influence on government policy was limited but he is credited with some role in the Anglo-French *Entente Cordiale* and in the cooling of relations with Germany, partly because of his dislike for his cousin, Kaiser Wilhelm II. After years of royal sobriety, Edward's nine years as King were a time of pomp and ceremony which helped to strengthen the constitutional role of the monarchy. His death in 1910 was deeply mourned with an estimated two million people lining the streets for his funeral. The equestrian monument that stands in Waterloo Place bears very little resemblance to the real King, who was exceedingly fat and only came near horses when attending the races. There is a second monument to Edward on Whitechapel High Street (see page 355).

## 9. Sir John Franklin (1786-1847)

*Location: Waterloo Place, SW1*
*Sculptor: Matthew Noble*
*Material: Bronze*
*Date: 1866*

Like Captain Scott, Sir John Franklin was an explorer in the heroic British tradition and one best known for his disastrous last voyage. Franklin joined the navy at 14 and fought at Copenhagen and Trafalgar. After leaving the navy in 1815, Franklin was given command of his first Arctic expedition in 1819 which reached the Arctic coast in 1821 and successfully mapped over 500 miles of uncharted territory. The expedition encountered many problems and ten members of the crew died; the rest only survived with the help of native Inuit people. Franklin's second expedition to the Arctic in 1825 was much easier and he successfully mapped a further 500 miles of territory. He was knighted for his services in 1829.

Franklin embarked on his last voyage to find the Northwest Passage in May 1845 with two ships, and a crew of 134. They were never seen again. As many as 40 ships searched for Franklin and his crew between 1848 and 1859 and over the years more men sacrificed their lives in the search than were lost in the expedition itself. Since then, enough wreckage, notes and bodies have been found to establish that the ships were trapped in the ice for two years and the crew died on board ship or attempting to make their escape. It is also thought that the canned provisions on board gave the crew lead poisoning. Much of the expedition still remains in the Arctic and expeditions continue to this day to find wreckage of the two fateful ships. Some of the remnants can be seen at the National Maritime Museum.

# 10. Field Marshal Sir Colin Campbell, 1st Baron Clyde (1792-1863)

*Location: Waterloo Place, SW1*
*Sculptor: Carlo Marochetti* ◆ *Material: Bronze*
*Date: 1867*

Campbell's father was a humble carpenter and he assumed his mother's maiden name when joining the army at the age of 16. Campbell soon saw action during the Napoleonic wars and was wounded several times, forcing his return to Britain where he was rewarded with promotion. So began his long career in the British army which included the quelling of the Demerara Insurrection (1823), the Chinese War (1842), and the Sikh War (1848-49). His role in the victory at Gujrat brought him considerable praise and he was made a KCB in 1849. During the Crimean War he accepted the command of the Highland Brigade, who distinguished themselves at the Battle of Alma and fought off the Russian attack at Balaklava. After the end of hostilities in the Crimea, Campbell had little time to rest on his laurels for he was sent by Lord Palmerston to quell the Indian Mutiny in July 1857, which he succeeded in doing with the capture of Lucknow in March 1858. On his return to England he was raised to the peerage and awarded a substantial pension and on his death buried in Westminster Abbey. His native town of Glasgow also has a statue in his honour.

# 11. Captain Robert Falcon Scott (1868-1912)

*Location: Waterloo Place, SW1*
*Sculptor: Lady Scott*
*Material: Bronze*
*Date: 1915*

Captain Scott became famous for his first expedition to the South Pole on the ship *Discovery* with Ernest Shackleton (see page 309) which got within 530 miles of the Pole. This monument is the work of Scott's widow and commemorates his last disastrous expedition to the South Pole which left in 1910. Scott was beaten to the Pole by a Norwegian expedition led by Amundsen, and his team were to die on their homeward journey. The bodies of Scott and two of his five fellow explorers were found in November 1912 along with Scott's journal which states "These rough notes and our dead bodies must tell the tale." Lady Scott was protective of her husband's reputation and edited his writings to present a more heroic image of the expedition. The reality was one of serious disagreements within the team and a lack of survival experience in Arctic conditions; Amundsen's men had gained weight during their expedition, Scott's men starved. The monument shows Scott in his full Arctic dress, but is intended as a memorial to all those that lost their lives in the fateful expedition.

## 12. Florence Nightingale (1820-1910)

*Location: Waterloo Place, SW1*
*Sculptor: Arthur Walker*
*Material: Bronze*
*Date: 1915*

Florence Nightingale proved an able student particularly gifted at mathematics and, against her wealthy parent's wishes, continued her studies to a very advanced level. In her late 20s, she determined to become a nurse, an occupation which had a very low status and no formal training in this country. Her wealth allowed her to travel widely and acquire nursing experience in Egypt and Germany.

When the Crimean War began in March 1854 reports soon came back of the poor medical care. The Secretary for War, Sir Sidney Herbert (see page opposite), was a friend of the Nightingale family and recruited Florence as a nursing administrator to improve the situation. When she arrived at the Scutari hospital in November 1854 injured soldiers were seven times more likely to die from disease in hospital than on the battlefield. Nightingale immediately improved the sanitary conditions and greatly increased the life expectancy of casualties. Using statistics that proved the need for better hygiene Nightingale campaigned for reform on her return to London and largely due to her efforts a Royal Commission was set up in 1857. Nightingale became the first female Fellow of the Royal Statistical Society in 1858. Her work was to have a major effect upon health care and was instrumental in improving the training and status of nurses. Nightingale outlived Queen Victoria and died at the age of 90.

## 13. Sidney Herbert, 1st Baron Herbert of Lea (1810-1861)

*Location: Waterloo Place, SW1*
*Sculptor: John Foley ◆ Material: Bronze*
*Date: 1857*

This statue first stood outside the old War Office on Pall Mall, but was moved to Waterloo Place in 1915 to stand among the other monuments associated with the Crimean War. Sidney Herbert was an aristocrat who entered parliament as a Conservative in 1832 and served as a minister under Robert Peel (see page 338). It was Herbert's mistress who leaked Robert Peel's change of mind over the Corn Laws in 1845 and so led to Peel's resignation. Herbert's indiscretion was overlooked and he served as Secretary of War in a number of Conservative administrations. When the Crimean War broke out he was quick to appoint his friend Florence Nightingale to improve the medical situation, but his general handling of the war was much criticised. Herbert was a conscientious minister and the pressure of his job began to take a toll on his health. He resigned from office in July 1861 and died just a month later. His death removed one of the key advocates for military reform and contributed to the stagnation of the British Army with the 2nd Duke of Cambridge as commander-in-chief (see page 40).

## 14. The Guards Monument

*Location: Waterloo Place, SW1*
*Sculptor: John Bell*
*Material: Bronze*
*Date: 1859*

The Crimean War was the most important and costly war of the Victorian era. This vast monument stands in commemoration of the 22,162 guardsmen who lost their lives in the conflict. The granite pedestal has three bronze figures of a Grenadier, a Fusilier and a Coldstream Guard. Upon a smaller block of granite at the back stand the actual broken Russian guns from Sevastopol. At the top of the monument is a bronze figure of Honour, with arms extended. The entire island is dedicated to the Crimean war, with statues of Florence Nightingale and Sidney Herbert standing either side of the main Guards Monument.

The war started in March 1854 when France and Britain declared war on Russia to defend the Ottoman Empire which had been the victim of Russian aggression for over a year. The Russians claimed to be acting to protect the Orthodox Christians living under Ottoman rule, but the long-term cause of the conflict was the evident decline of the Ottoman Empire. It was fear of Russian dominance in Eastern Europe and not a concern for justice that led Britain and France to go to the defence of the Turks.

In September 1854 Allied troops invaded the Crimea and began the siege of Sevastopol which was the main port for the Russian fleet. The Russians maintained a stiff resistance, sinking their ships and using the guns on land to beat off Allied attack. While the siege continued, several major battles were fought as the Russians attempted to liberate Sevastopol, including the Battle of Balaclava (October 1854) and the Battle of Inkerman (November 1854). The British public had expected an easy victory, but the war proved costly with more troops dying from disease and starvation than from battle. The Crimean was the first war to be influenced by the new medium of war reportage, with William Russell's reports for the *London Times* shocking the public with his accounts of the conditions and casualties. It was these revelations that encouraged Florence Nightingale (see page 104) and the less well known Mary Seacole to voyage to the Crimea and offer care to the wounded.

After two years of bloody and inconclusive war, Sevastopol finally fell to the Allied troops on 8th September 1855. The new Russian Emperor, Alexander II, agreed to sign a peace treaty at the Congress of Paris in 1856. The ultimate futility of the war was only proved in 1870 when Napoleon III fell from power and the new French Republic declined to uphold the Paris Treaty. The Russians were therefore able to establish a naval presence in the Mediterranean, the prevention of which had been the main achievement of the Paris Treaty. Key figures that fought in the Crimea include Sir Colin Campbell (see page 102) and the 2nd Duke of Cambridge (see page 40).

# 15. King William III (1650-1702)

*Location: St James's Square, SW1*
*Sculptor: John Bacon the Younger*
*Material: Bronze*
*Date: 1800*

The Dutch aristocrat William III deposed his father-in-law James II (see page 8) in what has become known as the Glorious Revolution, thus establishing Britain as a Protestant kingdom and ending James's often harsh attempt to catholicise his realm. After a brief interregnum the parliaments of England and Scotland recognised

108

James's eldest daughter Mary and her husband and cousin William as joint monarchs – although it was William that was to wield power. It was a compromise that divided the country's ruling class and in so doing created a two-party system of government, with Whigs supporting the monarchy and a sceptical Tory party introducing clauses to prevent William's heirs – should he re-marry – from claiming the throne.

William was less interested in establishing a royal dynasty than pursuing political power to confront the ambitions of France. His reign was entirely devoted to war with expansionist France, who had overrun his home country of Holland. To raise money to fund these wars William established the Bank of England and the National Debt and accepted regular parliaments to authorise further military funds. The Jacobite struggle to reclaim the throne also led to considerable bloodshed and bitterness, with the Battle of the Boyne still celebrated by the Protestants of Northern Ireland today (see William Duke of Cumberland on page 262). One consequence of William's reign was a considerable increase in the importation of Dutch Gin which was to have such a deleterious effect upon the poor of London as depicted in the pictures of Hogarth (see page 30). When later attempts were made to restrict the sale of gin there were riots. The loveless marriage of William and Mary produced no heir and after Mary's death in 1694 William reigned alone. His controversial rule ended in 1702 when he fell from his horse and caught a chill. It is said that the horse tripped on a molehill – Jacobites used to offer a toast to 'the little gentleman in the black velvet waistcoat'.

This fine equestrian monument was funded from the 1724 will of Samuel Travers, but was not erected for 80 years, the will having been lost. A grand monument to William also stands in the Bank of England which he helped to found, but this is not accessible to the public except on open days. There is another monument to him in the grounds of his former palace at St James's (see page 302). William was succeeded by his sister-in-law Anne who was the last of the Stuarts (see page63).

# 16. George Nathaniel, 1st Marquess Curzon of Kedleston (1859-1925)

*Location: Carlton Terrace, SW1*
*Sculptor: Sir Bertram Mackennal ◆ Material: Bronze*
*Date: 1931*

George Nathaniel Curzon lived for some time at number 1 Carlton Terrace just across from where his statue stands today. He was an aristocrat and a brilliant scholar, which helps explain his legendary conceit. His fellow students at Balliol College wrote of the young Curzon;

> *My name is George Nathaniel Curzon* .
> *I am a most superior person.*
> *My face is pink, my hair is sleek,*
> *I dine at Blenheim once a week.*

After his studies, Curzon travelled widely in the Middle-East and Asia and became a successful travel writer before entering politics as a Conservative MP and later as Viceroy of India (1899-1905). Curzon resigned as Viceroy after a dispute with Lord Kitchener (see page 55) and returned to England where he took his seat in the Lords and used his talents to fight against the suffragette movement and resist any reform of the second house. During the First World War, Curzon held a minor cabinet position but was promoted to Foreign Secretary in 1919 and held the post until 1924. His key achievement was the Treaty of Lausanne, negotiated with Turkey. Curzon was bitterly disappointed when passed over for the position of Prime Minister in 1924 in favour of Stanley Baldwin. He died in March 1925 having recently lost his job as Foreign Secretary. He was married twice and had three daughters, one of whom married the British fascist leader Oswald Mosley. His second daughter and his second wife were also to have affairs with Mosley.

110

# 17. General Charles André de Gaulle (1890-1970)

*Location: Carlton Terrace, SW1*
*Sculptor: Angela Conner*
*Material: Bronze*
*Date: 1994*

Charles de Gaulle began his career as a soldier and was decorated during the First World War and for his defence of the Polish nation against Soviets just after the war. He spent the interwar years campaigning for modernisation of the French army but his considerable height, arrogance and forceful personality made him many enemies and he was still only a colonel in 1939. De Gaulle was soon promoted to brigadier general, but the defeat of France was to mark the end of his military career and re-birth as a politician and figurehead of French resistance. The headquarters of the Free French was established in Carlton Terrace and de Gaulle gave his famous 'Appeal of June 18th' to the French people on BBC Radio. He moved his headquarters to Algiers in May 1943 and flew into Paris when France fell to the Allies to proclaim the continuation of the Third Republic. He was soon disillusioned with peacetime France and withdrew from politics in 1947. The collapse of the Fourth Republic under the pressure of the Algerian question saw de Gaulle's return. He became President in January 1959 and over the next ten years supervised the Independence of Algeria, established the Fifth Republic, withdrew from Nato and vetoed Britain joining the European Economic Union. De Gaulle's conservatism was increasingly against the spirit of the time, with the student riots of 1968 marking the effective end of his presidency. He resigned in 1969 and died suddenly in 1970. Unlike so many politicians who manage to enrich themselves while in office, de Gaulle died with considerable debts.

## 18. George VI (1895-1952)

*Location: Carlton Gardens, SW1*
*Sculptor: William Macmillan*
*Material: Stone*
*Date: 1955*

The second son of George V was a sickly youth neglected by his parents. The future George VI grew up in the shadow of his older and more glamorous brother and was never expected to take the throne. The prince served in the Royal Navy during the First World War and was made Duke of York in 1920. In the inter-war years he proved a conscientious member of the Royal family competing in the men's doubles at Wimbledon in 1926, visiting factories and mines and establishing the Duke of York's Camps which were a kind of summer camp for children of all classes. In all his work he was assisted by his young wife, Elizabeth Bowes-Lyon, with whom he had two daughters. Their happy life together was brought to an end with the abdication of Edward VIII and the Duke's unlooked-for coronation as George VI in December 1936. The new King was awkward and suffered from a stutter, so emphasis was placed on the 'family on the throne' which involved the Queen and the young princesses. George was in favour of Neville Chamberlain and his policy of Appeasement, and even offered to visit Hitler, Mussolini and Emperor Hirohito to try to avoid war. During the war George's political influence was limited but he and his family did serve a symbolic role for the country. The king's health had never been robust and in 1952 he died at the age of 56, ushering in the current reign of his daughter Queen Elizabeth. This statue shows the King in the uniform of Admiral of the Fleet and Garter robes.

## 19. Queen Alexandra (1844-1925)

*Location: Marlborough Road, SW1*
*Sculptor: Sir Alfred Gilbert*
*Material: Bronze*
*Date: 1926*

This art nouveau memorial stands in the wall of Marlborough House where Queen Alexandra lived as consort to Edward VII, although Sandringham in Norfolk was the main family residence. Alexandra was the daughter of King Christian IX of Denmark, and her sister married Tsar Alexander III of Russia. It was hoped that the beautiful Alexandra would help settle the young and reckless Prince Edward when they married in 1863. The marriage was generally happy and the couple had six children together, but this did not stop Edward having affairs with the actress Lillie Langtry, Winston Churchill's mother, Jennie Jerome, Alice Keppel and numerous others. Alexandra initially found Edward's philandering ways difficult to accept and they underwent a period of estrangement in the 1860s which was only ended when Alexandra nursed Edward after a serious illness in 1870. Alexandra eventually accepted her husband's infidelities and Alice Keppel was even allowed a place at Edward's deathbed in 1910. Alexandra remained a popular member of the Royal family until her death in 1925, founding Queen Alexandra's Nursing Corps during the Boer War and acting as a patron for many other charities. The sculptor, Sir Alfred Gilbert, is also responsible for Eros on Piccadilly (see page 33).

## 20. Queen Mary (1867-1953)

*Location: Marlborough Road, SW1*
*Sculptor: Sir William Reid Dick*
*Material: Slate Medallion*
*Date: 1967*

Mary Victoria of Treck was a German aristo-crat who married the future George V in 1893, having been previously engaged to the Duke of Clarence until his sudden death in 1892. She became the Queen consort in 1910, but was shy and avoided public attention. Queen Mary was known for her conservative dress sense and her interest in antiques and was notable for being the first Queen to visit the shops. Queen Mary was the Mother of Edward VIII and George VI and Grandmother of Queen Elizabeth.

## 21. Queen Victoria (1819-1901)

*Location: The Mall, SW1*
*Sculptor: Sir Thomas Brock, Sir Aston Webb (design)*
*Material: Marble*
*Date: 1911*

Princess Victoria of Kent was born to the Duke of Kent and Princess Victoria of Saxe-Coburge-Saalfield in May 1819, although there are some doubts about the Duke's involvement (see page 121). Following the death of William IV in June 1837, Victoria ascended to the thrown at the age of 18.

Queen Victoria's reign became synonymous with Britain's dominance and prosperity but the monarchy was far less powerful than during the reign of her grandfather, George III (see page 6). Prime Minister Lord Melbourne taught the young queen to question government policy but leave the final decision to politicians. She followed this advice throughout her long reign – even after her marriage to Prince Albert (see page 303) in 1840. The royal couple had little influence on government policy and were ignored on importan issues such as the Crimean War, when they favoured an alliance with Russia.

Following Prince Albert's death from typhoid in 1861, Victoria withdrew from public life and spent the rest of her life in mourning, although forming strong attachments to several of her male servants – most famously John Brown. Victoria was very susceptible to flattery and in the rivalry between Gladstone and Disraeli it was the later who won the Queen's favour by 'laying it on with a trowel'. Disraeli ingratiated himself further when he made Victoria Empress of India in 1876. Victoria died in 1901 having become Britain's longest serving monarch and establishing the form of modern British monarchy which survives to this day.

## 22. Field Marshal, 1st Earl Alexander of Tunis (1891-1969)

*Location: Guards Museum, Birdcage Walk, SW1*
*Sculptor: James Butler* ◆ *Material: Bronze*
*Date: 1985*

Harold Alexander was the third son of the 4th Earl of Caledon and educated at Harrow and Sandhurst. He was commissioned into the Irish Guards in 1911 and as part of the British Expeditionary Force (BEF) distinguished himself during the First World War, receiving the Military Cross in 1915, and by 1918 he was a Brigadier. By the start of the Second World War Alexander was a Major-General leading the withdrawal from Dunkirk and being the last British soldier to leave. He was then sent to command the withdrawal from Burma (see Field Marshal Slim page 45) and was made Commander-in-Chief in North Africa in August 1942, working with General Montgomery (see page 47) to secure the victory at El Alamein. In January 1943 he became deputy to Eisenhower and was put in command of the Allied Armies in Italy where he received the German surrender in April 1945. After the war, Alexander was created Viscount of Tunis for his command in Italy and North Africa and between 1946 and 1952 was a successful and popular Governor-General of Canada. His time as Minister of Defence in Churchill's government was less successful and he resigned from the position and from politics in 1954. This monument shows Alexander in full military dress, binoculars in hand, and stands within the courtyard of the Guards Museum.

# Embankment

# Embankment Part I
## Blackfriars to Waterloo

## Embankment Upper
1) Queen Victoria
2) City of London School
3) Queen Victoria (tablet)
4) Submarines Memorial
5) King's Reach
6) W.T. Stead
7) J.S. Mill
8) Lady Henry Somerset
9) William Edward Forster
10) Isambard Kingdom Brunel

# Embankment Part I: Blackfriars to Waterloo

It is fitting that Queen Victoria's monument is the first to be encountered on the journey west from Blackfriar's to Waterloo Bridge, because the roads, pathways and gardens along the route are all the product of her reign. It was Joseph Bazelgette (see page 143) who was given the task of improving London's decaying sewer system and as part of his plan built the Victoria, Albert and Chelsea Embankments between 1865 and 1870 under which vast sewer pipes carry the effluence of London out to sea. The inventive Victorians made good use of the reclaimed land to create wide roads, boulevards and several beautiful gardens.

The City of London School has Victorian statues to several great English men of former times – Bacon, Shakespeare, Milton and Newton – no doubt to inspire their young scholars. The other monuments in this area commemorate figures of the 18th and early 19th centuries, with the philosopher J. S. Mill and the engineer Brunel the only names that will be recognised by most people today. The tablet to W. T. Stead declares his virtues as a pioneering journalist, but in reality he was one of the first tabloid journalists who was imprisoned for fabricating a salacious story. There are several worthy but lesser figures commemorated here, including William Forster, who introduced state education and the philanthropist Lady Somerset. The Submarine Memorial, with its detailed reliefs and mosaic of anchors, is the most interesting of the monuments to be found on this stretch of the Embankment.

# 1. Queen Victoria (1819-1901)

*Location: New Bridge Street, EC4*
*Sculptor: C.B. Birch*
*Material: Bronze*
*Date: 1896*

This monument was erected towards the end of Victoria's reign, but depicts her in her regal prime with sceptre and orb. The monument is located at the start of the embankment which bears her name. A little further along the Embankment is a tablet commemorating the last visit of the Queen to the City of London in 1900 (see page 115 for further details about Queen Victoria).

# 2. City of London School

*Location: Victoria Embankment, EC4*
*Sculptor: J. Daymond and Son*
*Material: Stone*
*Date: 1882*

The City of London School has four monuments, to Francis Bacon (see page 195), William Shakespeare (see page 28), John Milton and Isaac Newton (see page 27) on the second floor of their grand Victorian building overlooking Blackfriars Bridge.

### 3. Victoria Tablet
*Location: Victoria Embankment, EC4*
*Sculptor: C. H. Mabey*
*Material: Marble Medallion*
*Date: 1902*

This stone was erected to commemorate Queen Victoria's last visit to the City of London in 1900. For a biography of Victoria see page 115.

### 4. Submarines Memorial
*Location: River Parapet, Victoria Embankment, WC2*
*Sculptor: F. Brook Hatch and A.H. Ryan Tenison*
*Material: Bronze*
*Date: 1922*

This monument was originally erected to commemorate those who lost their lives in Royal Navy submarines during the First World War. The First World War sadly was not the 'war to end all wars' and after 1945 further additions were made to recognise the sacrifice of submarine crews in the Second World War. The bronze relief lists the submarines lost in both wars and is flanked by the figures of Truth and Justice.

121

## 5. King's Reach
*Location: River Parapet,*
*Victoria Embankment, WC2*
*Material: Bronze plaque*
*Date: 1935*

This plaque was erected to commemorate the 25th anniversary of the accession to the throne of George V. For further information about George V see page 81.

# 6. W.T. Stead (1849-1912)

*Location: River Parapet, Victoria Embankment, WC2*
*Sculptor: Sir George Frampton*
*Material: Bronze plaque*
*Date: 1920*

Journalism was considered in the Victorian era to be a means of providing information, it was William Thomas Stead who identified the power of the press to shape public opinion and in so doing became the first truly modern journalist. As the son of a congregationalist minister, Stead was the first to realise that the moral indignation of the pulpit could be applied to the writing of newspaper copy, a practice that was most effective when combined with a good degree of sensationalism. In 1876, as editor of The Northern Echo, the young Stead was to employ his skills to engender righteous indignation against the Ottoman Turks for their brutality in Bulgaria. The long-term situation in Bulgaria was far from Stead's mind by the time he had become editor of the influential Pall Mall Gazette in 1883. It was in this position that Stead performed his most famous exploit – calling for the return of General Gordon (see page 148) to right the problems of the Sudan. It was Stead's campaign that persuaded Gladstone to appoint Gordon to a role for which he was unsuited and it was the disaster of this policy that led to the defeat of Gladstone's government in 1885. Stead eventually served three months in prison for publishing an entirely fictitious account of child prostitution which involved the actual kidnapping of a child in order to provide convincing pictures to accompany the story. On the anniversary of his imprisonment Stead would walk to work across Waterloo bridge in prison garb. He died on board the Titanic in 1912.

# 7. J. S. Mill (1806-1873)

*Location: Victoria Embankment – Temple Section, WC2*
*Sculptor: Thomas Woolner*
*Material: Bronze*
*Date: 1878*

John Stuart Mill received a rigorous education from his philosopher and historian father James Mill, and by the age of 12 had mastered Latin and Greek and was familiar with the works of classical philosophy. Jeremy Bentham, founder of Utilitarian philosophy, was Mill's godfather and it was under the influence of his writings that the young J. S. Mill became an enthusiastic advocate of the new science of morality, whose most popular principle was 'The greatest happiness for the greatest number'. The harsh rationalism of Mill's education was to launch him on a successful career as a thinker, essayist and reformer but had serious consequences for his emotional well-being. At the age of 21 Mill suffered a serious breakdown which he attributed to his upbringing and led to a change of mind and a more critical approach to the Utilitarian School. In the course of the next 50 years Mill was to write all manner of radical liberal works beginning with *A System of Logic* (1843) and ending with *The Subjection of Women* (1869). Mill's work *On Liberty* (1859) is probably the most famous and widely read of his books, setting out the liberal argument for limited state intervention in people's actions unless those actions are harmful to others. As well as a philosopher, Mill briefly became a radical MP for Westminster between 1865 and 1868, in which position he campaigned with Henry Fawcett (see page 135) for women's suffrage. Mill became the godfather of another famous philosopher, Bertrand Russell (see page 196).

124

## 8. Lady Henry Somerset (1851-1921)

*Location: Victoria Embankment,*
*Temple Section, WC2*
*Material: Bronze birdbath*
*Date: 1897*

This drinking fountain and birdbath was presented by the National British Women's Temperance Association in memory of its president, Lady Henry Somerset. Lady Somerset was born Isabel Cocks into an aristocratic family with an independent fortune. Her marriage to the impecunious Sir Henry Somerset was unhappy and short-lived. After the separation from her wayward husband Lady Somerset became a Methodist and devoted herself to the Temperance movement and other charitable causes.

# 9. William Edward Forster (1818-1886)

*Location: Victoria Embankment, Temple Section, WC2*
*Sculptor: H.R. Pinker*
*Material: Bronze*
*Date: 1890*

William Edward Forster was a Victorian philanthropist, reformer and politician. Forster received a Quaker education and as a young man became a vehement anti-slavery campaigner while training to be a lawyer. Forster took to business rather than law and made his fortune in the Bradford wool trade. He was expelled from the Quaker church when he married outside the religion in 1850 and then devoted much of his energy to the local Liberal Party. He was elected MP for Bradford in 1861 and was soon appointed to Gladstone's cabinet from which position he did much to carry the 1870 Education Act which was to ensure universal elementary education. Forster had a great interest in Irish politics and was appointed Chief Secretary for Ireland in 1880. He was a fierce supporter of the union and there were several assassination plots against him. When Gladstone changed his mind on home rule Forster resigned from office and became one of his most determined critics. This monument commemorates his role in education reform which was undoubtedly his greatest achievement.

# 10. Isambard Kingdom Brunel (1806-1859)

*Location: Victoria Embankment, Temple Section, WC2*
*Sculptor: Baron Carlo Marochetti, pedestal and surround Norman Shaw*
*Material: Bronze*
*Date: 1877*

Isambard Kingdom Brunel was born with engineering in his blood being the son of the famous French emigré engineer Marc Isambard Brunel. After a thorough scientific education, Isambard began work with his father on the ambitious Wapping to Rotherhithe Tunnel which encountered many problems and was only completed in 1843. Isambard won the competition to design the Clifton Suspension Bridge and soon after was appointed the chief engineer of the Great Western Railway, revolutionising rail travel with viaducts, bridges and wider gauge track which greatly increased the speed of rail travel. At the London end of the Western line he was given the task of designing a new station to rival that of Euston. Brunel's work can still be seen today in the vast glass edifice of Paddington Station. Among his other achievements were the design of a prefabricated 1,000 bed hospital for the Crimea and the design and building of three ships between 1837 and 1859, each larger and more revolutionary than the last. The construction of the last ship – The Great Eastern – on the banks of the Thames was fraught with financial and technical risks and the stress involved contributed to Brunel's fatal **stroke** on the ship's deck within days of its launch. Brunel's engineering achievements are some of the greatest of the Victorian era, the most impressive being the Clifton Suspension Bridge which was completed to Brunel's design after his death.

127

# Embankment Part II

## Waterloo Bridge to Westminster Bridge

1) Sir Walter Besant
2) Michael Faraday
3) Sir Arthur Seymour Sullivan
4) Herbert Francis Eaton
5) Robert Raikes
6) Henry Fawcett
7) Belgium War Monument
8) Cleopatra's Needle
9) Sir Wilfrid Lawson
10) Camel Corps
11) Robert Burns
12) York Watergate
13) William Schwenck Gilbert
14) Sir Joseph W. Bazalgette
15) Samuel Plimsoll
16) General Sir James Outram
17) Sir Henry Edward Bartle Frere
18) William Tyndale
19) General Charles G. Gordon
20) Lord Charles Portal
21) Fleet Air Arm Monument
22) Royal Air Force Memorial
23) Battle of Britain
24) Viscount Hugh Trenchard
25) Chindit Special Force Memorial
26) Queen Boudicca

128

# Embankment Part II: Waterloo Bridge to Westminster Bridge

It is impossible to feature the many monuments between Waterloo and Westminster Bridges without giving mention to the three Embankment gardens in and around which they stand. In the case of the Embankment Main Garden, monuments to Arthur Sullivan, Robert Raikes, Wilfred Lawson, Robert Burns and many others are randomly dotted about the garden with no discernable theme. Whitehall Garden is a more ordered affair, with only three monuments to General Outram, the colonial administrator Bartle Frere and the theologian William Tyndale taking central positions among the symmetrical flower beds. Whitehall Garden is the plainest and least attractive of the gardens, but its location behind the Ministry of Defence has given it a martial theme. General Gordon is the only 19th century military man to feature here, with Hugh Trenchard and Sir Charles Portal both playing a major role in the establishment of the Royal Air Force in the 20th century. Complementing these two men are monuments for The Royal Air Force and The Fleet Air Arm as well as one to the Chindit Special Forces which operated behind enemy lines in Burma during World War Two.

There are quite a number of monuments which stand outside the gardens and form a more direct route from Waterloo to Westminster Bridge. This more direct route begins with the now forgotten Victorian writer Sir Walter Besant and takes in Cleopatra's Needle, William Schwenck Gilbert (of Gilbert and Sullivan fame), the creator of the Embankment Sir Joseph Bazelgette and culminates with the enormous figure of Queen Boudicca astride her chariot and accompanied by her scantily clad daughters.

# 1. Sir Walter Besant (1836-1901)

*Location: Victoria Embankment, under Waterloo Bridge, WC2*
*Sculptor: Sir George Frampton*
*Material: Bronze bust*
*Date: 1902*

Sir Walter Besant is one of the famous names of the late-Victorian period consigned to the dustbin of history and his bestselling books are now only to be found in antiquarian bookshops. His early books were written with James Rice and were of a florid and romantic style with titles such as The Golden Butterfly (1876). After Rice's death in 1882, Besant continued to write books of a more serious nature and tackled social problems with titles such as All Sorts and Conditions of Men (1882) and Children of Gideon (1886) – which tackled the evils of child labour. He was also a scholarly historian who wrote many books about London's history, including the unfinished A Survey of London. Besant was an able campaigner who helped realise Barber Beaumont's dream of building a People's Palace on Mile End Road. The building was a great success as a leisure and educational centre for London's poor, but was burnt down in 1931. Besant was also instrumental in improving copyright law and was one of the founders of the Society of Authors in 1884. In 1895 he was knighted. The original of this bust was commissioned and erected in St Paul's Cathedral soon after Besant's death in 1901.

## 2. Michael Faraday (1791-1867)

*Location: Corner of Savoy Place, WC2*
*Sculptor: John Foley*
*Material: Bronze copy of a marble original*
*Date: 1988*

Michael Faraday was the son of a blacksmith who became the foremost scientist of his generation and discovered the principles of electro-magnetism. Faraday received very little formal education and became an apprentice bookbinder in London. The young Faraday attended the lectures of the chemist Humphry Davy and using his bookbinding skills bound the copied-out text into a fine volume which he sent to Davy along with a request for employment.

Faraday's efforts were successful and in 1813 he was employed as Davy's assistant. In this position Faraday travelled Europe and met many of the continent's leading scientists and returned in 1815 as a superintendent of the laboratories and mineral collection. Faraday published his first work on electromagnetic motors in 1821, but was unjustly accused of plagiarism which damaged his reputation. It was only after the death of Davy in 1829 that Faraday continued the work on electromagnetism that was to seal his reputation as the foremost scientist of his day. It was Faraday that established the principles behind electric motors, batteries, generators and transformers and created the words ion, cathode and anode which are still used today. At the time of his discoveries, people – including Gladstone – could not imagine what use could be made of electricity and yet within a few years of Faraday's death in 1867 the first electric lighting was being installed on London's streets. The bronze monument that stands outside the Institute of Electrical Engineers looking towards the Thames is a copy of John Foley's marble original.

## 3. Sir Arthur Seymour Sullivan (1842-1900)

*Location: Embankment Gardens, WC2*
*Sculptor: Sir William Goscombe John*
*Material: Bronze bust*
*Date: 1903*

Arthur S. Sullivan's father was the bandmaster at the Royal Military College. Young Arthur won several musical scholarships and attended the Royal Academy of Music, finishing his studies in Leipzig. He returned to England in 1861 and began his musical career which included composing *Onward Christian Soldiers* (1871) – his music was the first to be made into a phonograph record in England. Sullivan is best known for his 24 year partnership with librettist William S. Gilbert (see page 132) with whom he wrote 14 comic operettas. Many of the operettas were performed at the Savoy Theatre – built by the impresario Richard D'Oyly Carte. Relations between Gilbert and Sullivan were always fraught – Sullivan had grander ambitions than comic opera, ambitions that were bolstered by his knighthood in 1883. In this difficult atmosphere the two men produced some of their most popular works including *The Mikado* (1885) and *The Yeoman of the Guard* (1888), but in 1890 they separated acrimoniously. They reformed and produced three further operettas before Sullivan's premature death at the age of 58. Against his wishes he was buried in St Paul's Cathedral. The words of Gilbert from *The Yeoman of the Guard* are inscribed on Sullivan's bust;

*"Is life a boon?*
*If so, it must befall that Death,*
*when e'er he call,*
*must call too soon".*

## 4. Herbert Francis Eaton, 3rd Baron Cheylesmore (1848-1925)

*Location: Embankment Gardens, WC2*
*Sculptor: Sir Edwin Lutyens* ◆ *Material: Stone*
*Date: 1930*

Herbert Francis Eaton became the 3rd Baron Cheylesmore on the death of his brother in 1902. Herbert was educated at Eton and rose to the rank of major-general in the British Army. Although appearing a member of the establishment, his father – Henry William Eaton – was a humble omnibus driver who prospered after being offered a job in the city by one of his regular passengers impressed by his elegant appearance and manner. Henry Eaton's rise was spectacular, enabling him to acquire a fortune, an aristocratic title and his sons the requisite education of English aristocrats. It is said that after Henry Eaton's membership for White's Club was rejected he bought the club, increased the fees and still refused to become a member – a policy adopted by both his sons. Herbert Francis served on several committees concerning military reform and briefly as chairman of London County Council (1912-13). During the First World War he presided over several military courts one of which condemned the German spy Karl Loder to death. Herbert died in a motorcycle accident in 1925, becoming the first peer to die in such a manner.

## 5. Robert Raikes (1735-1811)

*Location: Embankment Gardens, WC2*
*Sculptor: Sir Thomas Brock*
*Material: Bronze*
*Date: 1880*

Robert Raikes inherited the Gloucester Journal from his father who had founded the paper in 1757. The young Raikes improved the paper and used his position as editor to pioneer the Sunday School movement in the 1780s. Raikes started his first Sunday School in Gloucester in 1780 and his reports of its progress helped the spread of the schools. In 1785 the Sunday School Society was established. At a time when there was very little education for the working-class, Sunday schools played an important educational role. Forty years after Raike's death, three-quarters of working-class children were attending Sunday School.

## 6. Henry Fawcett (1833-1884)
*Location: Embankment Gardens, WC2*
*Sculptor: Mary Grant*
*Material: Bronze medallion*
*Date: 1886*

Henry Fawcett was a draper's son who managed through his abilities to get a place at
Cambridge University. The young Henry
came under the influence of the radical political and economic thought of Jeremy Bentham and John Stuart Mill, but his plans for
a political career received a blow when he
was blinded by his father in a hunting accident. Henry Fawcett refused to be hindered
by his disability and at the age of 30 he was
appointed Professor of Political Economy at
Cambridge. In 1865 he became the Liberal
MP for Brighton joining a radical group of
MP's (including J.S.Mill) campaigning for
the vote for women. Fawcett had a romance with a prominent
suffragette, Elizabeth Garrett, and went on to marry her sister
Millicent in 1867. Henry Fawcett was appointed Post Master
General in 1880 by William Gladstone and it is in this capacity
that he really made his mark, introducing the parcel post, postal
orders, the sixpenny telegram and promoting the employment of
women within the Post Office. Fawcett became ill in 1882 and
after a brief recovery succumbed to pleurisy in 1884. Through
the work of his wife the name of Fawcett is commemorated in the
eponymous women's library and archive.

# 7. Belgium War Monument

*Location: Embankment, WC2*
*Sculptor: Sir Reginald Blomfield and Victor Rousseau*
*Material: Bronze*
*Date: 1920*

This monument was a gift from the Belgium government in thanks for Britain's help during the First World War. At the start of the war about 250,000 Belgians fled to this country.

# 8. Cleopatra's Needle

*Location: Embankment, WC2*
*Sculptor: Bronze Sphinxes by G.J. Vulliamy*
*Material: Pink granite*
*Date: 1878*

Many visitors assume Cleopatra's Needle is a Victorian copy, but it is in fact a genuine 68-foot high, 186 ton Egyptian obelisk dating from 1475 BC. The vast edifice was originally erected in Heliopolis for Pharaoh Thutmosis III, but was later moved to Alexandria. In 1819 the Turkish Viceroy of Egypt presented the now recumbent obelisk to the British. It remained in Alexandria for a further 58 years before a British engineer named John Dixon designed a huge iron pontoon to carry it by sea to England. The obelisk was envisaged as a monument to the British victory over Napoleon and money was raised by public subscription to fund the project. A storm off the Bay of Biscay cost the lives of six sailors but the Needle eventually reached its destination on the Thames Embankment in 1878 to be greeted by vast crowds. A plaque commemorating the sailors that drowned can be found at the base of the Needle with two very fine Victorian bronze sphinxes either side. Cleopatra's Needle is one of a trio of Egyptian obelisks that travelled to the west, the others can be found in Paris and New York.

# 9. Sir Wilfrid Lawson, 2nd Baronet (1829-1906)

*Location: Embankment Gardens, WC2*
*Sculptor: David McGill*
*Material: Bronze*
*Date: 1886*

The expression 'falling off the wagon' derives from the temperance wagons that would travel through the towns and cities of Britain advocating Christian sobriety. The politician Sir Wilfrid Lawson was one of the key figures in the temperance movement and spent much of his energies in parliament trying to pass a law that would allow residents to veto the granting of liquor licenses if they achieved a two-thirds majority. The law was never passed but Lawson's campaign helped to highlight the dangers of heavy alcohol consumption which were blighting many poor families. Anti-drug campaigns these days are largely run by those on the right of the political spectrum; Lawson was however a radical politician who believed in the disestablishment of the Church of England, abolition of the House of Lords and disarmament. In 1900 he lost his seat because of his determined opposition to the Boer War, only to return to parliament in 1903. Wilfrid Lawson died in 1906 having served over 40 years in parliament. The figures of Temperance, Peace, Charity and Fortitude that once adorned this monument were stolen in 1979.

## 10. Camel Corps

*Location: Embankment Main Gardens, WC2*
*Sculptor: Major Cecil Brown*
*Material: Bronze*
*Date: 1921*

This monument commemorates the short-lived Imperial Camel Corps who fought in Egypt, Sinai and Palestine between 1916 and 1918. The Camel Corps contained troops from many Commonwealth nations including Australia, New Zealand, Britain and India. On the side of the plinth is listed the many battles the Camel Corps were engaged in; 346 of their number died in the course of World War One. The sculptor of this monument was one of the surviving members.

# 11. Robert Burns (1759-1796)

*Location: Embankment Gardens, WC2*
*Sculptor:  Sir John Steel*
*Material: Bronze*
*Date: 1884*

Burns was the first of seven children of a poor Ayrshire farmer who became the Bard of Scotland and whose birthday of 25th January is celebrated with haggis, whisky and one of Burn's most famous poems 'Address to a haggis'.  Burns worked on his father's farm from childhood, but his father paid for a tutor to provide some education for his children and young Robert showed promise.  When his father died in 1784, Robert and his brother took over the running of the farm. A hard life at the plough was not suited to his nature and after a number of affairs the handsome young Robert was planning to flee to the West Indies.  It was the success of his first book of poetry that dissuaded him from his plans and led to a life roaming Scotland performing his poetry.  Burns did not earn enough as a poet and was forced to work as a tax collector to support his young wife and growing family while continuing to write in the evenings.  Burns became an increasingly troubled figure as his fame increased.  His radical politics, including open support for the French Revolution, alienated many of his less radical literary friends and his hedonistic habits began to seriously affect his health. When Burns suddenly died of heart disease at the age of 37 over 10,000 people attended his funeral. The monument that stands in Embankment Gardens was a gift from fellow Scott, John Gordon Crawford, and shows Burns in his romantic prime.

# 12. York Watergate

*Location: Embankment Gardens, WC2*
*Sculptor: Inigo Jones*
*Material: Stone*
*Date: 1625*

This stone tablet is all that remains of York House and marks the bank of the Thames before Joseph Bazelgette (see page 143) built the Embankment in the 1860s. York House was built in the early 17th century for the favourite and lover of James I, the 1st Duke of Buckingham – York Watergate still bears the Buckingham family arms. Buckingham continued to wield great power and influence after the death of James and the ascension to the throne of Charles I, but his charm at court was not matched by any political or military skill. Buckingham's clumsy diplomacy helped precipitate war with France and his leadership of the British fleet at La Rochelle in 1627 was to prove a disaster. He was assassinated by an infuriated former naval officer while reviewing the fleet in Portsmouth in 1728. The portrait of the Duke is one of the most impressive pictures in the National Portrait Gallery. York House was never fully completed and the Duke's son, George Villiers, sold it to developers on the condition that the new streets were named after him; hence Villiers, Duke, Buckingham and George Street.

# 13. William Schwenck Gilbert (1836-1911)

*Location: Embankment, WC2*
*Sculptor: Sir George Frampton*
*Material: Bronze plaque*
*Date: 1914*

William S. Gilbert began his professional career as a barrister, but supplemented his income with poetry published in a popular magazine. Gilbert began to acquire a reputation for his comic re-working of popular operas and became increasingly involved in the production of his work. He was a meticulous producer who changed the trend in British theatre by insisting that his actors follow his instructions and not play to the crowd. It was as a librettist with Arthur Sullivan and the producer Richard D'Oyly Carte that Gilbert achieved greatest success (see page 142). The relationship between the two men was a difficult one with numerous rows about whose work should take precedence. Sullivan's higher social status was further emphasized by his knighthood in 1883 which made their conflicts worse. It was only in 1907 – long after Sullivan's death – that Gilbert finally achieved equity when he was knighted for his work. Gilbert drowned after a heart attack in May 1911. It is worth noting that the difference between Gilbert and Sullivan's social status continued after their deaths – Sullivan commemorated with a bust, while Gilbert has this modest plaque.

## 14. Sir Joseph W. Bazalgette (1819-1891)

*Location: Northumberland Avenue, WC2*
*Sculptor: George Simonds*
*Material: Bronze bust*
*Date: 1899*

Joseph Bazalgette was one of the great Victorian engineers who transformed the landscape of London and eradicated the scourge of cholera with the building of a vast sewer system. Like his friend Brunel (see page 127), Bazalgette came from French stock and had an appetite for hard work. In 1856 he became the Chief Engineer of the Metropolitan Board of Works given the task of improving London's ramshackle sewer system. Between 1848 and 1854 over 30,000 Londoners died from cholera, but it was only when the raw effluent flowing into the Thames caused the 'Great Stink' of 1858 which affected Parliament that improvements were demanded. Bazalgette proved equal to the task, devising 82 miles of main sewers running along the Thames connected to over a thousand miles of smaller street sewers.

Bazalgette simultaneously made London a more attractive city – reclaiming vast tracts of land from the Thames to create the Victoria, Albert and Chelsea embankments below which run the main sewer pipes as well as new tube lines. The York Watergate (see page 141) marks the north bank of the Thames before the embankment was constructed. Many of the streets surrounding this bust are the work of Bazalgette including Northumberland Avenue and Charing Cross Road. Bazalgette was knighted for his work in 1875 having eradicated cholera from London. One of Joseph's great-great-grandsons is Peter Bazalgette, responsible for reality TV programmes such as Big Brother – pumping back into homes what his great-great-grandfather successfully removed.

# 15. Samuel Plimsoll (1824-1898)

*Location: Outside gates of Whitehall Gardens, SW1*
*Sculptor: Ferdinand V. Blundstone*
*Material: Bronze bust flanked by two figures*
*Date: 1929*

Samuel Plimsoll came from a working-class family and received only a rudimentary education. As a young man he worked in the coal industry, but failed in his business ventures and experienced several years of destitution. Plimsoll never forgot the suffering he endured in his youth and when he became MP for Derby in 1868 he embarked on a campaign to improve conditions for merchant seamen. The term 'coffin ships' was widely used at the time to describe unseaworthy vessels, overloaded with cargo. Plimsoll wrote a book entitled *Our Seamen* in 1873 outlining the injustice of a practice which benefited the heavily insured shipping companies but killed over 1,000 seamen every year. What Plimsoll lacked in his oratory and literary style he compensated for with passion and determination – he was even censured by parliament for using offensive language when Disraeli withdrew his promised bill of reform under pressure from the shipping companies. Public opinion was on Plimsoll's side and in 1875 the government was forced to pass the 'Unseaworthy Vessels Bill' and make amendments to existing law to improve the lot of merchant seamen. This monument was erected by the National Union of Seamen and the markings on the bow of ships to prevent overloading is called the Plimsoll Line in his memory.

# 16. General Sir James Outram, 1st Baronet (1803-1863)

*Location: Whitehall Gardens, WC2*
*Sculptor: Matthew Noble*
*Material: Bronze*
*Date: 1871*

James Outram was one of the great Victorian soldiers and spent most of his life in far flung parts of the British Empire. He departed for India as a skinny teenager in 1819 but soon acquired a reputation as a skilled and courageous wild game hunter and a natural leader of men. In 1838 he fought with distinction in the First Afghan war and the following year was promoted to Major and sent to the Indian province of Sind to serve under General Charles Napier (see page 22).

Outram strongly disagreed with Napier's heavy-handed approach but fought valiantly when the policy led to bloody conflict. This was not to be Outram's last conflict with authority and in 1856 he was removed from his responsibilities for too efficiently uncovering corruption in the Bombay Army. Outram was such a skilled soldier that within a year he was called back into service to assist Havelock (see page 18) in the relief of Lucknow. He again performed his duties with bravery and successfully held the city until the second relief force arrived. In 1858 Outram was made a baron and received the thanks of parliament. He returned to England in 1860, but his health was weakened by the rigors of war and he died in 1863. Outram gained the respect of all those who worked with him and acquired the nickname The Bayard of India after the medieval French knight renowned for his courage and honour.

# 17. Sir Henry Edward Bartle Frere (1815-1884)

*Location: Victoria Embankment Gardens, SW1*
*Sculptor: Sir Thomas Brock*
*Material: Bronze*
*Date: 1887*

Henry Frere was a colonial administrator who began his career in the Indian civil service in 1834. By 1850 Frere was appointed Chief Commissioner of the troubled Sind Province and in 1857 played a key role in suppressing the First War of Indian Independence – sending troops to Multan and the Punjab to prevent them being overrun. Frere was given a knighthood for his services and a place on the Viceroy Council in Calcutta. During the 1860s Frere adopted a paternalistic policy towards India – building colleges to educate the Indian elite and reversing the corrupt practices of the East India Company as First Governor of Bombay. Frere received considerable public criticism after the collapse of the Bombay Bank which hastened his returned to England in 1867. He maintained the trust of the crown and was appointed High Commissioner of South Africa in 1877. British rule in South Africa was facing difficulties and Frere made the situation worse – abandoning the enlightened policies of his time in India and confronting the Zulu tribes of Natal with brutal force. This heavy-handed approach was unpopular and Gladstone dismissed Frere as soon as he came into office in 1880. Frere came back to England and spent the last years of his life justifying his actions against critics which included Anthony Trollope. Frere is buried in St Paul's Cathedral and there is a mountain in Australia which bears his name.

# 18. William Tyndale (1484-1536)

*Location: Victoria Embankment Gardens, WC2*
*Sculptor: Sir Joseph Edgar Boehm*
*Material: Bronze*
*Date: 1884*

William Tyndale was a 16th-century priest and scholar who was the first person to translate the Bible from Latin and Hebrew into the English of his day. As a student at Cambridge Tyndale was strongly influenced by the teachings of Erasmus and became an advocate of the Reformation which questioned the teachings and practices of the Catholic Church. Tyndale's preaching soon caused controversy and in 1522 he was forced to flee Cambridge for London having been accused of heresy. He was by this stage convinced of the need for an English translation of the Bible so that it could be understood even by 'a boy that driveth the plough'. In London, Tyndale began his work but was soon forced to flee to Germany to evade his persecutors. It was in Cologne and later the town of Worms that Tyndale used the new process of printing to publish his work in 1525. Tyndale wrote commentaries on all aspects of scripture and it was his opposition to Henry VIII's divorce, and not his translation, that led the King to seek his arrest and return to England. Tynsdale was arrested in Antwerp and tried on the charge of heresy in 1536 and executed. Within a year his translation was being published in England with the encouragement of the King. Tyndale's work was the basis for the later King James Bible and has made a considerable contribution to the English language – introducing words such as 'scapegoat', 'atonement' and 'passover', and phrases such as 'the powers that be', 'my brother's keeper' and 'the salt of the earth'.

# 19. General Charles G. Gordon (1833-1885)

*Location: Whitehall Extension, SW1*
*Sculptor: Sir Hamo Thornycroft*
*Material: Bronze*
*Date: 1887 (Trafalgar Square) removed 1943, moved here 1953*

Charles G. Gordon was a career soldier who saw action in the Crimea and China during the Second Opium War where he participated in the destruction of the Summer Palace. In May 1862 he was assigned to strengthen Shanghai and did much with his native army to prevent the Taiping Rebellion. He returned to England in 1865 to great public acclaim and acquired the nick-name 'Chinese Gordon'. Britain was becoming increasingly involved in the political situation in Egypt and the Sudan and Gordon was appointed governor of the Sudanese province of Equatoria and did much to tackle the local slave trade and map the upper Nile. He returned to England in 1880 due to ill health, but was soon travelling in India, China and South Africa on colonial duties. Gordon was about to take an appointment as governor of the Congo on behalf of the Belgian government when events in Egypt and the Sudan reached crisis in 1884. Gordon's appointment owed much to the populist campaign of W. T. Stead (see page 123) and the indecisiveness of Gladstone's government. General Gordon returned to the Sudanese capital of Khartoum in February 1884 with a moral mission but no army to hold the Sudanese rebels at bay. He allowed the city to fall under siege rather than withdraw, as was his instruction. The siege lasted a year and ended with the overrunning of the city and the death of Gordon in January 1885, just two days before relief forces arrived. Gordon's death turned him into a national hero and contributed greatly to the end of Gladstone's administration in the election of 1885.

## 20. Lord Charles Portal,
## 1st Viscount Portal of Hungerford (1893-1971)
*Location: Whitehall Extension, SW1*
*Sculptor: Oscar Nemon*
*Material: Bronze ◆ Date: 1975*

Charles Portal was one of the key military figures of the Second World War but one largely
forgotten by the British public. Portal studied
at Oxford before joining the Royal Engineers
in August 1914. He flew many missions for
the Flying Corps and after the war joined the
newly established Royal Air Force. Portal was
Air Vice-Marshal by the start of World War
Two, but his intelligence and clear thinking
were soon to win him a place at Churchill's
side and promotion to Commander-in-Chief
of Bomber Command by April 1940. It
was Portal who adopted the policy of strategic bombing developed by Trenchard (see
page 152). This involved the bombing of German cities and towns
without any specific military target, with the intention of demoralis-
ing the enemy and limiting their ability to wage war. The British
bombing of Berlin on the 25th August 1940 was the first step in
the policy of 'Total War' which led to Germany's brutal retaliation
of the London Blitz in September 1940. Portal's determination to
win the war at any cost gained him promotion to Chief of Air Staff
and a knighthood. By early 1944 he wanted to reduce the role of
heavy bombing but was opposed by Arthur Harris (see page 172),
and Churchill supported the continuation of a policy which culmi-
nated in the bombing of Dresden, Berlin and other major cities in
early 1945. At the end of the war, Portal was rewarded with a baronetcy and worked as head of Atomic Energy and later the British
Aircraft Corporation. This monument by Oscar Nemon stands close
to his wartime offices.

## 21. Fleet Air Arm Monument

*Location: Victoria Embankment, SW1*
*Sculptor: James Butler*
*Material: Bronze*
*Date: 2000*

The Fleet Air Arm is that part of the Air Force which operates from aircraft carriers. During the Second World War it became the most important and effective part of the Royal Navy. This monument commemorates those who gave their lives in service of the Fleet Air Arm.

## 22. Royal Air Force Memorial

*Location: Victoria Embankment, SW1*
*Sculptor: Sir Reginald Blomfield and Sir William Reid Dick*
*Material: Bronze Eagle on stone column*
*Date: 1923*

This monument stands on the embankment and commemorates those that fought in the First World War in the Royal Flying Corps and the Royal Naval Air Service which amalgamated to become the Royal Air Force in 1918. The monument stands close to those for Trenchard and Portal both associated with the foundation of the modern Royal Air Force.

## 23. Battle of Britain

*Location: Victoria Embankment*
*Sculptor: Paul Day*
*Material: Granite and Bronze*
*Date: 2005*

This elaborate 25-metre-long monument is dedicated to the 2,936 airmen from 15 countries who fought to defend Britain from German air attack in what became known as the Battle of Britain. The battle is particularly important in British history because it represents a time when Britain stood alone against Germany after the fall of France in June 1940. On 10th July the battle began when the Luftwaffe launched 'Operation Eagle' with the intention of destroying Britain's air defences in preparation for a land invasion. The campaign started with attacks upon ports and convoys, but in August attention was turned to radar stations, airfields and aircraft factories in the south of England. The defence of Britain was directed by Sir Hugh Dowding (see page 175) who managed his limited resources with considerable care and economy – never committing more that half his aircraft to the defence of the south at any one time. By the end of August 1940 Dowding felt that the RAF were close to defeat and a serious disagreement broke out within Fighter Command as Sholto Douglas and Trafford Leigh-Mallory advocated more aggressive tactics. In the end the greatest ally of the British proved the erratic judgement of Hitler who, on the verge of victory, ordered the Luftwaffe to switch its attention to the bombing of civilian targets in retaliation for Charles Portal's bombing of Berlin. The start of the Blitz (see page 22) marked the effective end of the Battle of Britain. The words of Churchill are inscribed on this monument, 'Never in the field of human conflict was so much owed by so many to so few'.

# 24. Viscount Hugh Montague Trenchard (1873-1956)

*Location: Whitehall Extension, SW1*
*Sculptor: William Macmillan*
*Material: Bronze*
*Date: 1961*

Like his successor Charles Portal, Hugh Trenchard joined the army and only later transferred to the Flying Corps during the First World War. He was a straightforward character who acquired the nick name Boom Trenchard because of his loud voice. He became the first Chief of Staff of the Royal Air Force and was instrumental in its formation, in April 1918, from the disparate squadrons that existed at the time. Trenchard was one of the first to realise the importance of the Air Force in future conflicts and in the 1920s enthusiastically employed mustard gas dropped from aircraft to suppress Kurdish rebellion in Iraq and in Somaliland. Although some British soldiers and pilots were unhappy about the policy, one advocate was the young Arthur 'Bomber' Harris (see page 172). Trenchard was emboldened to devise the idea of 'strategic bombing', which justified the bombing of civilian areas to demoralise the enemy. Trenchard wrote a document advocating this policy and even suggesting that such a tactic could be used to suppress domestic industrial disputes. Churchill was alarmed by Trenchard's ideas and asked him never to put them in writing again. He resigned his position in 1929 and went onto become the Metropolitan Police Commissioner between 1931 and 1936 – thankfully avoiding the use of aircraft to deal with the capital's crime problem. Trenchard was too old to play any part in the Second World War, but lived to see many of his ideas put into practice by his successors.

# 25. Chindit Special Force Memorial
*Location: Whitehall Extension, SW1*
*Sculptor: David Price (architect), Frank Forster (sculptor)*
*Material: Bronze*
*Date: 1990*

This monument commemorates those special forces that fought the Japanese in Burma between 1943 and 1944 under the command of General Orde Wingate (1904-44). The bronze figure that sits upon the column is the Burmese mythological creature after which Wingate's force was named. Orde Wingate was a maverick who acquired experience of guerilla warfare in Palestine and Ethiopia before applying similar tactics behind enemy lines in Burma with his special force of British and Commonwealth soldiers. Both expeditions were incredibly costly in terms of lives and there is some argument as to their effectiveness when contrasted with the broader war being fought in Burma under General Slim (see page 45). What is certain is the morale boost that the Chindits' exploits gave to the Allied war effort, with four members of the multinational force receiving the Victoria Cross. The unit was soon disbanded after Orde Wingate's death in a plane crash in April 1944. Wingate is held in particularly high esteem in Israel for his efforts to form a Jewish state in the 1930s and wreaths from Jewish veteran groups are often to be found at the monument.

## 26. Queen Boudicca

*Location: Victoria Embankment, SW1*
*Sculptor: Thomas Thornycroft*
*Material: Bronze*
*Date: 1902*

Victoria Embankment begins on New Bridge Street with a monument of Queen Victoria and ends with an impressive statue to Boudicca with whom the 19th-century monarch was compared. Boudicca was the wife of Prasutagus – king of the Iceni Celtic tribe of Norfolk and Suffolk. When the Romans, under emperor Claudius, occupied Britain in AD43 Prastagus co-operated with them and prospered under the patronage of Rome. When Prasutagus died the Romans took the opportunity to overrun the Iceni – thrashing their queen and raping her daughters, but she was not the sort of woman to accept such abuse and rallied the Iceni and Trinovantian tribes to fight the Roman occupiers. Boudicca and her army succeeded initially as the greater part of the Roman army was away fighting the pagans in North Wales. The Roman settlements of St Albans, Colchester and London were razed to the ground by the Celtic army who slaughtered their inhabitants. The Ninth Legion, who came to their defence, were routed and the Britons briefly seemed in the ascendancy. Their success was short-lived, as the main Roman legions returned from Wales under the command of Suetonius Paullinus and crushed the Celtic army in battle. Boudicca killed herself to prevent being captured. The story of Boudicca is known through the writings of Roman historian Tacitus who is surprisingly even-handed in his account. Boudicca became a symbol of British strength during Victoria's reign and this monument was erected within a year of her death.

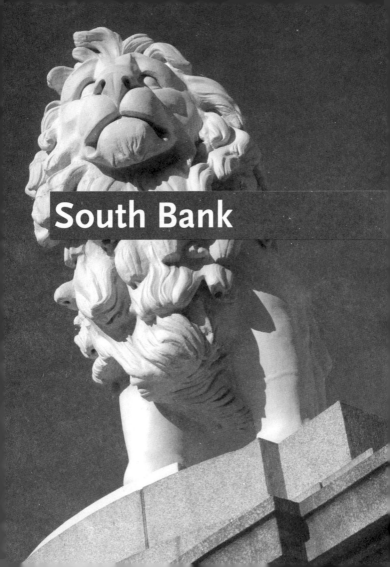

South Bank

1) Nelson Mandela
2) International Brigade
3) Coade Stone Lion
4) Edward VI
5) Edward VI
6) Queen Victoria
7) Florence Nightingale
8) Sir Robert Clayton

## South Bank

The south bank of the Thames from Waterloo Bridge to St Thomas's Hospital is one of the most attractive and popular pedestrian thoroughfares in London. This area was largely one of manufacturing and warehousing before the war but after heavy bombing during the Blitz many buildings, such as the old Lion Brewery, were demolished. Among the architecture that took their place was built the Royal Festival Hall which still stands here today.

The bust of Nelson Mandela is on the balcony of the Festival Hall building overlooking the Thames. The work is by Ian Walters and is well worth taking the steps to see. Further along, next to the old County Hall building and behind the London Eye, is another monument by Ian Walters to those British men and women who fought in the International Brigade. The two monuments were both commissioned and unveiled in 1985 as a last defiant gesture by the Greater London Council which resided in County Hall and was soon after abolished by the Conservative government. Further along is the Coade Stone Lion which once stood on the ramparts of the old Lion Brewery. Made in a long-closed factory close by, it is a last symbol of the south bank's industrial past.

The other monuments on this part of the south bank are concentrated in the grounds and buildings of St Thomas's Hospital and all those commemorated have some link with the place. Edward VI re-founded the hospital in 1552 and is remembered by two monuments in his honour. Robert Clayton funded the rebuilding of the hospital in the late 17th century, but his fine Grinling Gibbons statue now stands forgotten outside a disused building in the hospital grounds. Queen Victoria and Florence Nightingale were both patrons of St Thomas's and their monuments now stand in the modern surroundings of the hospital's central hall.

# 1. Nelson Mandela (1918-)

*Location: Riveside Walk close to the Royal Festival Hall, SE1*
*Sculptor: Ian Walters*
*Material: Bronze*
*Date: 1985*

Nelson Mandela is one of the few men to make the journey from terrorist/freedom fighter to respected elder statesman. He began his political career when a student at Fort Hare University from where he was expelled for his political activities; later he joined the African National Congress (ANC) while studying law in Johannesburg. He was further radicalised when the Afrikaaner-dominated National Party came to power in 1948 and introduced a system of racial discrimination known as apartheid. Mandela at first sought non-violent means to fight for black rights and with his friend Oliver Tambo provided legal aid to those suffering at the hands of the government. The authorities did not tolerate such interference and Mandela and his ANC colleagues were charged with treason and subjected to a long trial resulting in their acquittal in 1961. The pressures of the trial combined with the killing of protesters in what became known as the Sharpeville Massacre in 1960, persuaded Mandela that non-violent means would not bring an end to apartheid. From this point onwards he organised sabotage attacks upon military and government targets in which people were killed, and he continued to advocate such tactics after his arrest and imprisonment in August 1962.

Mandela came to represent the struggle against South Africa's apartheid system and became a hero to those who fought against it in the west – boycotting the country's products, disrupting sports events and protesting outside the South African Embassy in London. The political pressure continued to mount and in the spirit of change that also witnessed the demise of the Soviet Union, South Africa's President F.W. de Klerk unconditionally released Mandela in February 1990. The system of apartheid was later abolished in a referendum in March 1992. Mandela was awarded the Nobel Peace Prize (with de Klerk) in 1993 and became the country's first black president in a government of national unity in 1994. He retired from politics in 1999 but remains a respected international figure.

This imposing 8ft-high bust of Mandela is the work of the committed socialist sculptor Ian Walters, who is also responsible for the monuments to the International Brigade and Fenner Brockway (see pages 160 and 197). It was unveiled in October 1985 while Mandela was still serving the life sentence imposed on him in June 1964. At the time, Margaret Thatcher's Conservative government regarded Mandela as a terrorist and this monument was one of the last defiant gestures of the Labour-controlled Greater London Council (GLC), run by Ken Livingstone before its abolition in March 1986. These days very few people regard Mandela as a former terrorist or realise that this monument on the South Bank was once a matter for controversy.

## 2. The International Brigade

*Location: Jubilee Gardens, SE1*
*Sculptor: Ian Walters*
*Material: Bronze*
*Date: 1985*

The Spanish Civil War that raged between July 1936 and April 1939 was one that captured the interest of the world and divided opinion between those of the left and right. The war was between Spain's democratically elected Republican government and the Nationalist forces of General Francisco Franco who were supported by Fascist Italy and Nazi Germany. The Western governments did not come to the Republic's defence for fear of escalating the situation into a world war and it was left to the Soviet Union to provide support through its international Comintern organisation which established the International Brigade.

The International Brigade attracted nearly 60,000 volunteers from 55 countries to fight for the Republican cause including around 2,000 British volunteers. The many brave men and women that embarked on a clandestine journey across Europe to fight were inspired by a hatred of fascism but were not unified in their political allegiance – socialists and anarchists joining the largely Communist-run organisation. Their commitment to the cause was rewarded with harsh training, poor equipment and physical hardship, but they fought bravely alongside the Republican army against the better equipped and organised Nationalist forces.

The Brigade initially enjoyed some success with the 3,000 members of the 11th and 12th Brigade contributing to the successful defence of Madrid in November 1936. Divisions soon emerged within the Brigade as the Comintern attempted to keep control of the organisation and ousted rival organisations, leading to Republicans fighting each other in 1937. The Battle of Ebro in July 1938 was the last Republican offensive of the war as the Nationalist forces continued their advance. In September 1938 the International Brigade was disbanded by Spain's Republican government in an attempt to win the support of western democracies. The attempt failed and in April 1939, just five months before the start of the Second World War, Franco declared victory.

This monument is in memory of the British men and women who volunteered for the International Brigade, of whom 526 gave their lives in the struggle. The monument is a wonderful figurative piece by Ian Walters, who also made the bust of Mandela further along the south bank (see page 158). Many participants in the Spanish Civil War regarded it as part of the wider struggle against fascism and went on to fight bravely in the world war that followed. Among the British contingent was the author George Orwell who was driven out of the organisation by the Communists and came away from the battlefield with a more pessimistic view of politics which he expressed in his account *Homage to Catalonia*.

## 3. Coade Stone Lion

*Location: Westminster Bridge, SE1*
*Sculptor: W.F. Woodington*
*Material: Coade stone*
*Date: 1837 (moved here 1966)*

This is one of two lions that once stood upon the roof of the old Lion Brewery that was located next to Waterloo Bridge. The brewery was demolished in 1948 to make way for the the concrete edifice of the Royal Festival Hall. The lion was a feature of the Festival of Britain in 1951 but was unveiled on its present site, next to County Hall, in 1966.

The lion derives its name from the hard wearing artificial stone from which it is made. Coade stone was the invention of Mrs Eleanor Coade (1733-1821) who established her stone factory in Lambeth in 1769. The stone was a form of kiln-fired ceramic which proved very popular in public buildings such as Somerset House and the Royal Opera House. Mrs Coade had several untrustworthy business partners during her career and kept the exact formula and process for making her stone a closely guarded secret. She took the secret to her grave in 1821 and her factory, which stood remarkably close to where this lion stands today, subsequently closed in 1833. There have been several attempts to rediscover the Coade stone manufacturing process, but none have succeeded.

The lion wore a coat of red paint when it was a symbol of the Lion Brewery, but this has long ago been removed to reveal the wonderful and mysterious stone that lies beneath. The Coade stone lion has a prominent position looking across the Thames towards parliament, but the lion's genitals were considered too large and distracting and were reduced in size to keep the traffic flowing. The lion's more virile sibling now stands in Twickenham Rugby ground.

162

# 4. Edward VI (1537-1553)

*Location: St Thomas's Hospital, SE1*
*Sculptor: Thomas Cartwright*
*Material: Stone*
*Date: 1681 (moved here 1976)*

St Thomas's Hospital was established long before the reign of Edward VI, being founded
on Borough High Street in 1215 by the Bishop of Winchester. The hospital was run under
ecclesiastical governance and was therefore
closed when Henry VIII confiscated monas-
tic property during the English Reformation
(1538–41). It was left to his son and heir, the
young Edward VI, to refound the hospital in
1551 and provide it with a royal charter the
following year. The young king was stirred
into helping St Thomas's after a sermon by
the Bishop of London, his action being part of
a broader royal initiative which included the
founding of Christ's and Bridewell hospitals. Edward VI succeeded
to the throne at the age of ten and largely relied on Edward Seymour
and later John Dudley to carry out the business of government. The
founding of St Thomas's was one of the few things that bore the
mark of the young king's capacity to rule and it is fitting that two
monuments to Edward are to be found here.

163

## 5. Edward VI (1537-1553)
*Location: Central Hall, St Thomas's Hospital, SE1*
*Sculptor: Peter Scheemakers*
*Material: Bronze*
*Date: 1737*

This later monument to Edward VI has recently been moved inside the hospital and now resides in the north wing next to Florence Nightingale and Queen Victoria.

## 6. Queen Victoria (1819-1901)
*Location: Central Hall, St Thomas's Hospital, SE1*
*Sculptor: Matthew Noble*
*Material: Marble*
*Date: 1873 (presented to hospital 1898)*

Following St Thomas's move from Borough High Street, Queen Victoria laid the foundation stone of this building in 1868 and opened the hospital in 1871. The president of the hospital at the time, Sir John Musgrove, presented this monument to Victoria in 1873 and it was later given to the hospital by the company of Mercers on the 60th anniversary of the Queen's reign in 1898. There are several monuments to Victoria in London (see pages 115, 120 and 301).

# 7. Florence Nightingale (1820-1910)

*Location: Central Hall, St Thomas's Hospital, SE1*
*Sculptor: Frederick Mancini*
*Material: Metal composite*
*Date: 1958*

Florence Nightingale became involved with St Thomas's in 1859 and established her famous nursing school here a year later. The Florence Nightingale Museum is situated on the hospital site and contains many artefacts relating to her nursing career and time in the Crimea. The original bronze statue to Nightingale was unveiled in 1958 but was stolen in 1970. This replica is made of a less valuable composite metal and has recently been moved from the hospital entrance. It now stands within the main atrium of the hospital. The most prominent monument to Nightingale stands in Waterloo Place next to the Guards Memorial (see page 104).

# 8. Sir Robert Clayton (1629-1707)

*Location: St Thomas's Hospital, SE1*
*Sculptor: Grinling Gibbons*
*Material: Stone*
*Date: 1702 (moved here 1976)*

Robert Clayton was born in Nottingham, but came to London as an apprentice scrivener to his uncle. Scriveners were employed to transcribe legal and financial documents and were an essential part of London's commerce. It was while learning his trade that Clayton became friends with his fellow apprentice John Morris and the two men soon formed a business partnership which became the bank Clayton & Morris Co. Robert Clayton quickly made his fortune and in 1769 was awarded a baronetcy and in the same year had his portrait painted by Gainsborough. Clayton served as Lord Mayor in 1679 and as MP for the City of London from 1678 to 1681 and later allied himself to the Whig cause and the Hanoverian dynasty. He used his considerable fortune to advance many causes and one of his properties was the first meeting place for the London Institution for the Advancement of Literature. Clayton was also a patron of St Thomas's Hospital and largely paid for the hospital's rebuilding between 1693 and 1709. This rare example of a Grinling Gibbons statue was commissioned in 1702 to celebrate his great generosity and placed at the front of the hospital while Clayton was still alive. In the subsequent centuries the monument has moved several times and suffered wartime fire damage which turned the marble pink and destroyed both the statue's hands. Alabaster replacements were fitted during restoration work carried out in 1955, but these have since fallen off. Today Clayton's statue languishes outside an abandoned building at the back of the modern St Thomas's, unnoticed by most visitors to the hospital.

# Strand, Aldwych

# & Fleet Street

1) Count Peter of Savoy
2) Jewaharlal Nehru
3) Arthur Travers (Bomber) Harris
4) William Ewart Gladstone
5) Hugh Dowding, Air Chief Marshal
6) Dr Samuel Johnson
7) Robert Devereux, 2nd Earl of Essex
8) Temple Bar
9) Alfred Harmsworth, Lord Northcliffe
10) Queen Elizabeth I
11) John Wilkes
12) Robert Waithman
13) Thomas Power O'Connor
14) Edgar Wallace

# Strand, Aldwych & Fleet Street

The walk from Strand through Aldwych to Fleet Street is less than a mile in length but the monuments that stand along this ancient thoroughfare encompass almost 800 years of London's history. The monument to Count Peter of Savoy commemorates an ally of Henry III who, in 1263, built a grand palace on what is now the Strand. On Aldwych stand monuments to the first prime minister of India, Jewaharlal Nehru and two important figures from the Second World War; Hugh Dowding and Arthur 'Bomber' Harris. On a vast marble pillar towering above these two airmen stands one of the giants of the Victorian era – William Gladstone. Probably the greatest English man of letters, Samuel Johnson, can be found just behind St Clement Danes church where he once worshipped. Robert Devereux was a favourite of Queen Elizabeth I who fell from favour and was eventually executed for treason. His bust stands on the site of his former mansion. Within the boundaries of the old City of London, marked by Temple Bar, stands a monument to the queen that signed Devereux's death warrant. The monument to Elizabeth I is perhaps the oldest outdoor monument in London, dating from 1586 – although King Alfred's monument in Borough may be older (see page 359). Fleet Street was the birthplace of the printed word and all the monuments in this area have some association with newspapers. The press baron Lord Northcliffe has a bust alongside Queen Elizabeth at the entrance to St Dunstan's church, and further east is a monument to John Wilkes, who campaigned for press freedom. Robert Waithman was a Whig politician who, like Wilkes, fought for greater representation and press freedom and has a stone obelisk in his memory just off Fleet Street. The last two monuments in this area commemorate two of the 20th century's most famous journalists; T. P. O'Connor and Edgar Wallace.

# 1. Count Peter of Savoy (1203-1268)

*Location: The Savoy Hotel, Fleet Street, WC2*
*Sculptor: Frank Lynn Jenkins*
*Material: Bronze*
*Date: 1904*

The name of Savoy has been associated with this part of the Strand since 1241. Henry III married Eleanor of Provence in 1236 and her uncle, Peter of Savoy, was brought into alliance with the King, given the title Earl of Richmond and provided with land between the Strand and the Thames. Peter was to prove useful to the King in his battles with the barons led by Simon de Montfort. He did side with de Montfort for a brief period but in 1260 allied himself with the crown. On the death of his nephew Boniface in 1263, Peter assumed the title of Count of Savoy and in that same year built the Savoy Palace on the Strand. He died without an heir in 1268 and much of his estate passed to the crown. His grand palace was burnt down by Wat Tyler's men during the Peasant's Revolt of 1381 (see page 191). The Savoy hotel was built by Richard D'Oyly Carte to adjoin the Savoy Theatre in 1889 on the former site of the palace, and following the hotel's expansion between 1903-4 this gilt bronze statue of Count Peter was placed on the hotel's canopy where it has remained to this day.

## 2. Jawaharlal Nehru (1889-1964)

*Location: India Place, WC2*
*Sculptor:*
*Material: Bronze bust*
*Date:*

Jewaharlal Nehru was an English-educated lawyer who practised in India before dedicating himself to Indian independence after the Amritsar Massacre of 1919. Nehru became a follower and ally of Mahatma Gandhi (see page 247) and was elected President of the Congress Party in 1929 under Gandhi's leadership. In 1930 Nehru declared Indian Independence as the party's aspiration and spent many of the inter-war years in jail for his campaigns against British rule. When the Second World War started Nehru broke with Gandhi and advocated support for the British in return for independence. The offer was rejected and Nehru joined Gandhi's Quit India campaign which led to his arrest and imprisonment for the last two years of the war. The war's end saw Nehru's release and his ascendancy to the presidency of the Congress Party as Gandhi withdrew from direct participation in Indian politics. Nehru became Prime Minister during the difficult first years of Indian independence and presided over the country's partition, its first war with Pakistan (1947-9) and the military integration of the princely states. Nehru provided stablility for the fledgling Indian state after Gandhi's assassination and remained Prime Minister until his death from a heart attack in May 1964. He established a dynasty which was to see his formidable daughter, Indira Gandhi, become his successor and his grandson also led India. This bust stands just outside the High Commission of India.

171

## 3. Arthur Travers (Bomber) Harris (1892-1984)
*Location: Strand (west of St Clement Danes)*
*Sculptor: Faith Winter*
*Material: Bronze*
*Date: 1992*

Arthur Travers Harris joined the Royal Flying Corps in 1915 and became a pilot in the First World War at the head of 44 Squadron. In 1919 he was made a squadron leader in the newly formed Royal Air Force and saw action in India, Iraq and Iran. In Iraq Harris showed his preference for brutality by bombing villages to quell an Iraqi rebellion. Air Commodore Lionel Charlton resigned in protest after witnessing the casualties. Harris had no doubts about his policy and wrote of his actions, 'The Arab and Kurd now know what real bombing means, within 45 minutes a full-sized village can be practically wiped out'. His advocacy of a policy of strategic bombing developed by Hugh Trenchard (see page 152), and his lack of scruples was to earn Harris the nickname 'Bomber' or 'Butcher' within the RAF and the position of Air Vice Marshal by the start of World War Two. Harris served under Charles Portal (see page 149) as head of Bomber Command and worked unstintingly to cripple Germany's morale through strategic bombing of its major cities. As Allied victory became more certain it was Harris who successfully appealed to Churchill for the policy of strategic bombing to continue, culminating in the bombing of Dresden and other cities in February 1945. After the war Harris continued to defend his actions, but spent most of the post-war years living in South Africa. This monument was unveiled by the Queen Mother in 1992 amid controversy, with a crowd booing and throwing eggs in protest at the celebration of someone they considered a war criminal.

## 4. William Ewart Gladstone (1809-1898)

*Location: Strand (West of St Clement Danes)*
*Sculptor: Sir Hamo Thornycroft*
*Material: Bronze*
*Date: 1905*

William Gladstone was one of the great statesmen of the Victorian era and certainly the greatest reformer of the late-19th century. He was not born into radicalism, his father being a self-made Liverpool merchant and MP whose influence allowed his young son to enter parliament under the patronage of the Duke of Newcastle and to serve in the Conservative administration of Robert Peel (see page 67). The Repeal of the Corn Laws in 1846 divided the party, with Gladstone committed to free trade and Benjamin Disraeli (see 69) in favour of protectionism. Gladstone never forgave Disraeli for his betrayal of Peel and the genuine enmity between the two men was to shape the political landscape as these two great political figures rose to prominence. Gladstone became more radical with age and by 1859 he was Chancellor of the Exchequer in Palmerston's Liberal administration (see page 72). Palmerston was against parliamentary reform, but when he died in 1865 Gladstone became the driving force for a second reform bill which would extend the franchise and give more seats to urban areas. The bill that was passed in 1867 owed a great deal to Disraeli's change of heart on the matter, but the electorate realised it was the work of Gladstone and voted him into office in 1868.

Gladstone's first administration was to make many of the institutional changes necessary to accommodate the new democratic age, its greatest achievement being the 1870 Education Act (see Wil-

173

liam Forster page 126) and the introduction of the secret ballot. Gladstone was to lose power to his arch-rival Disraeli in 1874, but was to lead three further administrations, all of them continuing the process of parliamentary and social reform. Gladstone's moral crusading in domestic issues was always sure-footed, but the same approach to foreign policy was often to lead him into difficulties. His dispatch of General Gordon (see page 148) to Khartoum was to prove a disaster which ended his second administration, while his moral stand against the Turks and their treatment of Bulgarians was popular, but wrong-headed. Gladstone's career came to an end in March 1894 when his repeated attempts to introduce Home Rule for Ireland were defeated. He died in retirement four years later having established his reputation as one of the great political figures of his age. Like many moral and decent people, Gladstone had a reputation for being rather dull. He did spend his free time looking for prostitutes, but his only motive was to help them reform their ways. There is also a bronze monument to Gladstone in Bow Churchyard, erected in 1882 (see page 356).

# 5. Hugh Dowding, Air Chief Marshal (1882-1970)

*Location: Strand (west of St Clement Danes)*
*Sculptor: Faith Winter*
*Material: Bronze*
*Date: 1988*

Hugh Dowding started his career in the army but transferred to the Royal Flying Corps in 1913 and saw action in the First World War. During the war Dowding argued with General Hugh Trenchard over the issue of rest for pilots and was sent home, playing no further part in the conflict. Between the wars Dowding pursued his career in the newly formed Royal Air Force rising to the rank of Air-Marshal in 1933 and playing a key role in the development of the Spitfire and Hurricane fighter planes. He was also instrumental in promoting the use of radar systems which were to prove vital during the Second World War. When the war started it was Dowding's controversial decision to limit the use of fighter planes during the evacuation of Dunkirk in May 1940, that enabled the RAF to emerge victorious from the Battle of Britain (see page 151). Dowding's command during this key period of the war was vital in deterring Hitler from launching any further direct attack upon British soil, but Air Chief Marshal Portal (see page 149) was more critical of his decisions and Dowding was replaced in November 1941 by Vice-Marshal Sholto Douglas. Dowding retired from the RAF in July 1942 and was awarded a baronetcy in 1943. In his long years of retirement Dowding pursued rather unusual interests for a former Air Chief Marshal – writing books about spiritualism and fighting for the rights of animals. A lone Spitfire flew overhead when this monument was unveiled by the Queen Mother in October 1988.

# 6. Dr Samuel Johnson (1709-1784)

*Location: St Clement Danes, Strand, WC2*
*Sculptor: Percy Fitzgerald*
*Material: Stonebust*
*Date: 1910*

Samuel Johnson's father was a Lichfield book-seller and his son was to continue this fascination with words and books despite an early illness which caused the loss of one eye. As a young man Johnson attended Oxford University but could not afford to continue his studies. After some time as a teacher Johnson left for London in 1837 to make his fortune and found work as a writer of thinly disguised accounts of parliament (see John Wilkes on page 181), and other commissioned books. The work did not pay well and at one stage Johnson and his friend John Savage walked around St James's Square all night because they could not afford lodgings. Despite poverty, Johnson thrived in London society, embarking on a happy marriage with an older woman and enjoying some literary success. His greatest achievement was the compilation of the first comprehensive and detailed English language dictionary in 1755, which employed six scribes and took seven years to produce. Johnson was by then a widower and the most successful stage of his life was spent as a bachelor – working, drinking and socialising. He had a talent for friendship which is well documented by his friend and biographer James Boswell, who immortalised many of Johnson's most famous sayings. This monument was a gift from the sculptor and stands by St Clement Danes where Johnson worshipped. The inscription reads, 'Critic. Essayist. Philologist. Biographer. Wit. Poet. Moralist. Dramatist. Political Writer. Talker'. Dr Johnson's house – where he compiled his dictionary – is now a museum and is close by in Gough Square.

# 7. Robert Devereux, 2nd Earl of Essex (1567?-1601)

*Location: Devereux Inn, Devereux Court, WC2*
*Sculptor: Anonymous*
*Material: Stone bust*
*Date: 1676*

The Earl of Essex was one of the favourites of Queen Elizabeth and a patron of Francis Bacon (see page 177). Following the death of his father in 1576 his mother married the influential Earl of Leicester and it was he who arranged young Robert's education and his introduction at court. The handsome and tall young Devereux quickly became a favourite of Queen Elizabeth (see page 180) and established his reputation as a daring soldier on the battlefield against the French. Devereux could be a charming courtier and brave soldier but he lacked diplomacy and was prone to quarrels with his rivals which made enemies of Raleigh (see page 330), Blout and the Cecil family. Devereux's fall from grace began with his marriage to Sir Philip Sidney's widow, which displeased the Queen, and was completed with his disastrous expedition to Ireland in 1599. When Devereux and his army landed in Ireland he avoided battle with the Catholic rebellion and against orders made peace with the Earl of Tyron. Devereux was exiled from court in 1600 for his failure and embarked on a rash conspiracy with James VI of Scotland to overthrow the Queen. When arrested it was not his obvious enemies that worked for his conviction and execution, but his former friend Francis Bacon. Partly due to the efforts of Bacon, the 2nd Earl of Essex was executed for treason in February 1601. This bust is located in the area where the Earl's grand house once stood and in streets and courts which carry the family name.

177

## 8. Temple Bar

*Location: Fleet Street, EC4*
*Sculptor: Horace Jones (memorial),*
*Sir Joseph Boehm (Edward VII and other panels)*
*Material: Marble ◆ Date: 1880*

Temple Bar marks the boundary of the City of London and it is here that the Lord Mayor has greeted the monarch when visiting the City since the time of Elizabeth I. Temple Bar was a place where traitors' heads were displayed after execution – the last head to be displayed here being that of Jacobite Francis Towneley in 1746. This was also the site of a pillory where dissenters such as Titus Oates and Daniel Defoe were publicly humiliated. Although the original Temple Bar survived the Great Fire it was considered too modest for ceremonial purposes and a grand Portland stone gate was erected on the site in 1672 – reputedly to the design of Christopher Wren (see page 219). The gate was dismantled in January 1878 to improve the flow of traffic and a few years later this memorial by Horace Jones was placed on the site, with a statue to Edward VII and bronze reliefs by Sir Joseph Boehm added later. The old gate was bought by a wealthy brewer and reconstructed on his Hertfordshire estate, where it languished for many years until the City of London agreed to fund its restoration and return. The original gate now stands at the entrance to Paternoster Square next to St Paul's (see page 178).

# 9. Alfred Harmsworth, Lord Northcliffe (1865-1922)

*Location: St Dunstan-in-the-West, Fleet Street, EC4*
*Sculptor: Lady Scott*
*Material: Bronze bust*
*Date: 1930*

Alfred Harmsworth began his career as a writer for *Cycling News*, but soon went into newspaper publishing – launching a publication called *Answers to Correspondents* which proved a great success. Harmsworth changed British newspapers forever by introducing banner headlines, human interest stories, more photography and adopting an outraged populist style of writing. The formula was an instant success, transforming the *Evening News* within two years of buying it in 1894. In 1896 he launched the *Daily Mail* as a cheap condensed read based on US papers. He described his papers as standing 'for the power, the supremacy and the greatness of the British Empire' and this was best demonstrated in the build-up to the First World War. As early as 1897 the *Daily Mail* published a series of articles entitled 'Under the Iron Heel' which portrayed Germany as the great threat and campaigned for war. A rival paper wrote 'Next to the Kaiser, Lord Northcliffe has done more than any living man to bring about the war'. When the war started he used his papers to chastise those he considered responsible for the Allied casualties. Lord Kitchener (see page 179) was the main recipient of his criticism. Northcliffe was offered a place in cabinet by Lloyd George, but he declined the poisoned chalice. Harmsworth was made Lord Northcliffe in 1918 and his final campaign was against what he regarded as a Zionist plot within the British establishment. Suffering from stress, anxiety and paranoia he had a breakdown in 1922 and died in the same year.

# 10. Queen Elizabeth I (1533-1603)

*Location: St Dunstan-in-the-West, Fleet Street, EC4*
*Scuptor: William Kerwin*
*Material: Stone*
*Date: 1586*

Queen Elizabeth I was the last of the Tudor monarchs. She claimed the throne after the death of her half-sister Mary in 1558 and reigned for almost 45 years. Unlike Mary, Elizabeth had been brought up a Protestant and with the Act of Uniformity and Bill of Supremacy of 1559 effectively established the Protestant nature of her realm. This may explain the location of her monument in puritan London, originally located above Ludgate at the very entrance to the City. In the North of England there was considerable Catholic support and Elizabeth was to face what became known as the Northern Rebellion in 1569. Elizabeth's religion had consequences for her foreign policy leading to war with Catholic Spain in 1585. The defeat of the Spanish Armada and Elizabeth's speech to the troops at Tilbury became a landmark in English history, but the war continued against Spain and France for many more years. Relations with Ireland were also very difficult, with several rebellions leading to the eventual bloody suppression by Baron Mountjoy in 1601.

There were inevitable failings during Elizabeth's reign, particularly in the matter of state financing where Elizabeth resorted to the selling of monopolies to raise money, but her greatest achievement was to provide a stable commonwealth which allowed Britain's art and commerce to flourish. She died in February 1603 and the crown passed to her cousin James I. This small stone figure is considered the oldest outdoor monument in London and considerably pre-dates the church in which it stands.

## 11. John Wilkes (1727-1797)

*Location: Fetter Lane, EC4*
*Scuptor: James Butler*
*Material: Bronze*
*Date: 1988*

John Wilkes was one of the most influential radicals of his time and, as his monument proclaims, 'A champion of English Freedom'. As a young man he acquired the reputation as a rake but at the age of 30 became interested in politics and moderated his excesses becoming a member of Parliament for Aylesbury in 1757. In April 1763, Wilkes wrote an article which criticised George III's speech to parliament and the Treaty of Paris which it endorsed, claiming it was the work of the Earl of Bute. Wilkes was arrested for seditious libel and imprisoned for a week – being released because of public protest. In November he was shot and wounded in a duel with a friend of the King and fled to France in 1764 where he remained for four years. On his return he gained the seat for Middlesex, but was imprisoned which caused rioting on the streets of London. In the following years he was elected to several positions, including Lord Mayor of London, and was eventually permitted to sit in Parliament. Wilkes also successfully campaigned to report directly parliamentary speeches which was then prohibited. He continued to campaign on radical issues such as representative government and freedom of the press, but lost public sympathy when he headed the suppression of the Gordon Riots. He died in 1797 having withdrawn from politics for some years. Wilkes once wrote 'The liberty of the press is the birthright of a Briton'. This monument stands close to Fleet Street in recognition of his role in securing this birthright.

## 12. Robert Waithman (1764-1833)

*Location: Salisbury Square, EC4*
*Material: Stone*
*Date: 1833*

Robert Waithman was born in the Welsh town of Wrexham in 1764. His association with Wales was limited, for after the death of his father and remarriage of his mother he was sent to live with his uncle and was educated in Bath. At the age of 14 Waithman came to London to be apprenticed to a linen draper and by the age of 22 he had set up his own draper's shop on Fleet Street and proceeded to make his fortune. Although Waithman had little formal education he took a keen interest in politics and was an advocate of reform following the stagnation and repression that had held sway under Pitt the Younger (see page 259). Waithman was an honourable and popular man and was the MP for the City on several occasions and Mayor of London in 1823-4. He was an ally of Major John Cartwright (see page 250) and succeeded in promoting the cause of reform which resulted in the Parliamentary Reform Act passed just before Waithman's death in 1833. This stone obelisk was erected close to his shop soon after his death by his friends and bears the inscription 'The Friend of liberty in evil times.' He is buried nearby in St Bride's Church.

# 13. Thomas Power O'Connor (1848-1929)

*Location: 72 Fleet Street, EC4*
*Sculptor: F. Doyle-Jones*
*Material: Bronze bust*
*Date: 1934*

Thomas Power O'Connor was born in modest circumstances, being the son of a shopkeeper in Athlon, southern Ireland. O'Connor was a gifted student and gained a scholarship to Queen's College, Galway before embarking on a career in journalism and politics. He started his journalistic career in Dublin, but as a fluent speaker of French and German he was soon offered a job at the *Telegraph* when the Franco–Prussian War broke out in 1870. O'Connor – or T.P. as he was commonly known – became a popular figure on Fleet Street, but did not lose his interest in politics and the cause of Irish nationalism in which he was brought up. In 1880 he was elected MP for Galway as a representative of Parnell's Home Rule League and in 1885 was elected MP for Liverpool Scotland division due to Liverpool's large Irish immigrant population. O'Connor was to remain an MP for nearly 50 years as member of Parnell's party and, after the party's demise in 1918, as an independent. T.P. continued his career in journalism throughout his time in parliament, founding the then radical papers *The Star* (1887) and *The Sun* (1893) and *T.P's Weekly* (1902). As an old man T.P. became something of an establishment figure, returning to the *Telegraph* where he became a noted obituary writer and, as the longest serving MP, became Father of the House – a position he held until his own obituary was printed in November 1929. This bust stands opposite the Telegraph building where he worked and bears the inscription 'His pen could lay bare the bones of a book or the soul of a statesman in a few vivid lines'.

## 14. Edgar Wallace (1875-1932)

*Location: Ludgate Circus at the junction with Fleet Street, EC4*
*Sculptor: F. Doyle-Jones*
*Material: Bronze medallion*
*Date: 1934*

Edgar Wallace was a reckless young man who tried many jobs before enlisting in the army to escape his mounting gambling debts and unhappy engagement. He was sent to South Africa during the Second Boer War (see page 95) but left to become a war correspondent for the *Daily Mail* in 1898 and later the editor of the *Rand Daily Mail*. Wallace's returned to England with a new wife and a long list of creditors and was given a job at the *Daily Mail* by Alfred Harmsworth (see page 179).

While reporting the Russo-Japanese War Wallace began his first thriller *The Four Just Men*. The book was a great success but owing to a reckless competition which Wallace devised he lost money on the venture. Despite his debts Wallace had established his reputation and proceeded to write all kinds of thrillers from colonial tales such as *Sanders of the River* (1911) to further sequels in *The Four Just Men* series. The writing style and attitudes of Wallace's fiction were those of his Victorian childhood with decent English men fighting bravely against restless and scheming natives and untrustworthy continental types. Wallace's first marriage ended in 1918 and he married his young secretary in 1921 but his debts continued to mount. He moved to Hollywood to become a screenwriter, but died from complications resulting from diabetes soon after his arrival. Wallace's writing is now largely forgotten, but during the 1960s his racy plots and sharp dialogue were adapted for television and he is still a household name in Germany where many of these programmes were made.

Holborn

1) Sir Thomas Gresham
2) Holborn Viaduct Statues
3) Henry Fitz Eylwin
4) Sir William Walworth
5) Prince Albert
6) Charles Dickens
7) Prudential War Memorial
8) Royal Fusiliers, City of London Regiment
9) Holborn Bars
10) Francis Bacon (Viscount St Albans)
11) Bertrand Russell
12) Fenner Brockway
13) John Bunyan
14) John Hunter
15) Margaret Ethel MacDonald
16) William Fredrick Danvers Smith
17) Sir Thomas More

# Holborn

Contemporary Holborn consists largely of offices and shops with very few residents, but until the 17th century this area was dominated by the Holborn Road – an important thoroughfare into the City of London. Holborn Bars (see page 194) marks the entrance to the City of London where all visiting tradesmen were obliged to pay a toll before entering the City to sell their goods. Holborn was often busy with live cattle on their way for slaughter at Smithfield Market until the New Road (now Marylebone and Euston Roads) was built in 1756 to by-pass the inner city areas. Coaching inns of Holborn such as the Dagger, the Bull and Gate and Furnival's Inn were famous in their day but disappeared with the arrival of the railways which saw the end of the stagecoach. The gates and tolls that once protected the guilds of London have long disappeared, but the division between the old established City and the areas that were consumed by London's expansion are still in some way marked by the area's monuments.

Within the bounds of the City can be found two war memorials (see pages 193 and 194), an equestrian statue to Prince Albert (see page 192), several statues of former Lord Mayors and one to the financier Sir Thomas Gresham. Charles Dickens is the only radical to be commemorated within the boundary of the old City in Holborn and this is because he lived for a time at Furnival's Inn which once stood on the site of his memorial. The area features heavily in Great Expectations and in Nicholas Nickleby the eponymous hero leaves London via the stage coach at nearby Snow Hill. It is outside the City that more controversial figures such as the pacifist philosopher Bertrand Russell, the left-wing politician Fenner Brockway and the non-conformist preacher and writer John Bunyan are to be found.

# 1. Sir Thomas Gresham (1519-1579)

*Location: Gresham House, Holborn Viaduct, EC1*
*Sculptor: Henry Bursill*
*Material: Bronze*
*Date: 1868*

Thomas Gresham was born into a family of wealthy Norfolk merchants. Through family connections Gresham became a royal financial agent in Antwerp in 1551 and soon made a personal fortune and a reputation for financial acumen. It was Gresham that managed to raise the value of the Pound on the Antwerp market after its collapse in 1551 and so relieve many of Edward VI's debts. He became particularly important as financial advisor to Elizabeth I and spent some time as ambassador to Palma while maintaining his business interests in Antwerp. In 1567 Gresham moved to London to avoid the political instability in Holland prior to the Dutch Revolt and remained in the city until his sudden death in 1579. As he had no heir, he devoted his great fortune to public works such as Gresham College (founded by his uncle) and the Royal Exchange and is credited with having established Gresham's Law which states 'Bad money drives out good money'. The law applies to counterfeit or inferior coinage which will remain in circulations while good coinage is withdrawn by hoarders. It is certain that Gresham did not invent this law but merely adopted it. A further monument to Gresham stands in a niche of the Royal Exchange where it was placed in 1845.

## 2. Holborn Viaduct Statues

*Location: Holborn Viaduct, EC1*
*Sculptor: Henry Bursill, Farmer and Brindley*
*Material: Bronze*
*Date: 1868*

There are four bronze statues on Holborn Viaduct that were commissioned at the time of the viaduct's construction. Statues by Farmer and Brindley representing Commerce and Agriculture are on the north side, while on the south are two statues by Henry Bursill representing Fine Art and Science.

## 3. Henry Fitz Eylwin (d.1212)

*Location: Holborn Viaduct, EC1*
*Sculptor: Henry Bursill*
*Material: Stone*
*Date: 1868*

Henry Fitz Eylwin was a successful London draper who became the first Lord Mayor of London in 1192 and held the post until his death in 1212. Although Fitz Eylwin has drifted into the margins of history his appointment as the first mayor of the City of London does mark an important change in the status of the City. The granting to the City of a mayor with special rights and authority only superseded by the Crown was a major concession by Richard I to the powerful merchants of the capital, upon whom the king was dependent for revenue. Fitz Eylwin introduced the first building ordinances which specified the materials to be used and set building standards to minimise the spread of fire; prospective builders were obliged to present their plans for approval to the 'Fitzailwyn Assize'. Fitz Eylwin built his own city mansion in an area now occupied by Salters Hall Court and Oxford Court, near the Bank of England. It is said that he continued to trade as a draper while lord mayor and gave over several rooms within his house to the running of his business. Not long after Fitz Eylwin's death and partly due to his good governance, London was given further privileges under the City Charter of 1215 and a month later London's 'ancient liberties and free customs' were confirmed in the Magna Carta. This monument is a mid-Victorian creation and depicts Fitz Eylwin as a medieval knight, holding a vast battle axe, while in reality he was a prosperous draper more familiar with needle, thread and making money than with the weapons of medieval battle.

190

## 4. Sir William Walworth (d.1385)

*Location: Holborn Viaduct, EC1*
*Sculptor: Anonymous*
*Material: Stone*
*Date: 1868*

His family was from Durham but Sir William Walworth moved to London to follow the fishmonger trade and rose through the Fishmongers Guild to become Sheriff of London in 1370 and Lord Mayor in 1374. Walworth became famous for his actions during the Peasant's Revolt of 1381 when he raised a City bodyguard to defend London Bridge as the peasant armies of Kent and Essex marched on London with Wat Tyler as their leader. Walworth was forced to abandon the defence of the bridge when Tyler threatened to burn it down and as prisons were emptied and London's poor joined the rebel army the

14-year old King Richard was forced to give concessions to the rebels at Mile End. Some of the rebels dispersed having achieved what they wanted, but Tyler and his army remained in London settling old scores and waiting for further concessions. The armies met again at Smithfield when Walworth was so enraged by Tyler's arrogance towards the king that he pulled him from his horse and killed him with a dagger while Tyler's army looked on. Walworth was awarded a knighthood for his services and his actions have gone down in history. His dagger is kept at Fishmongers' Hall and at the east end of Mansion House there is a stained glass window depicting Tyler's killing. After serving two terms as lord mayor, Walworth died in 1385 and was buried in St Michael's Church, Crooked Lane. He was immortalised in verse by Richard Jonson in his 'Nine Worthies of London' published in 1392 and for some time remained a popular nursery rhyme hero in the same vein as Dick Whittington.

## 5. Prince Albert

*Location: Holborn Circus, EC1*
*Sculptor: Charles Bacon*
*Material: Bronze*
*Date: 1874*

This monument was presented to the City of London by Charles Oppenheim. The equestrian monument shows Prince Albert in field-marshal uniform and stands on an oblong plinth with plaques showing Britannia and the prince. He is kept company by bronze figures representing Commerce and Peace but the grandest monuments to Prince Albert are to be found either side of the Royal Albert Hall (see page 303).

## 6. Charles Dickens

*Location: Prudential Assurance Co., 142 Holborn Bars, EC1*
*Sculptor: Percy Fitzgerald*
*Material: Cupronised plaster*
*Date: 1907*

This bust stands on the site of the rooms Dickens lived in when he started his career as a writer. The area was the site of Furnival's Inn and which was populated by young lawyers and it is here that Dickens began one of his great works, *Pickwick Papers*. Dickens said in his will; 'I conjure my friends on no account to make me the subject of any monument, memorial, or testimonial whatever. I rest my claims to the remembrance of my country upon my published works'. There is also a bust of Dickens just off Parliament Square (see page 50).

# 7. Prudential Assurance War Memorial

*Location: Prudential Assurance Co., 142 Holborn Bars, EC1*
*Sculptor: F.V. Blunderstone*
*Material: Bronze*
*Date: 1922*

This fine monument was erected just after World War One to commemorate the 794 Prudential staff who lost their lives in the conflict. The main figures depict a fallen soldier being carried by two angels while four female figures at each corner of the pedestal hold symbols of the conflict; one holds a Howitzer machine gun, another a bi-plane. Close to the main monument are large bronze panels listing the names of the dead. The Prudential Company moved out of its Alfred Waterhouse-designed offices in the 1990s.

## 8. Royal Fusiliers, City of London Regiment

*Location: Holborn, EC1*
*Sculptor: Alfred Toft*
*Material: Stone*
*Date: 1922*

The Royal Fusiliers served in the First World War at Le Cateau, Mons, Marne, Aisne, Ypres, Somme, Arras, Passchendaele, Cambrai and Gallipoli. Members of the regiment became the first two soldiers to receive the Victoria Cross during the war. It was amalgamated in April 1968 with three other regiments to form the Royal Regiment of Fusiliers that has served in recent conflicts and took part in the invasion of Iraq in 2003. The Royal Fusiliers Museum is located in the Tower of London and gives a full account of the regiment's history.

## 9. Holborn Bars

*Location: The bottom of Gray's Inn Road, EC1*
*Sculptor:*
*Material: Stone*

Holborn Bars mark the entrance to the City of London where tolls were paid to enter the city with goods to trade. These gates to the city were originally established around 1130. The stone obelisks surmounted by silver griffins are a Victorian creation.

## 10. Francis Bacon, Viscount St Albans (1561-1626)

*Location: South Square, Gray's Inn, WC1*
*Sculptor: F.W. Pomeroy*
*Material: Coade Stone*
*Date: 1912*

Francis Bacon's reputation rests upon his achievements as a philosopher who advocated the use of scientific methods, observation and deduction to determine knowledge and truth. He argued against the abstract reasoning of Aristotle and in this way helped establish the philosophical ground upon which men such as Newton (see page 27) and Faraday (see page 131) could prosper. Bacon's life did not match the clarity and purity of his writings. His father was a successful member of the legal establishment and Francis was born within walking distance of this statue, but when his father died in 1579 his estate was divided between five brothers. Francis had extravagant tastes and despite becoming a barrister and member of court he was imprisoned briefly for debt in 1598. Ambition and lack of money led him to betray his friend and patron, the 2nd Earl of Essex (see page 177), in order to gain a position in court and even helped in the prosecution which led to the hapless earl's execution in 1601. Bacon became a favourite of James I and was made Lord Chancellor in 1618, but was dismissed for corruption in 1621. He was barred from office and spent the last years of his life writing. In 1626, while attempting to preserve the carcass of a chicken using snow – pre-empting Birdseye by several centuries – he contracted pneumonia and died. Bacon was also an enthusiastic gardener who did much work on the garden in which his monument stands, including the planting of the Catalpa Tree which can still be found here today. There is a smaller monument to Bacon on the 2nd floor of City of London School, Victoria Embankment.

# 11. Bertrand Russell, 3rd Earl Russell (1872-1970)

*Location: Red Lion Square, WC1*
*Sculptor: Marcelle Quinton*
*Material: Bronze*
*Date: 1980*

Bertrand Russell was a philosopher, logician, essayist and political campaigner who is considered – along with his colleague G.E. Moore – the founder of analytic philosophy. Russell's philosophy concerned itself with logic and reasoning and avoided the metaphysical concerns of continental philosophers such as Hegel and Nietzsche. As well as writing complicated philosophical texts, Russell also led a fascinating public and private life. He was a life-long pacifist who was dismissed from Trinity College in 1916 for his anti-war protests and imprisoned under the Defence of the Realm Act in 1918. He was also interested in education and, with his second wife, opened an experimental school in 1927, based on his unconventional libertarian ideas. In 1929 he wrote 'Marriage and Morals' which advocated sex before marriage, contraception and open marriages – his second marriage ended as both he and his wife put these ideas into practice. Despite a post being withheld from him in America because of his views, Russell continued to lecture and write and in 1950 won the Nobel prize for literature. He continued to campaign for peace and was the founding president of the Campaign for Nuclear Disarmament in 1958. Russell was imprisoned again for an illegal anti-nuclear protest in 1961 at the age of nearly 90 and continued to campaign against the Vietnam War throughout the final years of his life. He died in 1970 having been born in the middle of Victoria's reign and lived to see the end of the swinging 60s. This modest bust is close to Conway Hall where Russell often lectured.

## 12. Fenner Brockway, Baron Brockway (1888-1988)

*Location: Red Lion Square, WC1*
*Sculptor: Ian Walters*
*Material: Bronze*
*Date: 1985*

Fenner Brockway was a left-wing journalist and politician who started his political life as a liberal but became a socialist after interviewing Labour leader Keir Hardie. Like Bertrand Russell, Brockway was a pacifist who campaigned against the First World War and spent much of that time in prison. After the war Brockway became one of the founders of the India League, which campaigned for independence for India, and continued to write for left-wing publications as well as briefly becoming Labour MP for East Leyton. During the 1930s Brockway reconsidered his pacifist position and supported the International Brigade in the Spanish Civil War and Britain's involvement in the Second World War. After the war Brockway rejoined the Labour Party having spent many years as a member of the more left-wing Independent Labour Party. He won the seat of Eton and Slough in 1950 for Labour, but always remained on the left of the party, campaigning for independence for Britain's colonies, supporting CND and founding the charity War on Want. Brockway lost his seat in 1964 and accepted a life peerage from which position he offered critical support to the various Labour governments of the time. Brockway was 97 years old when this charming and animated monument was unveiled by Michael Foot.

197

# 13. John Bunyan (1628-1688)

*Location: Baptist Church House, Southampton Row, WC1*
*Sculptor: Richard Garbe*
*Material: Stone*
*Date: 1903*

John Bunyan was born into a tinker family in Bedfordshire at the high point of English puritanism. Bunyan was an extremely imaginative boy, who despite having very little formal education, transformed the religious fervour of the time into his own tales of fantasy. As a young man his fertile imagination and sensitivity were to lead him close to insanity. He fought in the parliamentary army during the English Civil War (1642-6), but his troubled mental state and religious fantasies continued. In 1653 he joined the Baptist Church and focused his imagination within an organised religion and proved himself a charismatic and powerful preacher. Charles II had ambitions to return Britain to the Catholic faith and Bunyan was prosecuted by the authorities in 1660 for preaching without a licence. He refused to renounce preaching and so spent 12 years in Bedford prison from where he started writing his famous religious allegorical tale *Pilgrim's Progress*. After a second period of imprisonment the book was completed and published to great acclaim. Bunyan's fame was to prevent his further prosecution by the authorities and he went on to write many more religious books and preach to vast audiences. Having contracted a cold on the way to London he died in 1688 and was buried at the non-conformist Bunhill Fields cemetery. This monument stands on the first floor of a Baptist Church and shows Bunyan holding a copy of his famous book.

## 14. John Hunter (1728-93)
*Location: Lincoln's Inn Fields, WC2*
*Sculptor: N.F. Boonham*
*Material: Bronze*
*Date: 1977*

See review on page 29.

## 15. Margaret Ethel MacDonald (1870 -1911)

*Location: Lincoln's Inn Fields, WC2*
*Sculptor: Richard Goulden*
*Material: Bronze*
*Date: 1914*

This monument commemorates the life of Margaret MacDonald, wife of the British Prime Minister Ramsey MacDonald. Margaret was the daughter of a doctor who became a socialist at the age of 20 and began working for various organisations concerned with improving the lot of the working-class and particularly women. She met Ramsey MacDonald in 1895 and they married in 1896. She bore six children but continued her work helping to establish trade schools for women and campaigning for women's suffrage. She died prematurely from blood poisoning in 1911 and this monument with the inscription 'She brought joy to those with whom she lived and worked' was erected soon after.

# 16. William Frederick Danvers Smith, 2nd Viscount of Hambleden (1868-1928)

*Location: Lincoln's Inn Fields, WC2*
*Sculptor: Plinth with bust removed*
*Material: Stone*

William Smith's father was the inheritor of the newspaper and bookselling business known as W.H. Smith and Son. By the time William assumed control it was a vast business empire which had prospered selling newspapers at the growing network of railway stations. This plinth stands close to where the business once had its offices in the Strand. William was the inheritor of a great fortune and the title of 2nd Viscount Hambleden, but he did work within the business to ensure its continued success. The bust which sat on this stone plinth and the entrepreneurial spirit which once drove the company have both disappeared, though the shops still prosper in high streets and railway stations around the country.

## 17. Sir Thomas More (1478-1535)

*Location: Carey Street, WC2*
*Sculptor: Robert Smith*
*Material: Stone*
*Date: 1866*

See review on page 322.

## 18. Pocahontas (1595-1617)

*Location: Formerly in Red Lion Square*
*Sculptor: David B. McFall*
*Date: 1955*
*Material: Bronze*

The statue of the native American princess Pocahontas was a feature of Red Lion Square for many years, having been commissioned by the map publisher Cassell's in 1955. The company, based in a former inn where Pocahontas had stayed in 1616, used the reclining figure of the princess as their logo. The sculpture was removed from the square when Cassell's moved and in 1996 it was sold at Christie's auction house and disappeared into private hands. For more information about Pocahontas' saving of John Smith refer to his monument in the City (page 217).

# The City

# London's Monuments • The City

1) Monument
2) Sir John Soane
3) The Duke of Wellington
4) William III
5) War Memorial to London Troops
6) Abraham Lincoln
7) James Henry Greathead
8) George Peabody
9) Paul Julius Reuter
10) Guildhall
11) Captain John Smith
12) Admiral Arthur Phillip
13) Sir Christopher Wren
14) John Wesley
15) Queen Anne
16) St Thomas Becket
17) Temple Bar
18) Blitz / Firefighters' Memorial
19) Postman's Park
20) Rowland Hill
21) Henry VIII
22) Sir William Wallace
23) Protestant Martyrs
24) Smithfield War Memorial
25) Golden Boy
26) Charles Lamb

# The City

Between Wren's monument to the Great Fire and the Golden Boy on Giltspur Street, where it is said the fire was extinguished, there are many monuments to admire. Bank is largely dominated by Victorian architecture and the monuments here are all dedicated to great Victorians – Wellington, Abraham Lincoln, James Greathead, George Peabody and Paul Reuter. The only exception is the architect Sir John Soane who was an old man when Victoria came to the throne in 1839

Further west towards St Paul's there are some fine monuments to be found in the grand medieval environs of the Guildhall and in and around the Church of St-Mary-le-Bow where the explorers Captain John Smith and Admiral Arthur Phillip are to be found. St Paul's Cathedral dominates the skyline and has around it monuments to the religious figures John Wesley and Thomas Becket, and the monarch Queen Anne whose reign witnessed the completion of the cathedral. It is appropriate that the memorial to the Blitz stands just opposite St Paul's whose survival came to symbolise the City's defiance of German bombing. Wren's Temple Bar, has recently been returned to the capital and now serves as a grand entrance to the modern shops and offices of Paternoster Square.

The inventor of the postage stamp, Rowland Hill, stands outside the old Post Office building and looks over Postman's Park. The park has a wall of painted tiles commemorating fatal acts of heroism by members of the public and was the inspiration of the sculptor George Watts.

Both William Wallace and the Protestant Martyrs are commemorated with tablets in the wall of St Bartholomew's Hospital close to where they were executed; the founder of the hospital, Henry VIII, has a monument above the entrance. On Giltspur Street can be found the Golden Boy statue and a bust of the Georgian writer and essayist Charles Lamb.

# 1. Monument

*Location: Monument Street and Fish Street Hill, EC2*
*Sculptor: Christopher Wren and Robert Hooke,*
*reliefs by Caius Gabriel Cibber*
*Material: Stone* ◆ *Date: 1677*

The Monument commemorates the Great Fire of London which started on the 2nd September 1666 and raged for four days, destroying two thirds of the City. The act of parliament which provided for the rebuilding of London also contained provision for a monument 'the better to preserve the memory of this dreadful Visitation'. The result was the work of Christopher Wren and Robert Hooke and consisted of a Doric order column made of Portland stone with a viewing tower. The tower is 202 feet tall which is the distance from the base of the monument to the shop on Pudding Lane where the fire started. There are panels at the base, the grandest of which is the West bas-relief by Cibber which gives an allegorical account of the City's reconstruction, with Charles II at its centre.

A French Catholic called Robert Hubert was quickly arrested, made to confess and hung at Tyburn and in 1681 the following words were added to the monument; 'But Popish frenzy, which wrought such horrors, is not yet quenched'. The inscription was removed in 1830 once the accidental nature of the fire was established. Another dark aspect of the monument's history was its use as a place of suicide, with a baker throwing himself from the viewing tower in 1788 and a further six people ending their lives in this bloody way before the balcony was enclosed in an iron cage in 1842. The Monument is still open to the public and the exhausting climb is worth it for the spectacular views of the City (phone 020 7626 2717 for further details).

## 2. Sir John Soane (1753-1837)

*Location: The Bank of England, Corner of Lothbury, EC2*
*Sculptor: Sir William Reid Dick*
*Material: Stone*
*Date: 1937*

Sir John Soane, the son of a bricklayer, was christened John Swan and became one of the most prominent neo-classical architects of his generation. Swan changed his name to Soane when he came to London to study at the Royal Academy in 1771. After studying in Italy for three years, Soane returned to England in 1780 and inherited a considerable fortune when he married in 1784.

His big break came when he became Surveyor of the Bank of England in 1788. He redesigned the Bank over many years and put his name to Dulwich College (1812), the Church of St Peter in Walworth (1823-25) and Holy Trinity on Marylebone Road (1828) during the next 40 years. Unfortunately much of his work has been lost and his greatest masterpiece, The Bank of England, was completely redeveloped by Sir Herbert Baker between 1921 and 1937. Some idea of Soane's original interior can be found at the Bank of England Museum where his Stock Office has been faithfully recreated. Sir John Soane is now best known for the museum bearing his name which is located in his former home at 12 Lincoln's Inn Fields and contains his huge collection of art and artifacts. One of the prize exhibits is the sarcophagus of Pharaoh Seti I, for which Soane held a three-day party when it arrived in 1825, with guests who included Samuel Taylor Coleridge. Soane donated his house and collection to the nation, partly to spite his surviving son whom he disliked.

## 3. Field Marshal Arthur Wellesley, 1st Duke of Wellington (1769-1852)

*Location: Royal Exchange, EC2*
*Sculptor: Chantrey ◆ Material: Bronze*
*Date: 1844*

The Duke of Wellington was born Arthur Wellesley, the fifth son of the 1st Earl of Mornington, who was a member of the Protestant squirearchy of Ireland. The young Arthur did not show any promise as a student at Eton and was without vocation until he was enlisted in the army. He spent several years as a dissolute young officer, but having been rejected in marriage he reformed his ways and began to seriously study military strategy. Wellesley first showed his talent in India during the Fourth Anglo-Mysore War (1799) and the Second Mahratta War (1803) and he returned to England in 1805 having become a Major-General and a Knight of the Bath. Wellesley's family was wealthy and he was able to buy a seat in Parliament and serve as Chief Secretary for Ireland before events on the continent forced his return to the battlefield against Napoleon's army.

Wellesley left Britain to command an expeditionary force against the French army in 1808 and was to spend the next six years fighting a series of key battles and sieges that were to drive the French army from the Iberian peninsular and culminate in the Battle of Toulouse in 1814 (see Cadiz Monument on page 56). By this time Wellesley had been awarded the title the Duke of Wellington and was appointed to attend the Congress of Vienna after Napoleon's surrender. The negotiations were cut short by Napoleon's escape and it was Wellington who led the allied forces that achieved the Emperor's ultimate defeat at Waterloo in June 1815.

Wellington returned to Britain as a hero and continued his career in politics, joining Lord Liverpool's government in 1819 and eventually becoming Prime Minister in 1828. Wellington arrived at Downing Street on his faithful horse Copenhagen but his wartime popularity was rapidly fading. He passed a Catholic Emancipation Act and Catholic Relief Act with the help of the Whigs and even fought a duel with Lord Winchilsea when the latter accused Wellington of treachery. Despite such reforms Wellington was a reactionary and refused to consider public demands for Parliamentary reform. The Duke became so reviled that his London home, Apsley House, was regularly stoned by angry mobs – he earned the epithet 'The Iron Duke' because of the iron shutters he installed rather than the strength of his character. His Tory administration fell in 1830 and was replaced by that of Earl Grey's Whigs, who passed the 1832 Parliamentary Reform Act in the face of Wellington's vehement opposition. Wellington continued in politics but was gradually superseded as leader by Robert Peel (see page 67) and retired from politics in 1846. He briefly returned to public life to organise an armed force to prevent insurrection during the revolutions of 1848, by which time he was nearly 80. Wellington was loved and hated in equal measure by his countrymen and is certainly one of the most celebrated figures in 19th century Britain with this statue and the one in Hyde Park Corner both erected within a few years of each other (see page 281). On his death in 1852, Wellington received a state funeral and was placed in a sarcophagus next to Nelson's in St Paul's Cathedral. Wellington is credited with the phrase 'publish and be damned', which was his response to the threat by the courtesan Harriette Wilson to reveal secrets of their affair. Wilson's memoir was a bestseller and revealed the Duke to be a jealous and boorish lover.

## 5. War Memorial to London Troops

*Location: Royal Exchange, EC2*
*Sculptor: Sir Aston Webb and Alfred Drury*
*Material: Bronze*
*Date: 1920*

## 6. Abraham Lincoln (1809-1865)

*Location: Inside Royal Exchange, EC2*
*Sculptor: Andrew O'Connor*
*Material: Stone bust*
*Date: 1930*

Located in the entrance to the Exchange shopping complex, this fine bust of Abraham Lincoln is easily missed. For more details of the 16th President of the United States see page 210.

# 7. James Henry Greathead (1844-1896)

*Location: Royal Exchange, EC2*
*Sculptor: James Butler RA*
*Material: Bronze*
*Date: 1994*

James Henry Greathead was one of the great Victorian engineers whose pioneering methods of tunnel construction enabled London's underground tube system to be built. Greathead was born in South Africa but came to England to study engineering. He began his career in 1864 working with engineer Peter W. Barlow and spent a brief period as assistant engineer on the Midland Railway. In 1869 Greathead and Barlow were appointed to engineer a train tunnel under the Thames from Tower Hill in the north to Vine Lane on the south bank. Greathead adapted the methods developed by Marc Brunel, involving a series of moving metal shields behind which the walls of the tunnel could be built. He employed hydraulic jacks and compressed air to greatly increase the rate of progress and the Tower Subway was opened in August 1870. The tunnel proved uneconomic and soon closed, but Greathead's skills as a tunnel engineer were widely recognised. He was appointed as the Chief Engineer responsible for building an underground railway line from Stockwell to the City of London which is now part of the Northern line. The underground was opened in 1890, by which time Greathead was already busy engineering the Central Line. He was only 52 and at the height of his powers when he died suddenly from stomach cancer. This monument was erected 98 years after Greathead's death and stands upon an airduct for the tube system which he did so much to build.

# 8. George Peabody (1795-1869)

*Location: Behind Royal Exchange, EC2*
*Sculptor: W.S. Story*
*Material: Bronze*
*Date: 1869*

George Peabody was born to a modest family in Massachusetts and left school at the age of 11 to help support his six siblings. Peabody fought against the British in the war of 1812 and afterwards established a wholesale business that made him a small fortune. He travelled to England in 1827 and over the next ten years built a successful banking business trading in currencies and American securities. In 1838 he intervened to stabilise US state bonds during a crisis. The states made good on their loans and Peabody's bonds made him a further fortune. In 1851 he profited from promoting American goods during the Great Exhibition and made further fortunes investing in US railways and trans-Atlantic cables.

Peabody was now a trusted figure and he came to the public's attention when he funded the search for the missing explorer Sir John Franklin (see page 212) in 1852. He was troubled by the poverty he saw and following the advice of Lord Shaftesbury (see page 33) the Peabody Donation Fund was established to build good cheap housing for the poor. The first Peabody estate was built on Commercial Street, Spitalfields in 1863 and many more estates were built over the years. In the last years of his life Peabody spent an estimated £8 million in his philanthropic work to improve housing and education in both America and his adopted home. This monument was unveiled by the Prince of Wales in July 1869, just a few months before Peabody's death. He was briefly laid to rest in Westminster Abbey before being returned with full honours to the United States.

# 9. Paul Julius Reuter (1816-1899)

*Location: Behind Royal Exchange, EC2*
*Sculptor: Michael Black*
*Material: Stone*
*Date: 1976*

The founder of Reuters News Agency was born in Germany, the son of a rabbi. He went to work as a clerk in his uncle's bank in Goettingen and soon became interested in the new technology of telegraphs to rapidly communicate important market information.

While living in London in October 1845 he converted to Christianity, changed his name and later married the daughter of a business colleague, Ida Magnus. Reuter and his wife established their first news agency in 1850 using carrier pigeons to bridge gaps in the telegram network and so provide information about the Paris stock market faster than by rail. Reuter's first London office was established close to this memorial in 1851.

Reuter's business maxim was 'follow the cable', meaning that wherever the cable network terminated a Reuters office was established to send and receive news. English papers were reluctant to use the service, but in 1858 *The Times* used a Reuters report of a speech by Napoleon III and Reuters became a recognised news source. It was Reuters that broke the news of Lincoln's assassination several hours before the ship carrying the news docked. In 1870, Reuter signed agreements with other agencies to provide the first worldwide news network, having begun his career using pigeons only 25 years before. In 1878, having been awarded a baronetcy, Reuter retired, leaving the business to his son. He died at his villa in the South of France at the turn of a century in which his company was to become the world's largest news agency.

Sir Winston Churchill

Horation Nelson

Wellington

William Beckford

Royal Fusiliers

William Pitt the Younger

William Pitt the Elder

# Guildhall EC2

*Gresham Street, EC2*
*Open: Monday-Friday 9.30-4pm*

The Guildhall dates from medieval times and is first mentioned in a property inventory of St Paul's in 1128. The building has been used as the venue for all manner of events, from grand receptions to famous trials such as those of Anne Askew (1546), Archbishop Cranmer (1563) and Henry Garnet (1605).

The Guildhall has not been without its own trials and tribulations. The Great Fire of 1666 destroyed the medieval roof and windows, but with the stone walls intact the building was quickly rebuilt, probably under the supervision of Wren. The roof and windows of the Guildhall were again destroyed by German bombing in December 1940. Again the building structure remained intact and after the war Sir Giles Gilbert Scott won the commission for the reconstruction. Scott's fine roof, with hidden steel supports and contemporary surrounding buildings, are still there today.

The Guildhall is a physical manifestation of over 800 years of local government in the City of London. It was the Common Council in the 18th century that proposed the erection of monuments to men of national importance and it is not surprising that the men they chose were figures of stout patriotism and conservative political views. If Bloomsbury can be regarded as a suitable place for the great Whig politician Charles James Fox, it is not surprising that the Guildhall should be the site of monuments to both Pitt the Elder and Younger who were the most conservative politicians of their day. As well as the two Pitts there are monuments to Horatio Nelson, Winston Churchill, the Duke of Wellington and a commemorative tablet to the City of London Royal Fusiliers who lost their lives in the Second South African War.

Two of the great men featured merit special attention as they are not featured anywhere else in the capital;

# William Beckford (1709-1770)

*Sculptor: Francis J. Moore*
*Date: 1772*
*Material: Stone*

Beckford was born in Jamaica into a plantation-owning family and continued their fortunes in the sugar trade. He came to London and enjoyed further success in ship-building and money-lending ventures. Beckword became an significant figure in the City of London and served as Lord Mayor twice as well as being an important ally of William Pitt the Elder in Parliament. Beckford married into aristocracy with the ambition of securing the fortunes and status of his family. His son, also called William, became a famous novelist and architect but was hopeless with money and managed to dissipate a great deal of the fortune left to him.

# William Pitt the Elder (1708-1778)

*Sculptor: John Bacon*
*Date: 1782*
*Material: Stone*

William Pitt the Elder dominated British politics for a generation, deriving his power and influence not from the crown but from the support of the people. Pitt entered politics in 1735 and formed a group of young Whigs, known as the 'Patriots', who were enemies of Sir Robert Walpole. Pitt did not gain office until he was appointed Paymaster General in 1746 establishing a reputation for honesty and probity. Pitt advocated war as a means of securing the country's economic interests and it was his sound leadership that secured Britain's victory during the Seven Years War (1754, 1756-1763). He resigned in dissaproval when the Treaty of Paris was signed and although he became prime minister again in 1766 he was never able to impose himself in peacetime as he had during a time of war. Pitt collapsed in the Lords in 1778 and died four days later. He created a legacy of aggressive foreign policy which was to be followed by his son (see page 259) and by later politicians such as Lord Palmerston.

## 11. Captain John Smith (1580-1631)

*Location: Outside St Mary-le-Bow Church, Cheapside, EC2*
*Sculptor: Charles Rennick*
*Material: Bronze*
*Date: 1960*

John Smith went to sea at 16 and fought as a mercenary against Spanish and Ottoman armies before escaping Turkish capture and travelling across Europe and North Africa. After his return to England, Smith was recruited by the Virginia Company and set sail from Blackwall in December 1606 with three ships to found a colony in America. Smith fell out with the captain and crew so badly during the voyage that he was imprisoned and destined to be executed. A letter from the Virginia Company appointing him one of the members of the colony's council saved his life.

The founding of Jamestown proved difficult and Smith was captured by one of the native tribes and only saved by the pleading of the chief's daughter, Pocahontas. Relations with the tribes and between the settlers soon deteriorated further and Smith returned to England in 1609, having been injured and fearful that some of the settlers were plotting to kill him. In 1614 he embarked on another voyage to America, sailing further north and producing detailed maps of the area he named New England. After a last unsuccessful voyage he settled in London and spent the rest of his life writing florid and self-serving accounts of his adventures. The interest in his stories was greatly increased when Pocahontas visited England in 1616. This statue is a copy of one that stands in Virginia and is close to St Sepulchre-without-Newgate, where he was laid to rest in 1631. The church has a plaque which reads 'Here lyes one conquered, that hath conquered Kings, Subdu'd large Territories, and done Things Which to the world impossible would seem'.

217

## 12. Admiral Arthur Phillip (1738-1814)

*Location: Inside St Mary-le-Bow Church, Cheapside, EC2*
*Sculptor: Charles Hartwell*
*Material: Bronze*
*Date: 1992*

Arthur Phillip joined the merchant navy at the age of 15 and was promoted to lieutenant during the Seven Years War. After intermittent commissions his appointment as captain of HMS Sirius, with responsibility for establishing a penal colony in New South Wales, was to make his name. He planned the expedition for over a year, but his requests for experienced farmers and craftsmen were refused and most of those who sailed from Portsmouth in May 1787 were convicts. The 11 ships followed Captain Cook's route (see page 93) and landed in Botany Bay in January 1788 before settling in a place they named Sydney Cove.

Phillips began a process of convict emancipation in return for hard work, saying 'In a new country there will be no slavery and hence no slaves'. He also attempted to treat the Aborigines fairly, although small pox brought by the settlers killed many of them.

Phillips proved himself as an administrator and by 1792 the colony had a small but growing farming community and a busy port. He left the colony in December 1792 due to ill health but recovered sufficiently to hold a series of commands during the Napoleonic Wars. This bust of the Admiral was first unveiled at St Mildred's Church, in 1932 and retrieved from the rubble when the church was destroyed during the Second World War. It spent time on the Bank of America building facing St Paul's before being restored and placed here in St Mary-le-Bow Church to commemorate the Australian Bicentenary in January 1998.

# 13. Sir Christopher Wren (1632-1723)

*Location: St Paul's Cathedral, Ludgate Hill, EC4*
*Architect: Sir Christopher Wren*
*Material: Stone*
*Date: 1675-1708*

St Paul's Cathedral is Christopher Wren's greatest masterpiece and – unlike many of his smaller churches – rooted in the Baroque and Renaissance tradition. A tablet near Wren's tomb within the Cathedral contains the words, 'Reader, if you seek his monument, look around you.' It is surprising that a statue of Wren does not exist in London, but as a statement of Wren's genius St Paul's is perhaps the greatest of all London's monuments. Christopher Wren was born into an established clerical family – his father was the Dean of Windsor and his uncle the Bishop of Norwich. He excelled at school and proved himself a brilliant student of the natural sciences at Wadham College, Oxford. He was appointed professor of astronomy at Gresham College in 1657 and conducted several experiments that influenced Isaac Newton's theory of gravity (see page 27).

Wren was one of the founding members of the Royal Academy in 1662, but at the age of 30 he had studied many subjects without finding one to occupy his attentions fully. It was architecture that was to capture his imagination and after designing the Sheldonian Theatre in Oxford, he studied architecture in earnest and travelled to Italy and France to educate himself in classical styles. After the Great Fire of London in September 1666 Wren became a key figure in planning the new city and was appointed Surveyor of Works responsible for the city's reconstruction in 1669. This herculean task was to occupy the rest of his professional life and create many buildings that are still standing today, including the Royal Exchange, the Royal Naval College, Drury Lane Theatre, Chelsea Hospital and the Monument to the Great Fire (see page 206). St Paul's Cathedral was the centre piece of the new City and from the laying of the foundation stone in 1675 it took Wren 35 years to complete his design which was finished in 1710. It is said that when Wren was too old to climb the 530 steps to the Golden Gallery he was carried up in a basket to survey the works.

Wren's achievements were never without difficulty and criticism and in his later years a younger generation resented his dominance and questioned his taste. He gradually lost control of the Fifty New Churches Commission established in 1711, and was dismissed from his post in 1718 in favour of William Benson, who proved a poor successor. When Wren died in 1723 he was the first person to be buried in St Paul's, followed by many of the country's most prominent men, including Nelson (see page 19) and Wellington (see page 208). There are also several major monuments within the Cathedral's walls, including one to Joshua Reynolds (see page 32).

# 14. John Wesley (1703-1791)

*Location: North side of St Paul's Churchyard, EC4*
*Sculptor: Samuel Manning and Son*
*Material: Bronze*
*Date: 1988 (based on an original marble statue of 1839)*

Raised in a pious Protestant household, John Wesley was one of 19 children of the rector of Epworth. It was at Oxford that Wesley formed a group of like-minded theologians called the 'Holy Club' which became known as the 'Methodists' for their adherence to a methodical religious life. Wesley defined a Methodist as 'one who loves the Lord his God with all his heart, and with all his soul' and avoided scriptural disagreements with the Church of England.

John Wesley failed to find a place within the church and left for the new colony of Georgia with his brother Charles in 1735. His preaching was not liked or fully understood by the settlers and after an unhappy love affair Wesley returned to England. He became certain of the injustice of slavery during the voyage and campaigned against it when he returned to Britain. Failing yet again to find a church, Wesley gave his first open-air sermon in April 1739. Wesley's call to challenge the evils of poverty and injustice drew large crowds and from 1739 a network of Methodist Societies sprang up around the country. In 1777 the City Road Methodist Chapel was built, by which time the society had become so accepted that George III gave navy timber to assist in the chapel's construction. Wesley spent the rest of his life leading the Methodist movement. He died at the age of 88 and was buried in the churchyard of the City Road Chapel where another monument to him stands (see page 353). Methodism, Pentecostalism and the Christian Movement are all based upon Wesley's teachings and are still active today.

## 15. Queen Anne (1665-1714)

*Location: Entrance to St Paul's Cathedral, EC4*
*Sculptor: Richard Belt (copy of original by Francis Bird erected in 1712)*
*Material: Stone*
*Date: 1886*

Queen Anne was the second daughter of James Duke of York, later James II (see page 8). Anne was brought up a strict Protestant and her faith was to become a major point of difference with her father, who publicly converted to Catholicism in 1673 and ascended to the throne in 1685. James II proved a despotic and unpopular King who was easily overthrown by his elder daughter Mary and her husband. Anne played no direct part in the events of 1688, but certainly knew of the plot and did nothing to prevent it.

Anne soon fell out with the royal couple and following the banning of her friends, the Churchills, from court for corresponding with the exiled King, she never spoke to her sister again. Anne's marriage to George of Denmark failed to produce an heir and she suffered 18 miscarriages, bearing only three children who died in childhood.

Anne was ill with gout and rheumatism and dependent on laudanum and alcohol when she was carried to her coronation in 1702, and spent her reign as an invalid. The original monument by Francis Bird was erected in 1712 to commemorate the completion of St Paul's, but the marble deteriorated over the years and was replaced by this Victorian copy in 1886. The original was saved by the writer Augustus Hare and now stands in St Leonard's-on-Sea. There is another monument to Queen Anne at Queen Anne's Gate (see page 63).

# 16. St Thomas Becket (1118-1170)

*Location: South side of St Paul's Cathedral, EC4*
*Sculptor: E. Bainbridge Copnall*
*Material: Stone*
*Date: 1973*

Thomas Becket received a sound clerical education before joining the staff of Theobald, the Archbishop of Canterbury. When Henry II came to the throne in 1155, determined to exert royal authority, Becket was appointed his Lord Chancellor. The two men became close friends and Becket proved himself a conscientious and able Chancellor. While serving the King Becket lived luxuriously and travelled with a vast retinue that rivalled that of his master. He is known to have led troops into battle against the French and was mentor to Henry's son.

Becket's relations with the King changed when he was appointed Archbishop of Canterbury in 1162. The King was soon angered by Becket's change of allegiance when his attempts to control clerical courts were rejected by Becket. Their differences came to a head at Clarendon Palace in January 1164 when Becket refused to accept the King's reforms and was forced to flee to France to avoid the King's wrath. He remained in exile for six years until a compromise was reached which allowed his return to Canterbury in December 1170. Becket soon disturbed the fragile peace by excommunicating several of the King's allies. Henry's words of rebuke were not a command for Becket's murder, but were enough to encourage four knights to slay Becket just a few weeks after his return to Canterbury. Becket was quickly canonized by Pope Alexander and his tomb became a popular place of pilgrimage until its destruction by Henry VIII. This modern sculpture outside St Paul's depicts Becket in the last moments before his martyrdom.

# 17. Temple Bar

*Location: Paternoster Square, EC4*
*Sculptor: John Bushnell, recent additions by Tim Crawley (design by Christopher Wren)* ◆ *Material: Portland stone*
*Date: 1672*

This Portland stone gate by Christopher Wren was originally erected in 1672 at one of the medieval entrances to the City of London. Temple Bar was intended as a symbol of royal authority but also used as a place to display the remains of executed traitors. The body parts of Sir Thomas Armstrong were displayed here in 1684 as were the heads of the Rye House Plotters, with the last head to be displayed being that of Jacobite, Francis Towneley in 1746. The dissenters Titus Oates and Daniel Defoe were also publicly chastised in stocks by Temple Bar.

Temple Bar was considered too narrow for the efficient flow of traffic by the unsentimental Victorians, who dismantled Wren's work in 1878 and replaced it with the more modest Temple Bar Memorial in 1880 (see page 178). The carefully dismantled parts of the old Temple Bar would have stayed in storage for many years were it not for the social ambitions of the former barmaid, Lady Henry Meux. She persuaded her husband to buy Temple Bar and unveil it at a grand party in the grounds of their country estate in Hertfordshire; Lady Meux is said to have dined with the future Edward VII inside the monument. Long after the Meux fortune had been spent, Temple Bar remained neglected and forgotten in Theobalds Park. In 1974, efforts were begun to restore and return Temple Bar to the City of London. The process took over 30 years and cost £3 million, but the renovated Temple Bar was finally unveiled at the entrance to Paternoster Square in 2004.

## 18. Blitz / Firefighters' Memorial

*Location: Old Change Court, opposite St Paul's Cathedral, EC4*
*Sculptor: John W. Mills*
*Material: Bronze*
*Date: 1991 (Blitz Memorial), re-dedicated to Firefighters 2003*

This clumsy bronze sculpture was first unveiled in 1991 as a memorial to the Blitz. The
bombing of London and other British cities
began on the September 7th 1940 and inflicted enormous death and destruction against a
population that was ill-prepared for the attack.
In the first few months of the campaign the
Luftwaffe dropped over 13,000 tons of bombs
on the capital both day and night while suffering few casualties themselves. From November 1940 until February 1941 Germany
concentrated on industrial cities and ports including London, which suffered a devastating
night of bombing on 29th December. The
photograph of St Paul's rising from the smoke of the incendiary
bombs on the following morning has become one of the iconic
images of London's resistance to the Blitz. The bombing continued
into 1941, but there were only seven attacks directed at the capital. The most devastating raid was launched on 10th May 1941. It
proved a last vicious gesture before Hitler turned his attention to the
invasion of the Soviet Union. In the last year of the war, Hermann
Goering launched a 'Little Blitz' against London, but Germany was
close to defeat and the attacks proved much less effective. It is estimated that during the Blitz 43,000 people were killed and over a
million homes destroyed. This monument was re-dedicated in 2003
to the 1,192 firefighters who have died in active service. For further
background concerning wartime bombing see the monuments to
Hugh Trenchard, Lord Portal and Arthur 'Bomber' Harris (pages 152,
149 and 172).

225

# 19. Postman's Park

*Location: Between King Edward Street & Aldersgate Street, EC1*
*Tel: 020 7374 4127*
*Open: Daily 8am-dusk*

This park's unique feature is a wall of ceramic tiles commemorating acts of heroism. The wall was the idea of the painter and sculptor George Watts who had become an established artist but who, coming from humble origins, had a considerable dislike of the upper classes. Watts was a colourful character who married the beautiful 16-year-old actress Ellen Terry in 1864 when he was in his 40s. The marriage lasted only a year, when Terry eloped with her lover.

In 1887 Watts petitioned *The Times* newspaper to create a wall commemorating those ordinary heroic men and women who had lost their lives while saving others. The paper remained unmoved by the idea and Watts was forced to take up the scheme himself, creating a 50-foot long Heroes' Wall within the former churchyard. The stories of selfless courage are told on hand-lettered ceramic tiles with decorative borders. The tales of heroism are told in florid Victorian prose which seem rather melodramatic today. One inscription reads, 'Sarah Smith, pantomime artiste. At Prince's Theatre died of terrible injuries received when attempting in her flammable dress to extinguish the flames which had enveloped her companion. January 24 1863'. The people commemorated are all everyday heroes who gave their lives to save others and rightly deserve to be remembered. Watts only established 13 tablets before his death. His second wife continued the work with a further 34 tablets. Upon her death the wall was left unaltered as a late Victorian creation commemorating heroes and heroines of that period.

## 20. Sir Rowland Hill (1795-1879)

*Location: King Edward Street, EC1*
*Sculptor: Onslow Ford*
*Material: Granite*
*Date: 1881, moved here in 1923*

Sir Rowland Hill is best known for his reform of the Post Office but he was also an influential educationalist and thinker. His father was a teacher and friend of the radical and scientist Joseph Priestley (see pages 241). Priestley's liberal educational ideas were applied with great success to Rowland's education and as a young man he established his own school to further Priestley's methods. Hill made his first impact on public thinking with a pamphlet on liberal education, but in 1833 he left teaching and took up a post as secretary in the South Australian Colonization Commission.

In 1837, while still working for the Commission, Hill wrote a paper suggesting reform of the complicated postal system and the introduction of postage stamps paid by the sender with charges based on weight rather than distance. Such clear thinking was not welcomed by the politicians but the business community campaigned for Hill's reforms. In 1839, he was given responsibility for introducing his reforms and within a year the postal system was revolutionized. Hill still had his enemies among the politicians and was sacked by Robert Peel (see page 67) in July 1842. He was immediately appointed director of the London and Brighton Railway and made considerable improvements to their service. He was re-appointed to the Post Office in 1846. By the time of his death Sir Rowland Hill was recognised as one of the great practical reformers of his generation and, having been awarded a knighthood in 1860, was buried in Westminster Abbey.

## 21. Henry VIII (1491-1547)
*Location: St Bartholomew's Hospital, EC2*
*Sculptor: Francis Bird*
*Material: Stone*
*Date: 1702*

This is the only monument to Henry VIII but two of his offspring, Edward VI and Elizabeth I, are commemorated in London (see pages 164 and 180) which is some indication of the big man's importance in British history. Henry was the second son of Henry VII and only became his heir on the death of his elder brother in 1502. His father died in April 1509 when Henry was not yet 18 and he spent the first years of his reign under the tutelage of a group of senior clerics among them William Warham, the Archbishop of Canterbury. He fulfilled his promise to his father by marrying Catherine of Aragon in June 1509, but the son born to them in January 1511 died in infancy.

Henry was a forceful and intelligent man and he soon took charge of his realm, replacing his old advisers with ambitious men such as Thomas Wolsey, and declaring war against France. Henry took a well-prepared army to France in 1513 and enjoyed victory in battle but was unable to derive any long-term advantage against a larger and wealthier adversary. Money soon ran out and Henry sued for peace in 1518, making much of his role as peacemaker in a war he had started.

The peace treaties and summits were to go down in history for their splendour but peace was shortlived and Henry's forces continued their campaign across northern France without any clear objective. At this time Henry gained favour with the Vatican for his refutation of Martin Luther, but when he sought an annulment of his marriage, having failed to produce a male heir, Pope Clement VIII was at the mercy of Catherine's nephew, Charles V, and could not grant his wish. Wolsey attempted an alliance with France in 1527, but the defeat of the French at Landriano in June 1529 brought an end to the plan, and to Wolsey, who died on his way to London to face charges of treason in 1530.

Henry had already separated from Catherine and was in love with Anne Boleyn. After the death of the Archbishop of Canterbury William Warham in August 1532, Henry replaced him with the more amenable Thomas Cranmer. In April 1533, Cranmer granted the divorce without recourse to Rome and Henry immediately married the pregnant Anne Boleyn. Henry's 'break with Rome' was the most controversial aspect of his reign and he swiftly moved to strengthen his position by passing The Act of Succession and Act of Supremacy in 1534. The acts recognised his new daughter as heir and Henry as 'Supreme Head of the Church of England' making it an act of treason to deny this new state of affairs. Prominent clergymen, such as John Fisher and Thomas More (see page 322), were victims of this new orthodoxy.

Henry increasingly exploited the advance of the Reformation and tolerated the spread of evangelical preaching that was to become recognised as Protestantism as a means to strengthen his independence from Rome. Anne Boleyn, Thomas Cranmer and Thomas Cromwell all favoured the evangelical movement and this tide of change was to lead to the dissolution of the monasteries between 1536 and 1540, the banning of many traditional forms of worship and, most significantly, the authorization of an English Bible. The north of England rose up against these changes and the heavy taxes that Henry had imposed. Henry was never one to have scruples when dealing with his enemies and he lured the rebels into negotiation and then arrested and executed the ring leaders in a public display of brutality that was to end any further attempts at rebellion.

Anne Boleyn's failure to produce a son was to see her suffer a similar fate having been accused of false charges of adultery in the spring of 1536. Within a fortnight of her execution Henry married the young Jane Seymour who was to bear him his long-awaited son, Edward, in 1537, but she died soon after. Henry now had less use for the Protestant movement and began reining in its more radical preachers, passing laws which recognised the Mass, confession and the celibacy of priests. For the rest of his reign Henry was content to halt any further religious reform and to play one religious faction against another in his court. The evangelical Cromwell was soon in the dock for treason having attempted to marry Henry to Anne of Cleves who Henry found unattractive. Cromwell, who had executed so many on Henry's behalf, was himself executed in July 1540. Henry found solace in the arms of the young and attractive Catherine Howard, who was the niece of Cromwell's rival, the Duke of Norfolk, but the evangelicals again won favour when they provided evidence of the young Queen's infidelity, leading to her execution in February 1542.

Henry married his sixth and final wife, the widow Catherine Parr, in June 1543. He spent the final years of his reign again seeking military glory in battle with France. The ebb and flow of battle achieved very little and cost the country dear, but when the French fleet were repelled from the coast of England, Henry was able to declare himself before parliament in December 1545 as the country's saviour. As the King's health declined it was the evangelicals that assumed the upper hand and as he lay dying in January 1547 it was a Protestant group of advisers that he chose to provide counsel to his young son. This monument of Henry VIII stands outside St Bartholomew's Hospital, which he founded in 1539 having shut down St Thomas's during his dissolution of the monasteries

## 22. Sir William Wallace (1270-1305)

*Location: St Bartholomew's Hospital, EC2*
*Date: 1956*
*Material: Stone tablet*

Willliam Wallace was a young man when John Balliol was declared King of Scotland in 1292. Wallace remained loyal to Balliol when King Edward I of England won victory at Dunbar in 1296 and forced Balliol's abdication to become *de facto* king of Scotland.

There are a great many versions of how Wallace became involved in the struggle. Ayrshire legend claims it was an argument about the selling of fish which led to a fight and the killing of two English soldiers, while in Dundee it is claimed that Wallace killed the son of the town's English governor. Whatever the exact events, Wallace soon found himself at the head of a Scottish army which defeated the English at Loudon Hill and Scone and freed the land north of the Forth from English rule. The greatest victory for Wallace's rebel army was at Stirling Bridge in September 1297, but by this time many of the Scottish nobility had made peace with the English. After losing the Battle of Falkirk in 1298, Wallace left for France to attempt an alliance with Phillip IV. He returned to Scotland in 1303, by which time Robert Bruce had been forced to make peace with Edward. Wallace narrowly escaped capture at Elcho Wood but was later betrayed and handed over to the English. This tablet was placed in the wall of St Batholomew's Hospital in 1956, close to where William Wallace was hung, drawn and quartered after a summary trial in 1305. Wallace's head was placed on a pike at London Bridge and his body parts displayed in Scotland as a warning. The plaque reads, 'His example of heroism and devotion inspired those who came after him...'.

231

## 23. Protestant Martyrs

*Location: St Bartholomew's Hospital, EC2*
*Date: 1870*
*Material: Stone tablet*

This simple stone tablet was placed on the wall of St Bartholomew's Hospital to commemorate the Protestant Martyrs who died here during the reign of Queen Mary. The memorial makes particular mention of three prominent clergymen – John Rogers, John Bradford and John Philpot – who were burned to death for their refusal to accept the Catholic faith. Mary I was the daughter of Henry VIII but was closer to her mother, Catherine of Aragon, who brought her up to be a devout Catholic. While her brother, Edward VI, passed laws favouring the Protestant faith, his half-sister privately observed Mass.

When Mary unexpectedly came to the throne she immediately sent key Protestants, such as the Duke of Northumberland, to the Tower and released Catholics such as the Bishop of Winchester. Protestant legislation was revoked in her first parliament and in November 1554 Cardinal Pole accepted her realm back into the Catholic faith. Mary's use of the 15th century Acts for the Burning of Heretics claimed the lives of nearly 300 Protestants and forced many more to flee to the continent to avoid persecution. Her brutal policy was remarkably successful, but after her death Elizabeth returned the country to the Protestant faith and 'Bloody Mary' became a symbol of Catholic repression summoned up whenever a monarch's Protestant commitment appeared to waver. John Foxe's book *Acts and Monuments* used the Protestant Martyrs to demonstrate the fundamental brutality of the Catholic Church and is one of the key texts for the Protestant Alliance which paid for this memorial.

## 24. Smithfield War Memorial
*Location: Grand Avenue,*
*Smithfield Market, EC1*
*Material: Bronze and stone*
*Date: 1921*

This memorial is dedicated to all those of Smithfield that lost their lives in the First World War and has the names of over 200 victims engraved upon it. An additional plaque is dedicated to those of the area that lost their lives in later conflict

## 25. Golden Boy
*Location: Corner of Cock Lane and Giltspur Street, EC1*
*Sculptor: not known   Date: not known*
*Material: Bronze*

Pye Corner, at the junction of Cock Lane and Giltspur Street, was an area known for prostitution in medieval times and has since then always been associated with sin. It is claimed that the Great Fire of London was extinguished here in September 1666 and Puritan preachers concluded that having started in Pudding Lane and ended at Pye Corner, the fire was a punishment for the capital's gluttony. This fat gilt boy was placed on the corner after the fire to remind Londoners of the perils of excess. The building on which the boy stands has changed several times, but until 1910 it was a famous public house, The Fortunes of War, which served as a meeting place for the Victorian body snatchers who provided cadavers for St Bartholomew's Hospital nearby.

# 26. Charles Lamb (1775-1834)

*Location: Giltspur Street, EC1*
*Sculptor: William Reynolds-Stephens*
*Material: Bronze*
*Date: 1962, originally at Christchurch Greyfriars*

The name of Charles Lamb is largely forgotten, but in his time he was a very widely read essayist, poet and novelist and friend to many other writers including Coleridge and Wordsworth. This bust once stood within Christ's Hospital where Lamb was a school boy. Lamb was obliged to leave school at 14 and seek employment in various clerical posts while also pursuing his literary interests.

Charles Lamb's life and work was inextricably linked with that of his older sister, Mary. The two siblings were bound by affection but also by the mental illness that afflicted both of them, and by the tragic circumstances of their mother's death. In September 1796, Mary suffered a severe attack of mania and murdered her mother with a carving knife. It was only due to the efforts of her brother that she was not sent to prison and he remained her guardian for the rest of his life.

Despite this tragedy Mary and Charles enjoyed their life together and attracted a circle of literary and radical friends such as Coleridge, Wordsworth, Hazlitt and Shelley. Charles was already recognised as a poet when he collaborated with his sister to write *Tales from Shakespeare,* which proved a great success when published in 1807. Using the pen name 'Elia', Charles found further fame as an essayist for *The London Magazine* in 1821. Lamb loved London and once wrote, 'The man must have a rare recipe for melancholy, who can be dull in Fleet-street. I am naturally inclined to hypochondria, but in London it vanishes like other ills.'

234

# Bloomsbury

1) George I
2) Charles James Fox
3) Francis Russell,
   5th Duke of Bedford
4) Joseph Priestley
5) Queen Charlotte
6) Thomas Coram
7) Dame Louisa Aldrich-Blake
8) Virginia Woolf
9) Mahatma Gandhi
10) Hiroshima Tree
11) Peace Stone
12) Major John Cartwright

# Bloomsbury

From the Bloomsbury Gang of Whig politicians formed in 1765 by the 4th Duke of Bedford to the Bloomsbury Group of the 1920s, Bloomsbury has always been associated with England's liberal elite. Among the grand squares are some of the country's leading academic institutions including University College London, Birkbeck College and the British Museum, all of which attract students and academics to the area who provide custom for Bloomsbury's many antiquarian and second-hand bookshops. With the exception of the monuments to George I and Queen Charlotte, the monuments here reflect the area's liberal history with pride of place given to Whig politician Charles James Fox (see page 239) who was able to keep the flame of liberty alive during the repressive administration of Pitt the Younger (see page 259). Fox looks north along Bedford Place to where his aristocratic patron the 5th Duke of Bedford stands. Just off Russell Square sits a modest statue to the chemist and radical thinker Joseph Priestley who was forced into exile for his sympathy for the French Revolution.

Major John Cartwright (see page 250) is the only military man to be commemorated in the area, but he was a kindred spirit of Priestley, who refused to fight against American independence and is recognised here for his campaigning for reform in this country rather than his military adventures abroad. Near to Cartwright is the figure of Thomas Coram who dedicated his later years to helping London's destitute children. The values of 19th-century radicalism are continued in several 20th-century memorials in Tavistock Square, with Mahatma Gandhi taking centre stage and the surgeon Louisa Aldrich-Blake and the writer Virginia Woolf keeping the old man company. The Peace Stone and Hiroshima Tree confirm that this is a place dedicated to non-violence despite the events of the 7th July 2005 when a suicide bomber killed himself and 13 innocent people.

# 1. George I (1660-1727)

*Location: St George's Church, WC1*
*Sculptor: Anonymous*
*Material: Stone*
*Date: 1730*

George I came to the throne in 1714 having spent the first 56 years of his life as elector of the German state of Hanover. He was not ideal material for the crown as he could speak very little English, was a public cuckold who had imprisoned his wife and boasted a number of mistresses. He found himself monarch because neither William nor Mary produced an heir and so he was constantly under threat from the Jacobite descendants of James II, who arguably had a greater claim to the throne. Despite these disadvantages, George proved a rather successful monarch who allowed parliament to claim greater powers than it had previously enjoyed and was pragmatic in his dealing with politicians – even allowing Walpole to take office despite his initial objections. He established the house of Hanover and his son acceded the throne with more certainty. Despite being mocked by the public, his death in 1727 – while travelling in a coach to Hanover – was widely mourned. This is the only monument to the King in the capital and stands upon the spire of a Hawksmoor church. Horace Walpole described the monument's location as a 'master-stroke of absurdity'. There was an equestrian monument to him placed at the centre of Leicester Square in 1748, but as the area declined so the statue fell into disrepair and was removed in 1872.

## 2. Charles James Fox (1749-1806)

*Location: Bloomsbury Square, WC1*
*Sculptor: Sir Richard Westmacott*
*Material: Bronze*
*Date: 1816*

Charles James Fox was one of the most important politicians of his generation and yet he held office only fleetingly and was responsible for only one law, and that relating to libel. His early career was distinguished by his ability to remain a key figure in the reforming Whig party through his oratory, flamboyance and ability to win powerful friends. It was only in his later career, when the French Revolution so polarised British public opinion, that Fox showed his mettle by continuing his commitment to reform. William Pitt used the war against revolutionary France as a justification for stifling reform, and adopting draconian measures against radicals and was helped by the support of influential Whig figures such as Edmund Burke. Between 1793 and 1797 Fox and his allies continued to press for reform of the rotten boroughs, but were always outvoted by the Tories and their parliamentary allies. Other radicals such as Joseph Priestley faced considerable danger at this time (see pages 241), but Fox, with his aristocratic wealth and parliamentary immunity, was able to continue the fight. Although he failed to achieve any significant reform, his staunch support for William Wilberforce's anti-slave-trade movement was to help in the trade's abolition in 1807. Fox's continued advocacy of reform during the repressive years of William Pitt's government was to provide an important legacy to the Whig reformers of the late 18th and early 19th century who eventually achieved some measure of parliamentary reform in 1832. This monument shows Fox in the garb of a Roman senator, one hand holding a copy of the Magna Carta.

239

# 3. Francis Russell, 5th Duke of Bedford (1765-1805)

*Location: Russell Square, WC1*
*Sculptor: Sir Richard Westmacott*
*Material: Bronze*
*Date: 1809*

This monument commemorates the aristocrat and politician Francis Russell who was a member of Charles James Fox's Whig government and an ally of the Prince of Wales (later George IV). The Duke's greatest legacy remains the planned streets and Georgian squares of Bloomsbury which were built on farm land belonging to the Bedford estate. Russell Square was laid out in 1800 under the Duke's patronage and the development of the east side of Tavistock Square was begun in 1803 shortly before his death. This monument eschews any association with the city the 5th Duke helped to create but instead concentrates on his interest in agriculture; ploughshare and a sheaf of corn form part of the main design and agricultural scenes are depicted on the plinth. The figure of the Duke looks down Bedford Place towards Fox, his friend and political ally. The current Duke of Bedford has inherited the family fortune and is ranked 102nd on the Sunday Times Rich List.

## 4. Joseph Priestley (1733-1804)

*Location: 30 Russell Square, WC1*
*Sculptor: Gilbert Bayes*
*Material: Stone*
*Date: 1914*

Joseph Priestley was one of the first scientific chemists, the discoverer of oxygen but also a non-conformist minister and radical thinker who was eventually forced into exile. He was brought up in his aunt's non-conformist, liberal home and despite illness proved himself a brilliant scholar, eventually attending a Dissenting Academy where he studied to become a minister, but also acquired an interest in the natural sciences. Throughout his career as a minister and teacher he conducted experiments and advocated the use of scientific method to determine truth. He was interested in all manner of subjects and wrote books on science, religion and politics, and formed friendships with radicals such as Richard Price and future US president Benjamin Franklin on his regular visits to London. Priestley's Unitarian views and support for the American colonies created controversy, but his support of the French Revolution so enraged the population of his Birmingham parish that a mob ransacked his home and he was forced to flee to London. The capital provided only temporary refuge and in April 1794 Priestley embarked for the newly independent United States where he spent the final years of his life. Passing this modest statue above a doorway of the Royal Institute of Chemistry few people would know that it commemorates an exiled revolutionary as well as an accomplished scientist.

## 5. Queen Charlotte (of Mecklenburg-Strelitz) (1744-1818)
*Location: Queen Square, WC1*
*Sculptor: Anonymous*
*Material: Lead*
*Date: 1780*

In the 19th century this was thought to be a statue of Queen Anne, but has since been recognised as Queen Charlotte, consort to George III. Born Charlotte Sophia of Mecklenburg-Strelitz, she married George III of England in 1761. She was not George's first choice, but the first to meet the exacting requirements of his mother. The marriage was nevertheless happy and long, with Charlotte bearing 15 children, 13 of which lived to adulthood and was only blighted by George's bouts of mental illness. The Queen was said to have African features inherited from the Moorish branch of the Portuguese royal family, to whom she was related. Allan Ramsay's painting is the only one to show Charlotte's African heritage and can be seen at the National Portrait Gallery.

# 6. Thomas Coram (1668-1751)

*Location: Brunswick Square, WC1*
*Sculptor: William MacMillan*
*Material: Bronze*
*Date: 1963*

Thomas Coram spent his early career as a sea captain in the American colonies and later made his fortune as a ship-builder and London merchant. He became a famous philanthropist having settled in London and been troubled by the number of abandoned children he encountered on his regular walks through the City. He campaigned for some time to establish a foundling hospital and school but initially found little enthusiasm for the idea. Eventually he gained the support of Queen Caroline and obtained a Royal Charter from George II establishing the Foundling Hospital in 1739. The hospital became one of the most popular charitable institutions with artists such as Hogarth and Handel donating works and performances and the public exhibitions of art providing the inspiration for the Royal Academy exhibitions. This monument stands outside The Foundling Museum on the site of one of the early foundling hospitals and is based on Hogarth's portrait. An earlier bust of Coram is located above the museum's doorway.

# 7. Dame Louisa Aldrich-Blake (1865-1925)

*Location: Tavistock Square, WC1*
*Sculptor: A.G. Walker, Column and base by Edwin Lutyens*
*Material: Stone*
*Date: 1927*

Louisa Aldrich-Blake was the daughter of the rector of Chingford. As a young girl Louisa had always shown an interest in medicine, but it required determination to become the country's first female surgeon in a male-dominated profession. She proved an outstanding student, graduating from the Royal Free Hospital and becoming the first woman to pass the surgery degree. She went on to become master surgeon at the Elizabeth Garrett Anderson Hospital and performed the first operation to remove cancer of the cervix. Aldrich-Blake was appointed dean of the school in 1914 and was made a dame in 1924. She died a year later at the age of 60 in 1925. This unusual monument has two busts of the surgeon on a simple plinth by Lutyens, architect of the Cenotaph in Whitehall.

# 8. Virginia Woolf (1882–1941)

*Location: Tavistock Square, WC1*
*Sculptor: Stephen Tomlin (copy)*
*Material: Bronze*
*Date: 2004*

Viginia Woolf was born into a literary family, her father being the eminent critic, editor and biographer Sir Leslie Stephen. The family home on Hyde Park was a frequent meeting place for writers including Henry James and George Eliot. Virginia was educated at home amid her father's vast library and was both nurtured and harmed by her cloistered upbringing. She was sexually abused by her half brother and experienced her first mental breakdown at the age of 13 when her mother died, and a further crisis when her sister Stella died two years later. Creativity, depression and mental breakdown were to be features of Virginia's life, and the death of her father in 1904 led to her admission to a mental institution.

Virginia and her siblings sold the family house and moved to Bloomsbury and it is here that she became the nucleus of the intellectual circle known as the Bloomsbury Group whose members included Lytton Strachey, Clive Bell, Duncan Grant, Leonard Woolf and John Maynard Keynes. Virginia married Leonard Woolf in 1912 and in the same year began writing for the *Times Literary Supplement,* so beginning the literary career that was to make her newly acquired name. Her first novel, *The Voyage Out*, was published in 1915 by her brother's publishing company, but in 1917 she and her husband founded the Hogarth Press which published all her subsequent books. These included *Mrs Dalloway* (1925), *To the Lighthouse* (1927) and *The Waves* (1931), establishing her reputation as one of the first great modernist writers exploring the interior life of characters and experimenting with disjointed narratives that escaped the Victorian conventions of her father's library.

Virginia and Leonard were a very close couple but both had affairs, most famously Virginia's with Vita Sackville-West who was to be the inspiration for the cross-gendered *Orlando* (1928). Despite her evident success, Virginia continued to be plagued by depression and insanity. In 1941, having left London to escape the bombing which had destroyed her Bloomsbury home, she committed suicide. This modest bust was erected by the Virginia Woolf Society of Great Britain, close to her former home on the south side of Tavistock Square.

## 9. Mahatma Gandhi (1869-1949)
*Location: Tavistock Square, WC1*
*Sculptor: Fredda Brilliant*
*Material: Bronze*
*Date: 1968*

One of the key political figures of the 20th century and the father of Indian independence from British colonial rule, Gandhi was born into a wealthy family and studied law at London University close to this monument. As a young man he showed little interest in politics but when working in South Africa he became involved in fighting for the rights of the minority Indian population and developed a political strategy based upon civil disobedience (satyagraha) and non-violence (ahimsa). This strategy was not just politically expedient, but evolved from Gandhi's growing Hindu faith, which regarded violence as profoundly immoral. When he returned to India in 1914 he soon became involved in politics, initially campaigning against specific injustices such as taxes and the mistreatment of farmers, but then going all out for full independence. Over these years of struggle Gandhi was beaten and imprisoned many times by the authorities but he never called for retaliation and withdrew from campaigning when violence occurred. Gandhi controversially refused to take sides during the Second World War and in 1942 launched the 'Quit India' campaign which was to lead to Independence in August 1947. The bloodshed that resulted from independence and the creation of Pakistan greatly troubled Gandhi and he sought to lessen the violence and encourage trust and co-operation between the two new states.

Gandhi was assassinated by a Hindu radical on 30th January 1948 after only six months of independence. His ideas have influenced many people and were adopted by both the civil rights movement in America and the ANC in South Africa. This large and rather ugly monument sits upon a hollow plinth where people still leave flowers and candles.

247

## 10. Hiroshima Tree

*Location: Tavistock Square, WC1*
*Material: Memorial Tree*
*Date: 1967*

This tree was planted in 1967 in memory of those who died when America dropped the first atomic bomb on the Japanese city of Hiroshima on 6th August 1945. It is estimated that approximately 150,000 people were killed by the bomb – called 'Little Boy' by the Americans – and 75 per cent of the city's buildings destroyed. Many thousands were to suffer from the later consequences of radiation and even today Hiroshima's population suffers from a high level of birth defects. It is argued that the use of atomic weapons at Hiroshima, and three days later at Nagasaki, helped bring an end to the Second World War and as a result saved lives, but it is now known that Roosevelt (see page 257) already knew of Emperor Hirohito's intention to surrender.

## 11. Peace Stone

*Location: Tavistock Square, WC1*
*Material: Stone with bronze plaque*
*Date: 1994*

This stone was dedicated in 1994 'To all those who have established and are maintaining the right to refuse to kill'. It is the only pacifist memorial to be found in the capital and is a welcome change from places like Trafalgar Square (see page 5) which are almost entirely dedicated to military men and their achievements.

## 12. Major John Cartwright (1740-1824)

*Location: Cartwright Gardens, WC1*
*Sculptor: George Clarke*
*Material: Bronze*
*Date: 1831*

John Cartwright came from a wealthy family and his brother Edmund was the inventor of the power loom. John joined the Royal Navy at the age of 18 and served with distinction in the colonies, although his career was hindered by his refusal to serve under the Duke of Cumberland (see page 262) against American Independence. Cartwright had great sympathy for the claims of the American people and when he returned to Britain he determined to argue for parliamentary reform in Britain. From the publication of his first book in 1776, he campaigned tirelessly for universal suffrage, annual parliaments and the general principles of liberty and representation. He founded several organisations with the purpose of spreading these ideas and used some of his fortune to fund radical publications. Cartwright was fighting for reform during the same repressive period in British politics as Joseph Priestley (see page 241) and Charles James Fox (see page 239) and was imprisoned for his troubles several times. He became known as the 'Father of Reform' and his efforts contributed greatly to the passing of the first Reform Act of 1832, just eight years after his death.

# Mayfair & Marylebone

JOHN NASH
1752 — 1835

ARCHITECT

1) Raoul Wallenberg
2) Dwight D. Eisenhower
3) American Eagle Squadron's Memorial
4) Franklin Delano Roosevelt
5) Roosevelt and Churchill – The Allies
6) William Pitt the Younger
7) William George
   Frederick Cavendish Bentinck
8) William Duke of Cumberland
9) John Nash
10) Quintin Hogg
11) Field Marshal Sir George White
12) General Sikorski
13) Joseph Lister
14) Edward Augustus, Duke of Kent
15) John Fitzgerald Kennedy

# Mayfair & Marylebone

The fine squares and symmetrical streets of Mayfair and Marylebone were all created during the building boom of the early 18th century. The stability provided by the Hanoverian accession combined with the rapidly increasing population of London was to be the impetus for wealthy landowners, such as the Earl of Oxford and Duke of Portland, to build on their farm estates. In 1700 there was nothing but fields and cattle in this area but by 1778 one would recognise the same squares and streets that exist today. The area was originally developed for London's rich but, like Bloomsbury (see page 237), the wealthy residents have moved out and the grand houses been converted to offices, shops and embassies.

The heavily fortified United States Embassy looks out over Grosvenor Square which has monuments to presidents Eisenhower and Roosevelt and one to the American Eagle Squadron who fought as volunteers in the Battle of Britain (see page 151). The 'special relationship' between Britain and America is recognised in the bronze figures of Roosevelt and Churchill sitting on a bench on New Bond Street.

An enclave of Tory politicians and military men lies to the north with William Pitt the Younger on Hanover Square, while on Cavendish Square stands the lesser figure of William Bentinck, and a plinth which is all that remains of an equestrian monument to the Duke of Cumberland. Portland Place owes much of its beauty and grandeur to the work of John Nash and his bust can be found in the portico of All Souls Church. The philanthropist and sportsman Quintin Hogg is commemorated close to the University of Westminster which he helped to found as the Regent Street Polytechnic. Given the fact that the Polish leader General Wladyslaw Sikorski was betrayed by the Allies it is perhaps fitting that his monument faces the rear end of the British soldier Field Marshal Sir George White's horse. At the junction with Park Crescent can be found monuments to the medical scientist Joseph Lister, the Duke of Kent and a bust of President John F. Kennedy.

# 1.Raoul Wallenberg (1912-1947?)
*Location: Great Cumberland Place, W1*
*Sculptor: Philip Jackson*
*Material: Bronze*
*Date: 1998*

There are several monuments to those whose date of birth is not known, but Raoul Wallenberg is the only person whose date of death is still a mystery. Wallenberg was Swedish and studied architecture in the United States. After graduation he worked briefly in Palestine where he met many Jewish refugees and heard of the Nazi atrocities.

Wallenberg was not Jewish, but worked for a company owned by a Jewish Hungarian and used his Swedish passport to avoid the restrictions imposed on Jewish businesses. The persecution of Jews in Hungary had begun in 1938 and escalated to mass deportation to concentration camps by May 1944. Wallenberg was given diplomatic status by the American and Swedish governments to help save Hungarian Jews by the issuing of protective passports (Schutzpass). These passports were not legal but deterred the Hungarian authorities from sending many Jews to their deaths. There are accounts of Wallenberg climbing onto a death camp train to issue Schutzpässe while being threatened by Nazi guards. He saved thousands more lives by creating areas of diplomatic refuge in Budapest and used the threat of war crimes prosecution to stop further killings. It was not the Nazis but the Soviets who arrested Wallenberg in 1945, suspecting him of being an American spy. The Soviets claim Wallenberg died of natural causes while in custody in July 1947, but recent evidence suggests he was executed. It is estimated that Wallenberg saved the lives of up to 200,000 Jews.

## 2. Dwight D. Eisenhower (1890-1969)
*Location: Grosvenor Square, W1*
*Sculptor: Robert Dean*
*Material: Bronze*
*Date: 1989*

Eisenhower was born to an established farming family of Mennonites and attended West Point Military Academy despite his family's pacifist beliefs. By the First World War he was appointed lieutenant colonel, but never saw action. In the interwar years Eisenhower attained the rank of general and served under famous military names such as Fox Connor, John Pershing, Douglas MacArthur and George Patton. His intelligence and administrative skill were recognised by the army, but it was during the Second World War that he rose to prominence. General Marshall appointed him as senior military strategist after Pearl Harbour and he went on to head military operations in Europe, then commanded 'Operation Torch' in north Africa, and oversaw the invasion of Italy which was successfully accomplished in February 1944. Eisenhower had won the trust of both Roosevelt and Churchill and was appointed to overall control of the successful invasion of Europe in June 1944. He retired from the army in 1948 and briefly held the position of Supreme Commander of NATO until he was persuaded to run as Republican candidate for president in 1952.

Dwight D. Eisenhower became the 34th President of the United States in January 1953 with the election slogan 'I like Ike'. During his two terms as President he ended the Korean War, developed America's nuclear arsenal, initiated the space race, increased the social security programmes begun by Roosevelt and built the interstate highway system. His 'Dynamic Conservatism' was liberal by today's standards as he began the process of desegregation in schools and the military and avoided involvement in Suez and Vietnam. Eisenhower's farewell speech in January 1961 is significant for it warned of the growing power of America's military. He coined the phrase 'military-industrial complex' to describe the dependency of America's economy upon military spending. Eisenhower spent much of his retirement playing golf, dying in 1969 at the age of 78. This fine monument stands on a marble pavement which lists his military achievements. It was unveiled by Prime Minister Margaret Thatcher in 1989.

## 3. American Eagle Squadron's Memorial

*Location: Grosvenor Square, W1*
*Sculptor: Dame Elizabeth Frink*
*Material: Bronze*
*Date: 1986*

This monument stands in grateful memory to Eagle Squadron which was formed in September 1940. Their number comprised of 244 American pilots who volunteered to join the Royal Air Force before their country entered the war as well as 16 British pilots. The Squadron played a major part in the Battle of Britain and continued to serve until September 1942 when it was incorporated into the USAAF. During its existence the squadron suffered very high casualties, loosing 77 American and 5 British pilots.

# 4. Franklin Delano Roosevelt (1882-1945)

*Location: Grosvenor Square, W1*
*Sculptor: Sir William Reid Dick*
*Material: Bronze*
*Date: 1948*

Franklin Delano Roosevelt (FDR) was the only child of a wealthy New York family and after studying law at Harvard and Columbia embarked on a political career that was to take him to the White House. FDR served his political apprenticeship after winning a seat on the New York State Senate for the Democrats and working as assistant secretary for the navy before unsuccessfully running for Vice-President in 1920. Roosevelt was struck down by polio in 1921 which left him paralysed from the waist down, but he was able to hide his disability with the aid of walking sticks and leg braces. He continued to build his support within the Democratic Party winning the governorship of New York in 1929 and becoming the 32nd President of the United States when he defeated the incumbent Herbert Hoover in 1932.

Roosevelt entered the White House on a wave of goodwill and a commitment to combat the Great Depression, declaring 'the only thing we have to fear is fear itself'. Roosevelt's administration greatly increased the role of government with a raft of policies, known as the New Deal, which regulated business practices, embarked on large public works to tackle unemployment, regulated agricultural prices and encouraged the establishment of trade unions, while at the same time reducing military spending. The policies were a success and Roosevelt's ebullient and confident personality created a New Deal Coalition of ethnic minorities, trade unionists, urban workers and southern Democrats that was to see him elected president an unprecedented four times.

257

This grand statue to FDR was raised by public subscription in this country in recognition of his support during the Second World War. Roosevelt was careful not to arouse America's strong isolationist sentiments, but introduced a series of measures – 'Arsenal for Democracy' and 'Lend Lease' – designed to assist Britain, France and China in their battle against the Axis Powers. Japan's attacked on Pearl Harbour in December 1941 gave Roosevelt the opportunity to join the Allies as he had always intended.

FDR won a fourth term in office in 1944 but was already very frail and died just a few months before the declaration of victory in Europe which he did so much to secure. One of Roosevelt's greatest achievements was the founding of the United Nations which was designed as a forum for international relations and to limit conflict.

## 5. Roosevelt and Churchill – The Allies

*Location: Bond Street, W1*
*Sculptor: Lawrence Holofcener*
*Material: Bronze*
*Date: 1995*

This monument was erected by the Bond Street Association to commemorate fifty years of peace in Europe. The relationship between Roosevelt and Churchill was a complex one and fraught with difficulties, particularly concerning the third ally – Stalin. This clumsy sculpture is entitled 'The Allies', but has avoided featuring 'Uncle Joe'. Unpleasant historical realities, such as making alliance with one murderous dictator in order to defeat another, have been conveniently forgotten. These two giants of 20th-century history both have much finer monuments in London (see page 258 and 75).

# 6. William Pitt the Younger (1759-1806)

*Location: Hanover Square, W1*
*Sculptor: Francis Legatt Chantrey*
*Material: Bronze*
*Date: 1831*

William Pitt the Younger became this country's youngest Prime Minister at the age of 24 in 1783 and proceeded to dominate British politics for 20 years. Pitt began his precocious career as a Whig ally of Charles James Fox (see page 239) calling for peace with the American colonies. Pitt and Fox soon became bitter rivals and when Pitt became Prime Minister it was with the support of the Tories and George III and in opposition to Fox and his Whig Party. Pitt's hold on power was initially tenuous but he was popular among the people and won a decisive electoral victory in 1784, keeping power for nearly 19 years.

The first period of his administration was incredibly successful as he stabilised the country's finances, reduced the national debt and improved Britain's administration of India through the India Act of 1784. Pitt even attempted some limited reform of the corrupt electoral system, but this was rejected by many of his own party and was abandoned. The second phase of Pitt's government was concerned with the consequences of the French Revolution which eventually led to war with Napoleon in February 1793. Pitt was a strong leader in time of war, but he increasingly regarded any representation of worker's rights in Britain as a form of Jacobinism. As war raged on the continent, he suspended *habeas corpus* and passed a series of harsh laws which outlawed trade unions and all forms of radical political organisation. These measures remained in place for many years and put the cause of domestic reform back a generation.

Pitt was forced to resign in February 1801 when he attempted to pass a Catholic Emancipation Act to accompany the 1800 Act of Union which brought Ireland within the United Kingdom. He was returned to office in 1804 and despite the victory at Trafalgar was soon cast into despondency by Napoleon's victories at Alma and Austerlitz. The disappointments of war and his heavy drinking took a great toll on his fragile health and he died in office in January 1806 aged 46. Pitt was a hero to many for his leadership during the Napoleonic Wars and an enemy to others for his reactionary policies. When this monument was erected – 25 years after his death – a group of radical Whigs attempted to pull it down. Pitt the Younger died unmarried and insolvent but Parliament voted to pay his debts. He is buried in his father's grave in Westminster Abbey.

## 7. William George Frederick Cavendish-Scott-Bentinck (1802-1848)

*Location: Cavendish Square, W1*
*Sculptor: Thomas Campbell ◆ Material: Bronze*
*Date: 1851*

William (usually known as George) Bentinck was the second surviving son of the Fourth Duke of Portland. He was educated at home before spending a brief period in the army. He retired from the Hussars in 1822 and began working as a private secretary to his uncle, the Foreign Secretary George Canning (see page 63). In 1828 Bentinck inherited his father's seat in the House of Commons as a moderate Whig supporting parliamentary reform and Catholic emancipation. He later joined Robert Peel's (see page 67) Conservative party but took little part in politics, preferring to concentrate on his racing stables. The issue that brought Bentinck onto the political stage was Peel's proposed repeal of the Corn Laws. Disraeli and Bentinck joined forces and fought fiercely to prevent the end of corn tariffs.

It is difficult now to understand the level of passion that this issue aroused in the hearts of Conservatives, and although Bentinck and Disraeli failed to stop the law's repeal in 1846, they ended Peel's political career. Bentinck was too liberal in his thinking for the Conservative party, of which he was now leader, and he resigned in 1847 – dying of a heart attack soon after in September 1848. Bentinck was a decent man, but his grand monument, which stands in a square baring his family name, owes more to his wealth than his achievements as a politician.

## 8. Prince William Duke of Cumberland (1721-1765)

*Location: Cavendish Square, W1*
*Sculptor: not known*
*Material: Stone plinth, lead statue (missing)*
*Date: 1770 (removed 1868)*

The plinth that stands in the centre of Cavendish Square is all that remains of the equestrian statue of William Duke of Cumberland that stood here for nearly 100 years. The third son of George II (see page 262) William Augustus was created Duke of Cumberland in 1726. He joined the army in 1742 and was soon involved in military events on the continent, taking part in the War of Austrian Succession (1740-1748) against the French. After his defeat at the Battle of Fontenoy (1745) he was sent home to deal with the French-inspired Jacobite uprising and succeeded in driving Charles Stuart and his army back into Scotland before fighting the decisive battle of Culloden in April 1746. The Duke's conduct of the battle earned him the title 'Butcher Cumberland' in Scotland, but he was widely praised and awarded a substantial income for his victory.

He never enjoyed similar success against the French, losing the Battle of Lauffeld (1747) and ten years later the battle of Hastenbeck, and he returned home in ignominy having been forced to sign the Convention of Kloster-Zeven which his furious father rejected. Cumberland retired from public life to pursue his interest in botany, and introduced many new species to Windsor Great Park. He continued to take some part in politics behind the scenes and was instrumental in attempts to return William Pitt to the premiership, before his premature death in October 1765. Cumberland was popular with his men and the monument that once stood here was erected by Lieutenant General William Strode who served under him.

# 9. John Nash (1752-1835)

*Location: All Souls, Langham Place, W1*
*Sculptor: Cecil Thomas*
*Material: Stone wall-bust*
*Date: 1956*

The most important architect of his generation – the son of a humble London millwright – John Nash did more than any man since Wren (see page 219) to influence the landscape of London. Nash was apprenticed to the architect Sir Robert Taylor as a young man, but abandoned his work and settled in Wales when he inherited a fortune from a wealthy uncle. The fortune was lost through unwise investments and he was forced to return to his architectural work, establishing a successful country practice with the landscape gardener Humphrey Repton. Nash returned to London in 1792 and became rich designing stucco-clad, Palladian houses made from brick for London's rich and famous. He was nearly 60 when he came to the attention of the Prince of Wales and was appointed architect to develop the farmland called Marylebone Park. Over the next 18 years, assisted by James Pennethorne and Decimus Burton, extensive tracts of central London were developed under Nash's guidance. Parks were landscaped, while streets, terraces, crescents, town houses and villas sprang up in a golden age of architecture. Much of his legacy can still be seen, including Regent's Park and the grand terraces that enclose it, Portland Place, Regent Street, Carlton House Terrace, The Mall and finally St James's Park. His were the initial designs for Trafalgar Square, nearby Haymarket Theatre and the Royal Mews. He was also director of the company responsible for Regent's Canal which extends across London from West to East.

263

Outside London, Nash built Brighton Pavilion, the onion-domed oriental fantasy about which the Reverend Sydney Smith said 'The dome of St. Paul's must have come down... and pupped'. It continues to remain the most significant feature of the city today. Nash's greatest failure was his work on Buckingham Palace which began in 1825 and was altered many times due to the changing whims of the King. Nash received considerable public ridicule as the costs mounted and he was replaced by Edward Blore after the King's death in 1830. Today only the west wing remains from his original design. One of Nash's most prominent achievements is Marble Arch, originally designed as a triumphant arch for Pall Mall but moved to its current location at the end of Oxford Street during the reign of Queen Victoria. Nash retired to his grand estate on the Isle of Wight and died there in 1835. This fine bust stands in a niche of Nash's All Soul's Church and just ten minutes walk north are some of his finest buildings. As in his own time, these grand crescents are almost exclusively owned by the very rich.

# 10. Quintin Hogg (1845-1903)

*Location: Langham Place, W1*
*Sculptor: Sir George Frampton*
*Material: Bronze*
*Date: 1906*

Quintin Hogg was the Eton-educated son of James Hogg, the last director of the East India Company. Just like Thomas Coram a century before (see page 243), Hogg was troubled by the poverty and suffering he saw in London and started his philanthropic work by teaching children in the street. With the help of his friend Arthur Kinnaird and his sister Annie, Hogg opened his first school in a rented room near Charing Cross in 1864 which proved a great success. Hogg was a fine sportsman and had a sense of fun often giving street children rides in his father's carriage. His work was not always easy and on several occasions he was nearly killed by street robbers.

Hogg not only continued to extend the scope of his philanthropic work but prospered in his business dealings as a successful tea and sugar merchant. The passing of the 1870 Education Act by William Forster (see page 126) made the Ragged Schools less important and in 1882 he opened the Regent Street Polytechnic to provide educational, sporting and social facilities for working adults. The polytechnic was very popular and Hogg soon introduced morning classes and then a day school. As one of the first aldermen of London County Council, Quintin Hogg promoted the idea of polytechnics and helped establish 12 by the time of his early death in 1903. This monument is close to the University of Westminster which was the original site of his polytechnic. Hogg was the grandfather of the Conservative politician Quintin Hogg who became Lord Hailsham.

## 11. Field Marshal Sir George White (1835-1912)

*Location: Portland Place, W1*
*Sculptor: John Tweed*
*Material: Bronze*
*Date: 1922*

Educated at Sandhurst, this son of Irish gentry joined the Inniskillings in 1853 and soon saw action during the Indian Mutiny of 1857. White was promoted to second-in-command of the Gordon Highlanders and during the Second Afghan War (1878-80) overran several positions when outnumbered by the enemy. For his heroics at Charasiah and Kandahar White was awarded the Victoria Cross. He participated in the Nile Expedition (1884-5) with the Gordon Highlanders and was promoted to major-general for his service during the Burmese War (1885-7). Having succeeded Lord Roberts (see page 57) in Burma, White took over from him in India as Commander-in-Chief. He was knighted in 1897 and returned to England a year later but was soon dispatched to Natal at the start of the Second Boer War (see page 95) in 1899. After several victories against the Boers his forces were surrounded at Ladysmith and forced to endure a siege of 119 days. White returned to England after the war in ill health but was appointed governor of Gibraltar (1900-04) and promoted to field marshal in 1903. He became governor of Chelsea Hospital in1905 and died there in 1912. Sir George White's only son, Jack White, followed his father into the army and was decorated, but became disillusioned with the military and became a radical figure – fighting for the Republican cause in Ireland and for the International Brigade in the Spanish Civil War (see page 160).

## 12. General Wladyslaw Sikorski (1881-1943)

*Location: Portland Place, W1*
*Sculptor: Faith Winter*
*Material: Bronze*
*Date: 2000*

General Wladyslaw Sikorski was one of Poland's great military and political figures whose life and death were to have a dramatic effect upon the fate of the Polish nation. Sikorski was born in a country that had been partitioned between Russia, Prussia and Austro-Hungary since the time of Napoleon. During the First World War he abandoned his engineering studies to fight for the Austro-Hungarian army against Russia, believing that the defeat of Russia would afford the best opportunity of establishing Polish independence. Sikorski proved an able soldier and soon adapted his skill to fight directly for independence which was achieved with the collapse of the partitioning powers in 1918. The Second Polish Republic was immediately embroiled in the Polish Soviet War (1919-21) and, under the leadership of Jozef Pilsudski, Sikorski played a major role in the battle of Warsaw which secured peace in 1921. Within a year Sikorski became prime minister on a wave of popular support and served in several governments before Pilsudski, his former ally, took power in a coup in May 1926 and he was forced from public office.

Sikorski was exiled in Paris when Germany invaded Poland in 1939 and he became the head of the exiled Polish government. The army of over 80,000 exiled Poles was vital to Britain's survival during the first years of the war and Polish pilots played a key part in the Battle of Britain. Sikorski became the symbol of a future independent Polish nation in the same way as De Gaulle (see page

267

111) represented French liberation. When the Soviet Union joined the Allies Sikorski was persuaded to make a pact with Stalin and thousands of Polish prisoners of war were released from Soviet camps to join the allied campaign in North Africa. In January 1942 Sikorski was told of Stalin's plans to occupy large areas of Poland and serious divisions began to arose in the Allied camp. In April 1943 details emerged of the Soviet massacre of Poles in Katyn at the start of the war and the ensuing row gave Stalin the pretext to cut diplomatic contacts with Sikorski's government and threaten Britain and America with Soviet withdrawal from the Allied struggle. The brave Poles with Sikorski as their leader who had been vital in 1940, were now a major hindrance to Allied unity.

In July 1943 General Sikorski's plane mysteriously crashed just after taking off from Gibralter and with his death the problem of Poland was resolved. One Polish airman who witnessed the crash exclaimed 'this is the end of Poland', and so it was to be. Sikorski's successor, Stanislaw Mikolajczyk, lacked authority and was excluded from the conferences of Tehran, Yalta and Potsdam, when Poland was effectively given to the Soviet Union. The exact cause of the plane crash that killed Sikorski has never been established. The un-veiling of this statue to him just after the collapse of the Soviet Union does nothing to erase the betrayal of the Polish people which his name evokes.

## 13. Joseph Lister (1827-1912)
*Location: Upper Portland Place, W1*
*Sculptor: Thomas Brock*
*Material: Bronze*
*Date: 1924*

Joseph Lister was the son of a physicist but originally studied the arts before taking up medicine and graduating with honours in 1852. In 1856 Lister was appointed assistant surgeon to James Syme at Edinburgh Royal Infirmary and married Syme's daughter. After becoming a surgeon at the infirmary in 1861 Lister started work trying to reduce the level of infection in the operating theatre. At that time post-operative infection, called ward fever, killed nearly half of all patients. Lister was influenced by the work of the Hungarian surgeon, Ignaz Semmelweiss, who made the link between hygiene and infection, and Louis Pasteur's scientific paper suggesting that living organisms in the air caused infection.

By 1867 Lister had developed a carbolic acid spray which almost eradicated infection. In England Lister's results were treated with scepticism but they were well received in Prussia and his methods used to great affect during the Franco-Prussian War of 1870. Lister demonstrated his methods in Germany and the United States, but it was not until he accepted the chair of Clinical Surgery at King's College London in 1877 that his methods gained acceptance in Britain. He was recognised for his achievements with a baronetcy in 1883 and received of the Order of Merit in 1902. The last years of Lister's life were marred by the death of his wife in 1893 which effectively marked the end of his active career. This monument to the medical pioneer stands close to his London home at 12 Park Crescent.

## 14. Edward Augustus, Duke of Kent (1767-1820)

*Location: Park Crescent, W1*
*Sculptor: S.S. Gahagan*
*Material: Bronze*
*Date: 1827*

Like his siblings, Edward Augustus, fourth son of George III, had a difficult relationship with his father. He joined the army in 1785 and trained in Germany under a hated governor. His flight back to England only exacerbated his father's disapproval. He was promptly despatched to Gibraltar with the 7th Royal Fusiliers, with whom he travelled to Canada and North America. By 1799 he had been made Commander-in-Chief of British forces in North America and enjoyed a comfortable life with his long-term French mistress.

After a short spell back in Gibraltar as governor, he was ordered home in 1803 having nearly caused a mutiny. His life changed irrevocably on the death of Princess Charlotte, George IV's daughter, in 1817, which placed the Hanoverian succession in jeopardy. All Charlotte's uncles now attempted to sire an heir. The Duke gave up his mistress – for the greater good – and married Princess Victoire of Leiningen in 1818, a daughter arriving the following year. He died in 1820 and so failed to see his infant daughter Victoria become the Queen who would rule Britain and her empire at the height of its powers (see page 115).

While fathering the heir to the throne is perhaps the Duke's greatest achievement, there is considerable doubt about Victoria's parentage. It is known that Princess Victoire had a long affair with her secretary, Sir John Conroy, and her daughter introduced the haemophilia gene to the Royal family where it had not previously existed on either side.

# 15. John Fitzgerald Kennedy (1917-1963)

*Location: Marylebone Road, W1*
*Sculptor: Jacques Lipchitz*
*Material: Bronze bust*
*Date: 1965*

John Fitzgerald Kennedy was the charismatic 35th president of the United States whose rapid ascent to the White House and brief period in office are forever marred by his assassination on the streets of Dallas in 1963. JFK had all the attributes of a presidential candidate including a Harvard education, distinguished war record, good looks and a way with words, but this would have amounted to nothing without the money and political influence of his father Joseph. Joseph Kennedy was one of America's richest men, having made his fortune on the money markets, the selling of liquor and his control of several movie studios. Kennedy Snr was a close friend and financial supporter of Roosevelt (see page 257) and was determined to see one of his sons become president. The death of Joseph's eldest son during the Second World War placed all expectations on JFK and he duly became a Democratic congressman for Boston and was elected to the Senate in 1953, the same year he married Jacqueline Bouvier.

JFK was occasionally required to compromise his principles for the sake of family and political alliances – he did not vote for civil rights legislation in order to keep southern senators' support and avoided all criticism of Republican senator Joseph McCarthy because he was a family friend. In July 1960 JFK won the Democratic nomination for president and with his father financing and organising the campaign he became the youngest-ever and first Catholic president. The Kennedy administration lasted for just over a thou-

271

sand days but in that time acquired a glamorous reputation; the media referred to Kennedy's White House as 'Camelot'. His domestic policy was called the 'New Frontier' and was marked by support for civil rights legislation, reflation of the economy and increased federal funding for medical care and education. In reality, JFK was restricted on the domestic front by a Republican Congress, but many of his reforms were passed after his death under President Johnson.

Kennedy's foreign policy revolved around the politics of the Cold War. It began with his unsuccessful support for the overthrow of Castro which resulted in the Bay of Pigs incident and escalated to the Cuban Missile Crisis, when Kennedy blockaded Cuba to prevent the installation of Soviet missiles. In Europe, America was forced to resort to airlifts to prevent the blockade of Berlin and Kennedy made his famous speech in that city. Kennedy was becoming more adept at handling the Soviets by the autumn of 1963, but his support of the South Vietnamese government and introduction of 18,000 troops to the region was to lead to a disastrous war in years to come.

Many facts have emerged since November 1963 about Kennedy's presidency and character. It is now known that he suffered from chronic back pain and several other illnesses that were hidden from the public, and that he conducted numerous affairs behind the walls of the White House. Kennedy also had some troubling connections with organised crime through his friendship with Frank Sinatra. This bust stands as a monument to the more noble public face of John F. Kennedy and was unveiled by his brothers Robert and Edward a few years after his tragic death.

# Hyde Park Corner
# Belgravia & Victoria

1)  Animals In War Memorial
2)  Achilles
3)  George Gordon Byron, 6th Baron Byron
4)  Royal Artillery War Memorial
5)  Arthur Wellesley, 1st Duke of Wellington
6)  Machine Gun Corps (Boy David Memorial)
7)  Constitution Arch (Formerly Wellington Arch)
8)  Australian War Memorial
9)  New Zealand
10) Sir Robert Grosvenor
11) General Don Jose De San Martin
12) Prince Henry The Navigator
13) Christopher Columbus
14) Simon Bolivar
15) Marshal Ferdinand Foch

# Hyde Park Corner

When Kensington and Knightsbridge were villages on the outskirts of London Hyde Park Corner was the site of a modest toll gate into the city. The area was transformed by the ambitions of George IV to create a grand entrance into Hyde Park and by the arrival of the Duke of Wellington who bought nearby Apsley House in 1817. The Duke's grand house was to become surrounded by monuments to the great man, with Achilles arriving in 1822, closely followed by Wellington Arch (now Constitution Arch) and finally a vast statue of the Duke was placed on top of the arch in 1846.

It was not until 1887 – over 30 years after the Duke's death – that politicians found the courage to remove his statue to Aldershot, replacing it with one of more modest proportions and renaming the arch. The monuments that have been erected in the last hundred years have all been of a military nature culminating in the Australian and New Zealand War Memorials of recent years. Lord Byron's monument stands apart from the rest to the north, which is perhaps fitting given his dislike for Wellington and the Duke's conservative politics. A recent addition is the Animal War Memorial which commemorates the contribution made by animals during wartime.

Just a few minutes walk from Hyde Park Corner is Belgrave Square, which contains a recent monument to the Second Earl of Grosvenor who commissioned Thomas Cubitt to build houses for London's wealthy here in the 1820s. The several Latin American embassies in the area help to explain the other monuments on the square which all have an association with that part of the world, from explorers such as Henry the Navigator to Simon Bolivar. The grand equestrian monument to Marshal Foch stands alone on Buckingham Palace Road, but as one of the great military men of the First World War is worth making some effort to visit.

# 1. Animals In War Memorial

*Location: Brook Gate, Park Lane, W1*
*Sculptor: David Backhouse*
*Material: Bronze and Portland stone*
*Date: 2004*

This memorial to the animals that died in wars and conflict in the 20th century was inspired by Jilly Cooper's book, *Animals in War*. The author and other like-minded animal lovers started a fund in 1998 which raised over £1 million for the project. The monument consists of a semicircular wall of Portland stone depicting all kinds of animals serving man in wartime, from glow worms (used for light in the trenches) to carrier pigeons. The central area is occupied by statues of two heavily laden mules struggling to reach a breach in the wall where a bronze dog and horse are waiting. The monument seems to divide people between those that think such a monument is long overdue and is a reflection of a wiser less man-centred view of the world, and those that think it is a testament to the mawkish sentimentality of the British when it comes to animals. The reader can decide on which side of the line they stand.

## 2. Achilles

*Location: Park Lane, W1*
*Sculptor: Sir Richard Westmacott RA*
*Material: Bronze*
*Date: 1822*

This huge monument was erected through public subscription by 'the women of England to Arthur Duke of Wellington and his brave companions.' The 20-foot high bronze sculpture represents Achilles in martial pose with sword and shield in hand, but is actually a copy of one of the horse tamers on the Monte Catallo in Rome. The monument cost the vast sum of £10,000 and was cast from French cannon won at Salamanca, Vittoria, Toulouse and Waterloo. Achilles was the first public monument to depict a nude man and caused such controversy that a fig leaf was later added to save the warrior's modesty which in subsequent years has been removed by vandals on several occasions. Achilles was also the first of many public monuments to Wellington and as such was criticised and lampooned by radicals who disliked the Duke and the reactionary politics he represented. Lord Byron's friend, the radical journalist Leigh Hunt, described Achilles as 'manifesting the most furious intentions of self defence against the hero whose abode it is looking at'.

# 3. George Gordon Byron, 6th Baron Byron (1788-1824)

*Location: Hyde Park Corner, SW1*
*Sculptor: Richard C. Belt ◆ Material: Bronze*
*Date: 1880*

Lord George Gordon Byron was born on the eve of the French Revolution and like many of his English contemporaries his imagination was inspired by the idea of revolution and by a rejection of the political and social order in his own country. Byron was to become one the most recognised romantic poets of his generation, but he was also to become a figure of scandal who embodied the impulsive creativity of his poetry in his dramatic personal life. Byron's family was both aristocratic and chaotic – his father, John 'Mad Jack' Byron, spent the family fortune and young Gordon was brought up in modest circumstances in Aberdeen, with the further disadvantage of a club foot which was to trouble him throughout his life. At the age of ten Byron inherited his great-uncle's fortune and was able to complete his education at Harrow and Trinity College, Cambridge. Despite his disfigurement, Byron was a seductive character who embarked on a series of affairs including a passionate love affair with a junior choir boy.

In 1809 Byron published his first book of poetry which was indifferently received, but his comic poem ridiculing his critics was a success and he embarked on a tour of southern Europe with a burgeoning reputation. Between 1809 and 1811 Byron travelled across the Mediterranean enjoying numerous affairs and writing of his adventures in *Childe Harold's Pilgrimage* (1812) which was a great success and followed by *The Giaour*, *The Bride of Abydos*, *The Corsair* and *Lara*, all published soon after his return to England.

Byron assumed his seat in the Lords on his return and used his position to argue for radical causes such as the Luddites and against reactionary politicians such as Lord Castlereagh and the Duke of Wellington; both of whom he lambasted in his poetry. Byron's complicated private life led him into a short lived marriage and the scandal surrounding his separation was to drive him into permanent exile in 1816. Byron fled to Venice and began writing *Don Juan* (1819-24) which was loosely based on his own romantic adventures – he claimed to have slept with 250 woman in his first year in the City. He was joined in Italy by his radical friend Leigh Hunt and Shelley and together they published a radical journal called *The Liberal* to avoid the repressive laws in England at the time. Byron was always attracted by radical causes and through the family of one of his lovers he joined the Carbonari to fight for Italian independence.

By 1823 Byron was bored of his life in Italy and welcomed the chance to leave and join the fight for Greek independence against Ottoman rule. Byron landed in Missolonghi and spent his own money refitting the Greek fleet and establishing a brigade of fighters under his command. Byron was never to see battle as he fell ill and died of fever in April 1824. Lady Caroline Lamb described Byron as 'mad, bad and dangerous to know' and despite his recognised genius as a poet he was not commemorated in Westminster Abbey until the 1960s. The marble for this monument was provided by the Greek government in recognition of his efforts, and shows the poet with his favourite dog 'Boatswain'. Byron's friend Trelawny claimed the statue bore no resemblance to the poet.

## 4. Royal Artillery War Memorial

*Location: Hyde Park Corner, SW1*
*Sculptor: Charles Sargeant Jagger and Lionel Pearson*
*Material: Bronze and marble*
*Date: 1925*

This marble memorial with a bronze figure on each side and a vast howitzer gun at its centre is dedicated to those of the Royal Regiment of Artillery who were killed or injured in World War One. The monument is notable for its depiction of the harsh realities of war. One of the figures depicts the body of a soldier draped in his greatcoat with the words 'Here was a Royal fellowship of Death' taken from Shakespeare's Henry V. During the Second World War, 30,000 members of the Royal Artillery were killed and in 1949 a further three panels were added to commemorate their loss. It is claimed that the stone gun on this memorial is aimed towards the Somme in northern France.

# 5. Arthur Wellesley,
# 1st Duke of Wellington (1769-1852)

*Location: Hyde Park Corner, SW1*
*Sculptor: Sir Joseph Edgar Boehm ◆ Material: Bronze*
*Date: 1887*

This monument stands on the site where Constitution Arch was originally sited and replaces the vast equestrian statue by Matthew Cotes Wyatt that stood on top of the arch until 1883 (see Constitution Arch below). This monument shows the Duke upon his favourite horse, Copenhagen, and surrounded below by soldiers from the 1st Guards, 42nd Royal Highlanders, 23rd Royal Welsh Fusiliers and the 6th Inniskilling Dragoons. For further details of the Duke of Wellington's life see his monument outside the Bank of England (page 208).

# 6. Machine Gun Corps (Boy David Memorial)

*Location: Hyde Park Corner, SW1*
*Sculptor: Francis Derwent Wood RA*
*Material: Bronze*
*Date: 1922*

By the start of the First World War machine guns was used in all infantry battalions. The army introduced special training centres in November 1914 to develop tactics for the use of these new weapons and in October 1915 the Machine Gun Corps (MGC) was established and attached to every army brigade. The MGC were equipped with the new and powerful Vickers guns and throughout the war cut a deadly swathe through the battlefields of northern France. The effectiveness of the new weapons made the machine gunners particular targets for enemy fire and they were called 'The Suicide Club' for the heavy casualties they suffered during the conflict with over 60,000 killed or injured. After the war, machine guns became lighter and more widely deployed within the army and the MGC was no longer necessary as a unique fighting force. The corps was disbanded in 1922 and this memorial erected in the same year. It shows the naked figure of David resting upon a sword with two Vickers guns on either side. The biblical inscription reads, 'Saul has slain his thousands; But David his tens of thousands'. Questions were asked in the House about the monument amid complaints that it glorified war.

# 7. Constitution Arch (Formerly Wellington Arch)
*Location: Hyde Park Corner, SW1*
*Sculptor: Decimus Burton*
*Material: Bronze*
*Date: 1828 (moved here 1883)*

This grand arch was commissioned by George IV in 1825 along with Marble Arch to commemorate victory over Napoleon. Decimus Burton began work in 1826 but as the King's funds depleted, the elaborate exterior was abandoned for a simpler and cheaper design. It was erected opposite Wellington's residence, Apsley House, in 1828 and became known as Wellington Arch. In 1846 Matthew Cotes Wyatt's massive 8.5-metre high equestrian monument to the Duke was transported from his workshops on Harrow Road to Hyde Park Corner with a military escort of 500 guardsmen and placed on top of the arch. Decimus Burton, who had planned a quadriga for the top of the arch, objected to the lack of proportion of the statue and others complained that the horse did not resemble the Duke's famous Copenhagen. The arch and the monument parted ways when the arch was moved to the top of Constitution Hill, and Wyatt's monument was eventually dispatched to Aldershot where it stands to this day. Constitution Arch underwent a further transformation in 1912 when Burton's initial plan for a quadriga was completed by the soldier turned sculptor, Captain Adrian Jones. The work was funded by the Jewish businessman, Lord Michelham, in memory of Edward VII who had promoted the interests of the Jewish community during his reign. There are several other monuments to Edward VII (see p. 99).

283

## 8. Australian War Memorial

*Location: Hyde Park Corner, SW1*
*Sculptor: Janet Laurence and architectural firm Tonkin Zulaikha Greer*
*Material: Granite*
*Date: November 2003*

This beautiful monument was funded by the Australian government who commissioned the design of Australian artist Janet Laurence in partnership with the architectural practice Tonkin Zulaikha Greer in 2002. The monument consists of a 40-metre long sweeping curve of granite which is 3.4 metres at its highest point and weighs 200 tons. The monument commemorates the sacrifice of over 100,000 Australian lives in the two World Wars. The 24,000 Australian towns from which these people came are inscribed in small type, while the 47 battlegrounds upon which they shed their blood is inscribed in a much larger type, making them visible from some distance. The main inscription reads 'Whatever burden you are to carry we also will shoulder that burden'. The monument has a constant flow of water over the stone and at night lights illuminate it from below. Large crowds gathered to see the unveiling of the monument by Queen Elizabeth and Australian Prime Minister John Howard.

## 9. New Zealand War Memorial
*Location: Hyde Park Corner*
*Sculptor: Paul Dibble, John Hardwick-Smith (Architect)*
*Date: November 2006*
*Material: Bronze*

Consisting of 16 cross shaped columns rising at an angle from a grass verge, this monument is one of the most original to be found in the capital. From a distance the crucifix shape is evident at the top of each column, but closer up can be seen detailed markings which include text and symbols representing the links between Britain and New Zealand. The memorial was unveiled on Armistice Day, which gives some indication that while this is not only a war memorial, the sacrifice made by New Zealand soldiers in two world wars and other conflicts, is an important part of the annual commemoration. History has undergone some editing to emphasise the friendly links between Britain and New Zealand. The 1840 Treaty of Waitangi, which granted Maori land rights, is engraved upon one of the columns, but there is no mention that the treaty was largely ignored, resulting in 25 years of intermittent conflict. For more details of this conflict see the New Zealand memorial in Greenwich (page 326).

## 10. Sir Robert Grosvenor, 1st Marquess of Westminster (1767-1845)

*Location: Belgrave Square, SW1*
*Sculptor: Jonathan Wylder*
*Material: Bronze     Date: 1999*

Sir Robert Grosvenor was the 2nd Earl of Grosvenor and acquired the title 1st Marquess of Westminster in 1831 from William IV in return for his change of allegiance to the Whig cause. Robert Grosvenor was an established member of the aristocracy who spent much of his time and energy on his lands near Chester and in rebuilding the family's country home of Eaton Hall. Through the employment of the master builder Thomas Cubitt, Grosvenor transformed the farmland that he acquired through marriage into the grand Regency squares of Mayfair, Belgravia and Pimlico. The Grosvenor family have remained a prominent and wealthy aristocratic family to this day and the statue was commissioned by the current 6th Duke of Westminster and unveiled in May 1999. The plinth bears the Ruskin quote 'When we build we build for ever', which is apt given the unspoilt nature of the square.

# 11. General Don Jose De San Martin (1778-1850)

*Location: Belgrave Square, SW1*
*Sculptor: Juan Carlos Ferraro*
*Material: Bronze*
*Date: 1994*

Don Jose De San Martin was born in a province of what is now Argentina, but at the time of his birth was a colony of Spain. San Martin was educated in Spain and joined the Spanish army, seeing battle against the French in Africa and Spain. He rose to the rank of lieutenant colonel before fleeing Spain in 1811 to join the revolutionary army of Argentina fighting Spanish rule. When San Martin arrived in Buenos Aires in 1812, the fledgling government was under threat from the Spanish forces and he was employed to build an army to defend the city. He soon devised an audacious plan to drive out the Spanish by crossing the Andes into Chile and attacking the Spanish stronghold in Peru.

San Martin formed an alliance with Bernardo O'Higgins – the deposed leader of Chile – and between 1817 and 1821 began the arduous series of battles that were to liberate Chile, Peru and his beloved Argentina from Spanish rule. San Martin had no political ambition and he retired in 1824 to briefly live on his farm in Chile, before leaving for France after the death of his wife. He was to spend his remaining years in Europe and only returned once to South America before his death in 1850. This rather ugly monument was a gift of the British community in Argentina.

## 12. Prince Henry The Navigator (1394-1460)

*Location: Belgrave Square, SW1*
*Material: Bronze*
*Date: 2001*

Prince Henry the Navigator was the third son of King John I of Portugal. Henry persuaded his father to mount an attack upon the Muslim port of Ceuta, on the North African coast. The Portuguese successfully took the city in August 1415 and Henry was able to oversee the vast riches that flowed through the Saharan trade routes. In 1420, Henry was appointed as governor of the order of Christ which was based at Tomar at the southern tip of Portugal. As well as practicing a devout Catholic faith, Henry established a centre for navigation and map-making at Sagres and financed numerous voyages of exploration. These voyages succeeded in discovering and occupying the Madeira Islands, the Azores and helped establish trade routes in Africa which circumnavigated Muslim lands. Within 30 years of Henry's death Portuguese ships had sailed beyond the southern tip of Africa and soon established trade routes with the Indies. Henry was far less successful as a soldier and his expedition to Tangier in 1437 was a military failure, but his achievements at Sagres were to change the world. The monument lies within the gardens of Belgrave Square and can only be seen through the gates.

## 13. Christopher Columbus (1446-1506)
*Location: Belgrave Square, SW1*
*Sculptor: Tomas Banuelos*
*Material: Bronze*
*Date: 1992*

Christopher Columbus is thought to be Italian in origin, but his early life is not well documented and there is still some disagreement as to his year of birth – this monument states it to be 1446. It is fairly certain that he spent his early years as a merchant seaman and acquired skills in navigation and map-making. In the late 15th century the disintegration of the Mogul Empire and the rise of Islam threatened the long-established trade routes with India and attempts were made to find new routes eastward through Africa. Columbus devised a plan to voyage west across the Atlantic Ocean to India based upon a false calculation of the earth's size and very poor knowledge of its landmass. Columbus spent years partitioning the Spanish crown and in 1492 they granted the ships and provisions he required. After five weeks of sailing Columbus and his crew discovered land on 12th October and went on to explore the islands that are now known as San Salvador and Cuba. Columbus believed these lands to be part of the Indian subcontinent – a misconception he held till his death. He returned to Spain as a hero and embarked on a further three voyages, but was to prove a less successful administrator than explorer and was removed from his position as governor in 1500. Columbus is a hero to many who regard him as the discoverer of the Americas, but others have criticised the conquest of these lands. This bronze statue of a seated Columbus was a gift of the Spanish government to commemorate the 500th anniversary of the discovery of the New World.

289

## 14. Simon Bolivar (1783-1830)
*Location: Belgrave Square, SW1*
*Sculptor: Daini*
*Material: Bronze*
*Date: 1973*

Simon Bolivar came from a wealthy and privileged background, and inherited a fortune when he was left an orphan as a child. He was educated by tutors and inculcated with the ideas of the European Enlightenment. As a young man Bolivar travelled in Europe and for a while became a figure in the court of Napoleon. On his return to Venezuela he allied himself to the revolutionary cause and through military victory drove the Spanish forces out and declared independence in 1813. The success was short-lived and civil war allowed the royalist army to again claim Venezuela for the Spanish crown in 1815.

Bolivar fled to Jamaica, where he formed a new revolutionary army and again returned to do battle with the Spanish, culminating in victory and the establishment of Greater Columbia (which included present-day Columbia, Panama, Ecuador and Venezuela) in 1819, with Bolivar as its first president. Bolivar went on to drive the Spanish from Peru. He was less successful as a politician than a revolutionary soldier and he failed to unite the continent as one nation and encountered rebellion and an attempt on his life. He died of tuberculosis just months after relinquishing power in 1830 having established himself in South America as El Libertador. The monument, which stands on the corner of Belgrave Square, does very little justice to the great man and looks more like a toy soldier adopting a ludicrously wooden posture.

# 15. Marshal Ferdinand Foch (1851-1929)

*Location: Grosvenor Gardens, SW1*
*Sculptor: G. Malissard*
*Material: Bronze*
*Date: 1930*

Ferdinand Foch was the son of a civil servant whose childhood was filled with stories of his forefathers' battles in Napoleon's army told by his great aunt. At the start of the Franco-Prussian War (1870) Foch enlisted in the 4th Infantry Regiment and as a young man experienced the bitterness of defeat and German occupation. Foch became a career soldier and determined to re-establish French military pride. He quickly attained the rank of captain and entered staff college in 1885. Foch was to become a college instructor and in this position had a considerable influence upon the military strategy of the French Army. By the start of World War One, Foch had reached the rank of lieutenant general and assumed command of the XX Corps. Despite initial retreat he managed to hold the German advance and prevent them crossing the Meurthe. Following this success Foch was appointed head of the Ninth Army and again stemmed the German advance and counter-attacked during the Battle of the Marne which greatly strengthened Allied resolve. In October 1914 Foch became commander of the northern section of the front and held his line before suffering heavy casualties at the Battle of the Somme (1916) which was to cause his brief removal from the front. The failure of Foch's successor, General Nivelle, and the support of Prime Minister Clemenceau saw Foch's return and by March 1918 he was Allied Supreme Commander in which position he accepted German surrender on 11th November 1918. Foch was as tough at the negotiating table as he had been on the battlefield and the harsh terms of the Treaty of Versailles was largely due to the force of his character.

Foch became a national hero in France and was the only foreign soldier to be made a field marshal in the British army in recognition of his contribution to the defeat of Germany. In the years since his death in 1929, Foch has received some criticism for his offensive strategy, which some blame for the heavy French losses at the start of the war. This point is open to question and there is little doubt that Foch was a great soldier. King Albert of Belgium said of Foch, 'that man could make the dead stand up and fight!'. This fine equestrian monument is a copy of one that stands in Cassel, France.

# Kensington & Knightsbridge

1) Dr Edward Jenner
2) Reginald Brabazon
3) John Hanning Speke
4) Peter Pan
5) Physical Energy - Cecil Rhodes
6) Queen Victoria
7) King William III
8) Prince Albert – The Albert Memorial
9) Prince Albert
10) Field Marshal Lord Napier of Magdala
11) Sir Clements Markham
12) David Livingstone
13) Sir Ernest Shackleton
14) Sir Julius Wernher & Alfred Beit
15) General Lord Baden-Powell
16) Cavalry of Empire

# Kensington & Knightsbridge

Most of the monuments in and around Hyde Park and Kensington Gardens have a royal or imperial theme. The Albert Memorial is the largest in London and as much an expression of a widow's grief as it is a statement of the Prince Consort's achievements. A further grand monument to the prince stands behind the Albert Hall. Queen Victoria's monument by Kensington Palace shows her as the young Queen Albert married in 1840. A more recent monument to a much earlier monarch, William III, stands in Kensington Palace.

Victoria's reign was much concerned with the British Empire and there are a great many monuments which touch on this theme. Reginald Brabazon established the Empire Movement and was helped in his patriotic mission by Lord Baden-Powell who has a monument on Queen's Gate. Field Marshal Napier of Magdala fought in many of the most important wars of empire, including the defeat of the Abyssinian king in 1868.

The Royal Geographical Society commemorates a more benign aspect of Victoria's reign with monuments to a number of famous explorers. Wernher and Beit made their fortune in the South African diamond mines and gave part of their fortune to Imperial College's Department of Mining, outside which their busts stand. Both men knew and worked with the founder of Rhodesia, Cecil Rhodes, who is commemorated in the large equestrian figure, 'Physical Energy'. The monuments to Peter Pan and the pioneer of vaccination, Dr Edward Jenner, are all the more charming for having no connection with royalty or empire. The last monument is a depiction of George slaying the dragon and is a memorial to the Cavalry of Empire.

# 1. Dr Edward Jenner (1749-1823)
*Location: Italian Garden, Kensington Gardens, W8*
*Sculptor: W. Calder Marshall*
*Material: Bronze*
*Date: erected in Trafalgar Square in 1858, moved here in 1862*

Edward Jenner was a country doctor who pioneered and promoted the inoculation of cowpox virus against the widespread and deadly scourge of smallpox. The word he used for this treatment was 'vaccination' (from the Latin for cow), which was later adopted by Pasteur for all forms of immunisation. Despite his critics, Jenner proved the efficacy of his treatment from his country practice in Gloucestershire and eventually won the support of Parliament for widespread vaccination. Jenner saved many millions of lives with his research, but his interests were far wider than medicine. He was an enthusiastic geologist and fossil-finder and in 1819 found the first remains of a dinosaur now known as a Plesiosaur. He became a member of the Royal Society not for his medical work but for his paper on the nesting habits of cuckoos. He was taught by the famous John Hunter (see page 29) as a medical student and they remained life-long friends, working together on subjects such as hibernation and migration. Jenner was also fascinated by balloon flight and launched one of the first hydrogen balloons in 1784, the sight of which is said to have terrified local labourers. Jenner was an incredible man and one untouched by vanity or pomp. He would no doubt have been indifferent to the movement of his statue from Trafalgar Square to its present site in the Italian Garden of Kensington Gardens in 1862. His place on the square was taken by a monument to the soldier Sir Henry Havelock (see page 18).

## 2. Reginald Brabazon, 12th Earl of Meath (1841-1929)

*Location: Lancaster Gate, W2*
*Sculptor: Herman Cowthra* ◆ *Material: Stone*
*Date: 1934*

Brabazon started his career as a soldier and after a brief period in the diplomatic service, with postings in Germany, Holland and France, he retired while still in his 30s to devote himself to good causes. Brabazon founded the Metropolitan Public Gardens Society in 1880 which promoted parks and green spaces and introduced the now familiar idea of a green belt around London to limit the capital's expansion – Meath Garden in Bethnal Green still bears his name. Those readers who have terrible memories of compulsory games during their time at school have Brabazon to blame – his Physical Education Bill of 1890 was rejected by Parliament, but persuaded school governors to introduce physical education into the weekly curriculum. Brabazon became a supporter of the Scout movement and a friend and ally of its founder, Baden-Powell (see page 311). He founded his own movement, the Legion of Frontiersmen, in 1904 and later established The Duty and Discipline Movement, which had the rather vague purpose of combating 'indiscipline' and giving 'support to all legitimate authority'.

The Earl of Meath will be best remembered for his Empire Movement, which sought to promote 'Responsibility, Sympathy, Duty and Self-Sacrifice' and introduced Empire day, a patriotic celebration on 25th May. Brabazon's emphasis upon physical and mental discipline and respect for authority seems anachronistic in the 21st century, but there is no doubt that he was a generous and kind man.

## 3. John Hanning Speke (1827-1864)

*Location: Italian Garden,*
*Kensington Gardens, W8*
*Material: Granite obelisk*
*Date: 1864*

John Hanning Speke was a commissioned officer who served in the Punjab and the Crimea and travelled in the Himalayas and Tibet before being injured while exploring Somaliland. In December 1856 he joined Richard Burton's expedition to search for the great lakes of Africa and the source of the Nile. In February 1858 they were the first Europeans to reach Lake Tanganyika. Speke later set out on his own and in July 1858 became the first explorer to reach the source of the Nile, which he named Lake Victoria. Speke's claims were rejected by Burton and he set out again with Captain James Grant to prove his discovery. On his return to England in 1862, Speke was fêted by the British public, but because of his poor notes he failed to convince several key figures, including his rival Burton. On the day they were scheduled to meet to debate the matter publicly, Speke was killed by his own gun while grouse shooting. Although Speke achieved where David Livingstone had failed (see page 308), his journal reveals him to be a lesser character: 'Now I had made up my mind never to sit upon the ground as the natives and Arabs are obliged to do, nor to make my obeisance in any other manner than is customary in England.' Speke left a bloody legacy in the form of his Hamitic hypothesis which claimed that Tutsi people (Hamites) were a superior race to the Hutus (Bantus). This theory was a divisive element in the genocide that took place in Rwanda in the 1990s.

## 4. Peter Pan

*Location: Kensington Gardens, SW7*
*Sculptor: Sir George Frampton*
*Material: Bronze*
*Date: 1912*

Situated on the west bank of the Long Water, this statue of the boy who never grew up is one of the few in London to be dedicated to a fictional character. It was commissioned by the author of Peter Pan, J.M. Barrie, who had recently enjoyed great success with the stage play. The statue appeared on the 1st of May 1912 as if by magic having been installed at the dead of night. It was the author's intention to make the appearance of the statue as magical as the tale. The location of the statue is also of significance, for it is here that Peter Pan first appears to Wendy. Barrie lived on Bayswater Road and used his local park and the children that played there as inspiration for his play.

The art nouveau style of the sculpture and its sudden appearance led to some disquiet. It was thought by some to be a piece of self-publicity by Barrie to promote his book and questions about the statue were asked in the House of Commons. It was only the popularity of the statue, particularly with children, that ensured its survival. There are seven other replica statues distributed throughout the world, although the one in Liverpool has recently been taken down due to vandalism. The London statue has been damaged many times; perhaps the vandals are inspired by the mischievous Greek god of the woodland from which Peter Pan gets his name?

# 5. Physical Energy – Cecil Rhodes (1853-1902)

*Location: Lancaster Walk, Kensington Gardens, SW7*
*Sculptor: George Frederic Watts*
*Material: Bronze*
*Date: 1908*

This sculpture is the work of G.F. Watts who created the 'Heroes Wall' in Postman's Park (see page 226). Watts regarded his work as representing the energy of the 'age of empire' and it was used as the centrepiece for the memorial to Cecil Rhodes in Cape Town. The monument's association with the man has faded with time, but still offers an opportunity to mention the most successful empire-builder of the late 19th century.

Sent away to Africa because of his frail health, Cecil Rhodes established a successful fruit farming business before turning to the Kimberley diamond mines in 1871 and founding the De Beers Mining Company in April 1880, the basis of his fortune. It was at this time that Rhodes entered politics, becoming prime minister of the Cape in 1890 and passing measures to serve the interests of the mining industry, such as the Glen Grey Act, which deprived the black population of their land. In 1895, and with the financial support of Beit (see page 310), Rhodes attempted a disastrous coup in the Transvaal to overthrow the Boer government and helped bring about the Second Boer War a few years later. Undaunted, Rhodes established the British South Africa Company, which went on to occupy the Mashonaland, defeating the indigenous tribes and so creating Rhodesia in 1897. Ironically, it was a disturbed stalker, Catherine Radziwill, who gave Rhodes his greatest problems. Her false accusations were to lead to a court case which contributed to Rhodes's final illness and premature death.

# 6. Queen Victoria (1819-1901)

*Location: Broad Walk, Kensington Gardens, SW7*
*Sculptor: Princess Louise*
*Material: Marble*
*Date: 1893*

This is one of the seven statues dedicated to Queen Victoria in London. It is remarkable because it is the work of her daughter, Princess Louise, who was a skilled sculptor and a pupil of Joseph Boehm. The statue is close to that of her beloved Prince Albert and shows the Queen as a young monarch. The largest and most extravagant monument to Victoria can be found in front of Buckingham Palace (see page 115).

# 7. King William III (1650-1702)

*Location: Kensington Palace, W8*
*Sculptor: Heinrich Baucke*
*Date: 1907*
*Material: Bronze*

This statue commemorates William III, who deposed James II in 1688 – an event that has become known as the 'Glorious Revolution'. The monument is, however, less about the politics of 1688 and far more about the politics of the early 20th century. It was presented by Kaiser Wilhelm II to his uncle Edward VII, no doubt to remind him of the historic links between the two nations that were by then on opposite sides of international alliances. The attempt proved a failure and only seven years after this gift was presented the two countries were confronting each other accross northern Europe. Edward VII was the last monarch of the House of Saxe-Coburg-Gotha; his successor, King George V, replaced the German-sounding title with the more British Windsor during the First World War. For a more detailed account of the Glorious Revolution of 1688 and William III's part in it, refer to his monument on St James's Square (page 108) and the monument to James II on Trafalgar Square (page 8).

# 8. Prince Albert - The Albert Memorial (1819-1861)

*Location: Kensington Gardens, opposite Royal Albert Hall, SW7*
*Architect: Sir G. Gilbert Scott (monument)*
*Sculptors: John Foley (statue), P. Macdowell (Europe),*
*John Bell (America), J. H. Foley (Asia), W. Theed (Africa),*
*W. Calder Marshall (Agriculture), Thomas Thornycroft (Commerce),*
*J. Lawlor (Engineering), J. Weekes (Manufacturing),*
*H.H. Armstead, J. Birnie Philip, J.F. Redfern (Friezes & other sculpture).*
*Material: Red, Pink and Grey Granite; Marble; Bronze Gilt*
*Date: 1875*

There is no larger or more extravagant monument to be found in the capital than that to the memory of Prince Albert, consort to Queen Victoria. Prince Albert was a great influence upon the Queen and can take credit for many of the achievements of her reign. Britain had embarked on the world's first industrial revolution when George III was king, but it was not until the coronation of Victoria, with the considerable encouragement of Prince Albert, that the royal family embraced the middle-class virtues of industry and progress.

It was Prince Albert who organised the Great Exhibition to celebrate Britain's industry, which took place in Hyde Park in 1851. When it was suggested that a memorial be erected to the Prince at the time of the exhibition he dismissed the idea, writing: '... I would much rather not be made the prominent feature of such a monument, as it would both disturb my quiet rides in Rotten Row to see my own face staring at me, and if (as is very likely) it became an artistic monstrosity, like most of our monuments, it would upset my equanimity to be permanently ridiculed and laughed at in effigy.'

This monument, constructed after Albert's sudden death from typhoid at the age of only 42, is as much an expression of a widow's grief as it is a celebration of Albert's achievements. Standing 180 feet in height and involving the work of a vast number of the county's leading sculptors and craftsmen, the work took over 20 years to complete and cost £120,000, an enormous sum. The Prince is depicted by John Foley sitting with a catalogue of the Great Exhibition in hand and is the centre of a vast Gothic shrine with friezes depicting artists, musicians and writers (both English and German) while above him are depictions of the celestial. At each corner of the shrine, separate sculptures represent Agriculture, Commerce, Engineering and Manufacture and a further group of four statues stands further out, representing Europe, America, Asia and Africa. It is arguable whether the monument is a grand Victorian statement or the 'artistic monstrosity' which Albert dreaded. There are certainly elements of kitsch and pomposity to the work and very little to suggest progress amid these classical figures. By the 1990s the monument was falling into disrepair perhaps, in some part, due to the two wars fought with Germany and the increasing anglicisation of the royal family (see details of William III's statue on page 108). The monument was covered in scaffolding for several years and there were even plans for its demolition. In 1994 English Heritage took charge of its restoration at a cost of over £10 million and the monument can again be seen in all its bombastic glory. There is a second statue commemorating Prince Albert in Holborn (see page 192).

## 9. Prince Albert

*Location: Steps of Albert Hall, SW7*
*Sculptor: Joseph Durham*
*Material: Bronze*
*Date: 1858*

This monument is easily forgotten, being located behind the Royal Albert Hall and so close to the much grander Albert Memorial. It was first placed in the gardens of The Royal Horticultural Society, but was moved to its present site in 1899.

# 10. Field Marshal Lord Napier of Magdala (1810-90)

*Location: Queen's Gate, SW7*
*Sculptor: Sir Joseph Boehm*
*Material: Bronze*
*Date: erected in Carlton House Gardens in 1891, moved here in 1920*

Robert Cornelis Napier was born in Ceylon at the height of the British Empire. Despite not being a member of the famous Napier military family, he rose rapidly within the British army and gained a reputation as a skilled administrator and brave soldier. The Indian population was beginning to rebel against the yoke of British rule and Napier was involved in the Sikh Wars (1845–49) and took part in the relief of Lucknow (1858) during the Indian Mutiny under General Outram (see page 145). He later served in the North West Frontier District and saw action in Peshawar and Afghanistan. His most famous military campaign was the expedition to Ethiopia in April 1868 to release hostages held by the Abyssinian king Tewodros II and capture Magdala. This swift resolution made Napier a national hero and he was raised to the peerage. The situation was a little more complicated than the British public's adulation might suggest because Napier had defeated a poorly equipped army with the use of modern guns and the Abyssinians were trying to gain the protection of Britain from other Muslim neighbours and not seeking to go to war. To make matters worse, after victory Napier had supervised the removal of a valuable treasure from Magdala. The prime minister, William Gladstone, expressed dismay at Napier's actions but did nothing for fear of a scandal. Today there is still a campaign to return the Abyssinian treasures nearly 150 years after they were looted. This equestrian statue of Napier is a replica of one that formerly stood in Calcutta.

# 11. Sir Clements Markham (1830-1916)

*Location: Royal Geographical Society, Exhibition Road, SW7*
*Sculptor: F.W. Pomeroy*
*Material: Bronze*
*Date: 1921*

Sir Clements Robert Markham was born into a highly regarded clerical family, his great grandfather having served as Archbishop of Canterbury. Markham had a brief spell in the Navy before he travelled to Peru to explore the eastern slopes of the Andes and developed an abiding interest in the country and its history. After his travels, Markham joined the Indian civil service and while acting as an administrator also explored the sub-continent. In 1875 he went on his only Arctic expedition which made him an enthusiast for polar exploration and an important supporter of later Arctic expeditions when he became president of the Royal Geographic Society.

Markham was the key proponent of the Discovery expedition and supervised the building of the ship in Scotland and chose the crew, which included Captain Scott and Shackleton (see pages 103 and 309). It was Lady Markham who launched the Discovery on the Tay in March 1901. Markham was not only an explorer but also an influential historian who wrote on all manner of subjects, from the Greek traveller Pytheas to the reign of Richard III, as well as several important books about the culture and history of Peru. His knowledge of Peruvian medicine enabled him to save many lives by introducing the use of quinine as a cure for malaria in colonial India. This bust of Markham was a gift from the Peruvian government in recognition of his work and stands outside the Royal Geographic Society which he served for many years.

## 12. David Livingstone (1813-1873)

*Location: Royal Geographical Society, Exhibition Road, SW7*
*Sculptor: T.B. Huxley-Jones*
*Material: Bronze*
*Date: 1953*

Livingstone was a Scottish missionary who became the greatest African explorer of his generation. He spent over 30 years of his life exploring the continent, acting as missionary, doctor, explorer, scientist and anti-slavery activist. As a child, Livingstone worked in a cotton mill while continuing his education through evening classes, eventually qualifying as a medical doctor. It was his Methodist faith that persuaded him to become a missionary doctor in southern Africa in 1840. After settling in Africa and marrying the daughter of a fellow missionary it was from there that Livingstone began exploring the continent. Unlike John Speke (see page 298), Livingstone considered the Africans as his equals and in the course of his travels learnt several native languages. He covered almost a third of the continent and received a gold medal from the Royal Geographical Society for crossing the entire African continent from west to east. He was the first European to see Victoria Falls and contributed to the discovery of the source of the Nile. It was in November 1871 that Henry Stanley uttered the famous words 'Dr Livingstone, I presume?', having been sent by the New York Herald Tribune to provide assistance to Livingstone in his last, troubled expedition. Stanley provided Livingstone with vital supplies, but the years of struggle had begun to take their toll. Livingstone died in April 1872. In accordance with his wishes his heart was buried in Africa while his body was laid to rest in Westminster Abbey. This bronze statue was erected 80 years after his death.

# 13. Sir Ernest Shackleton (1874-1922)

*Location: Royal Geographical Society, Exhibition Road, SW7*
*Sculptor: C. Sargeant Jagger*
*Material: Bronze*
*Date: 1932*

Ernest Shackleton determined to lead a life of exploration from an early age and went to sea at 16 against the wishes of his father, who wanted him to train as a doctor. On leave in London in 1900, Shackleton was chosen to go with Captain Robert Scott (see page 103) to the South Pole on the famous Discovery expedition. On 30th December 1902 Scott, Shackleton and Wilson came within 400 miles of the South Pole, the furthest South then achieved. The reaching of the South Pole had captured the public's imagination and Shackleton now became determined to make it to the Pole with his own expedition, setting out in command of the Nimrod in 1907. He set out to cross the ice with a small team and reached within 97 miles of the South Pole in January 1909, before turning back after running out of food. Shackleton was awarded the Royal Geographic Society gold medal for his heroic failure but his achievement was soon eclipsed by Roald Amundsen's successful arrival at the South Pole in December 1911. Shackleton commanded another voyage to circumnavigate the South Pole between 1914–16 on the appropriately named Endurance. The ship became trapped in the ice in 1915 and Shackleton was forced to make an incredible journey across 800 frozen miles to South Georgia to get aid. It was this dramatic rescue which assured Shackleton's place in history as a great British hero. He died of a heart attack after embarking on a third expedition in January 1922.

## 14. Sir Julius Wernher (1850-1912) & Alfred Beit (1853-1906)

*Location: Royal School of Mines, Prince Consort Road, SW7*
*Sculptor: Paul Montford ◆ Material: Stone*
*Date: 1910*

The busts of Julius Wernher and Alfred Beit commemorate two men whose lives were intertwined. Both came from Germany in the 1870s after the Franco-Prussian War and both began their careers in the diamond and gold company of Jules Porges. They amassed vast fortunes for themselves and their patron in South Africa. When Porges retired, his successors formed Wernher, Beit and Co. which became De Beers in 1888.

The two men were strong allies in business but lived very different lives. Wernher married a society beauty and held lavish parties at their home in Piccadilly and bought a grand country house in Bedfordshire which he filled with one of the world's largest personal art collections. In contrast, Beit was a quiet, modest character who also had a grand London home but remained unmarried and made no attempt to gain recognition in British society. He spent much of his time and a good deal of his money attempting to further British colonial interests in Africa. He was a close ally of Cecil Rhodes (see page 300) and helped finance the Jameson Raid in 1895, which attempted to establish British rule in the South African Republic. He later provided money to support the British army during the Second South African War (see page 95). Wernher and Beit were both men of fabulous wealth and gave substantial sums to various educational and colonial causes including the Royal School of Mines outside which their busts stand. A good deal of Julius Wernher's art collection can be seen at Ranger's House in Greenwich.

## 15. Robert Baden-Powell, 1st Baron Baden-Powell (1857-1941)

*Location: Queen's Gate (near Hyde Park Gate), SW7*
*Sculptor: Donald Potter*
*Material: Granite ♦ Date: 1961*

This monument stands outside the head quarters of the British Scout movement which Baden-Powell founded in 1908. Baden-Powell was always interested in the outdoor life and as a boy would escape from his boarding school to camp in the nearby woods. He put his survival skills to good use as a soldier during the Second Boer War and became a hero of the Siege of Mafeking (1899-1900). He used his new-found celebrity to write books about military scouting and trained new recruits, who lacked the skills of self-sufficiency, common-sense and initiative, to be useful soldiers. Like many Victorian military men, Baden-Powell found the new century a bewildering place. He became concerned that society was becoming weak and degenerate and that people were losing their individuality and enjoyment of life. It was from his concern for the young and a desire to share some of his scouting experiences as a soldier, that Baden-Powell wrote *Scouting for Boys* in 1908. Widespread interest in this book led to the formation of the Boy Scouts and Girl Guides movements, with the first World Scout Jamboree taking place in Olympia in 1920. Today it is easy to mock Baden-Powell and his movement, but there are still millions of scouts with the Queen's Gate offices still busy with scouts from around the world. Some of Baden-Powell's attitudes continue in modern essentialist thinking such as the recent 'Iron John' movement in the US. Baden-Powell was a skilled artist and also an enthusiastic thespian.

## 16. Cavalry of Empire

*Location: Hyde Park, SW7*
*Sculptor: Captain Adrian Jones*
*Material: Bronze*
*Date: 1924*

This brutal depiction of St George's slaying of the dragon is dedicated to the cavalry regiments that fought in the First World War. The cavalry were for many centuries considered the most prestigious regiments of the army compared to the ordinary foot soldier. Even into the late 19th century cavalry regiments were important in the Crimean and South African Wars. The First World War was the first to employ mechanised tanks, aircraft and static trench positions. This new form of warfare left the cavalry without a role, and with the exception of one or two engagements they played little part in the conflict. It is appropriate that the sculptor used an ancient myth to represent the bravery of the cavalry, as they played no part in the Second World War and have since largely been used for ceremonial purposes.

Chelsea

1) Amadeus Mozart
2) King Charles II
3) Sir Hans Sloane
4) D.G Rossetti
5) Thomas Carlyle
6) Sir Thomas More

# Chelsea

Chelsea was probably founded as a settlement by the Saxons and there are records of the manor of Chelsea which precede the Domesday Book. The manor was acquired by Henry VIII in 1536 and has enjoyed royal associations since that time and has always been an area favoured by the wealthy. The monuments to Sir Thomas More and Sir Hans Sloane reflect the status of Chelsea as a residential area. Both men were buried in Chelsea Old Church – where More's monument stands – alongside many prominent figures of the 17th and 18th centuries. Chelsea Royal Hospital was completed by Wren in 1694 and is a further reminder of the area's royal associations and contains a monument to Charles II – after which the King's Road is named. It was not until the 19th century that Chelsea ceased to be a separate village and was subsumed into the capital during a period of rapid expansion. It was during the late-19th century that Chelsea became known as an artist's colony with painters Rossetti, Turner, Whistler and Singer Sargent, and writers George Meredith, Algernon Swinburne, Leigh Hunt and Thomas Carlyle among the artists to call Chelsea their home. The monuments to Rossetti and Carlyle stand on Cheyne Walk where both men lived and where the Pre-Raphaelite movement was born. Chelsea's bohemian reputation began to decline at the beginning of the 20th century as property prices in the area increased and those with a talent for making money rather than making art colonised the smart terraced houses. These days visitors will enjoy walking the streets of Chelsea to see its monuments, but are more likely to rub shoulders with merchant bankers and company directors than artists.

# 1. Wolfgang Amadeus Mozart (1756-1791)

*Location: Orange Square, SW3*
*Sculptor: Philip Jackson*
*Material: Bronze*
*Date: 1994*

Wolfgang Amadeus Mozart was a rare example of a genius born into circumstances which developed his talents to their full potential. Mozart's father, Leopold, was a recognised musician and teacher and both young Wolfgang and his sister were given a rigorous musical education. The Mozart family toured Europe and Amadeus and his sister performed for many royal courts and spent time in both Paris and London. In April 1764 the Mozart family briefly settled in London and Amadeus performed for George III (see page 6) on the fourth anniversary of his ascension to the throne. Mozart learned a great deal in London, being influenced by the Italian music that was so popular in the capital, and making a life-long friend of the composer Johann Christian Bach who was 30 at the time of their first meeting. London's interest in 'the little German boy' began to wane and the family left England for the continent in August 1765. Wolfgang was never to return to these shores, making his reputation and establishing his genius in Vienna and Prague. Having spent his youth under the strict but loving control of his father, Mozart was to lead a troubled, chaotic but remarkably creative adult life. He died from a mysterious fever at the age of 35 in December 1791, leaving behind him over 600 musical compositions, from symphonies and operas to piano sonatas and quartets. This diminutive 20th-century monument depicts Mozart as the child prodigy during his time in London and stands not far from where the family lived in Chelsea.

## 2. King Charles II (1630-1685)

*Location: South Court, Chelsea Hospital, Royal Hospital Road, SW3*
*Sculptor: Grinling Gibbons (1648-1721)*
*Material: Bronze*
*Date: 1676 (erected 1692)*

This monument to King Charles II in Roman costume was presented to the King by his loyal servant Tobias Rustat, who also presented a second equestrian statue which stands in Windsor Castle, and a third statue to commemorate his brother James II (see page 7). This marks Rustat as one of history's greatest royal sycophants, but his loyalty was to be rewarded when Charles II returned to the throne in May 1660. Rustat was given a well paid place at court and became a wealthy business man who funded many worthy causes, including Jesus College, Cambridge. The preference for Roman costume to depict British monarchs may stem from the idea in Roman Law of Divine Right, rather than British Common Law which defines the monarch's power as stemming from the will of his subjects. It was this difference in law which was at dispute during Charles I's trial. This interpretation is given further weight by the fact that the statue of Charles II shows him holding a baton, which is a symbol of imperial authority. Every year on May 29th the statue is wreathed in oak leaves to commemorate the king's escape from the battle of Worcester in 1651, when it is said he hid in Boscobel Oak to avoid Cromwell's troops. Originally gilded, it was bronzed in 1782 and re-gilded in 2002. Charles II sired at least 14 illegitimate children, many of whom were given an aristocratic title. Both Camilla Parker-Bowles and Princess Diana descend from Charles II's illegitimate offspring. Prince William will be the first monarch since Queen Anne in 1714 to have a direct hereditary line to the Stuarts.

# 3. Sir Hans Sloane (1660-1753)

*Location: Chelsea Physic Garden, Royal Hospital Road, SW3*
*Sculptor: John Michael Rysbrack (1693-1770)*
*Material: White marble*
*Date: 1732*

Hans Sloane was a scientist, naturalist and physician who gave this site to the Apothecaries' Society in 1722 on condition that they supply the Royal Society with specimens. If the establishment of this fine botanical garden had been Sloane's only achievement it would have been noteworthy, but this was only a small part of this incredible man's exploits. During his long life Sloane travelled widely and amassed one of the greatest collections of plants, animals, antiquities, coins and many other objects of his time which became so large that it filled much of his house and required a full-time curator. Sloane opened his collection to many leading naturalists and so helped the development of many fields of natural science. On his death at the age of 93, his collection formed the founding core of the British Museum and later the Natural History Museum. The original of this sculpture stands in the foyer of The British Museum in recognition of his importance in the founding of this great institution. Those with a love of chocolate should also be thankful to Hans Sloane. As a young man he journeyed to Jamaica and was introduced to the cocoa bean which he found unpalatable. It was Sloane who formulated a recipe for milk chocolate which was later to be used by the Cadbury brothers.

# 4. Dante Gabriel Rossetti (1828-1882)
*Location: Chelsea Embankment Gardens, SW3*
*Architect: J. P. Seddon* ◆ *Artist: Ford Madox Brown*
*Material: Bronze and Stone*
*Date: 1887*

Fountains are not really the subject of this book, but this ornate piece does include a fine bronze medallion representing Rossetti holding a quill pen, by his fellow Pre-Raphaelite and teacher Ford Madox Brown. Dante Gabriel Rossetti was born in 1828 to an illustrious family. His father was the exiled Italian patriot and scholar, Gabriele Rossetti and his sister, Christina, was a renowned poet.

Rossetti was both a painter and poet, whose work sought to recapture the richness and purity of medieval art. In both his paintings and his poetry his main theme was love, but he also tackled Christian subjects. As a student at the Royal Academy he met William Holman Hunt and John Millais, with whom he founded the Pre-Raphaelite Brotherhood in 1848.

As befits a romantic artist, Rossetti had many lovers. His most famous muse was Elizabeth Siddal, who became his wife in 1860. When she died of laudanum poisoning after only two years of marriage, Rossetti was consumed with grief and buried her at Highgate cemetery with the only draft of a book of his poems. Seven years later, and facing penury, Rossetti was granted permission to disinter her body and remove the book for publication.

After Elizabeth's death, Rossetti moved to 16 Cheyne Walk (close to this fountain) and established what he described as a 'temple to aestheticism'. This involved living with a great many exotic animals including a zebra, raccoon and kangaroo. He died in poverty in 1882. His paintings can be seen in Tate Britain.

# 5. Thomas Carlyle (1795-1881)

*Location: Chelsea Embankment, SW3*
*Sculptor: Sir Joseph Boehm*
*Material: Bronze*
*Date: 1882*

This monument commemorates the Scottish-born historian and essayist Thomas Carlyle, who was one of the leading intellectual figures of the Victorian Era. In an age of reason and progress Carlyle struck a sceptical tone, influenced by his Scottish Calvinist upbringing and his interest in German philosophy. His idiosyncratic style of writing captured the public imagination, contrasting as it did with the detached style of historians such as Macaulay. Carlyle moved to London with his formidable wife in order to write his three volume history of the French Revolution which appeared in 1837. The first draft of the work was mistakenly burned by the maid servant of his friend John Stuart Mill – a mistake for which Mill paid his friend £100. A stone medallion on 24 Cheyne Row marks his long residence at the address where he established his reputation with philosophical works such as *Sartor Restartus* (1834), and *On Heroes and Hero Worship* (1841). Like his near neighbour, Rossetti, Carlyle was deeply affected by the death of his wife in 1866 and virtually disappeared from public life. Ironically for a historian, history has not been kind to Carlyle. His praise of heroes as the driving force of history was to be discredited in the 20th century by the rise of Fascism and Soviet Communism, particularly when it was discovered that Hitler was a keen reader of Carlyle and kept a copy of his biography of Fredrick II by his bedside. The writer Henry James rather cruelly described the elderly Carlyle as 'the same old sausage, fizzing and sputtering in its own grease.'

# 6. Sir Thomas More (1478-1535)

*Location: Chelsea Embankment, SW3*
*Sculptor: L. Cubitt Bevis*
*Material: Bronze*
*Date: 1969*

This unusual painted statue is a contemporary work situated outside Chelsea Old Church where More worshiped and close to the farm house where he lived when Chelsea was still a rural hamlet. More was a scholar who as a young man wrote *Utopia* (1516) and became a close friend of Desiderius Erasmus and Hans Holbein. He considered joining the priesthood, but his talents and temperament led him to a political career within the court of Henry VIII. In 1518 he became a Privy Councillor and by 1529 he had risen to the position of Lord Chancellor. His fall came when Henry demanded changes that would sanction his divorce. More was an ardent Catholic and could not accommodate his master and so resigned in 1532. In April 1534 More was imprisoned for failing to swear to the Act of Succession and the Oath of Supremacy and in 1535 was executed for treason. His final words were: 'The King's good servant, but God's First.' More has become a Catholic martyr and was canonised in 1935 – 400 years after his death. This statue was unveiled by one of his successors as Speaker of the House, Dr Henry King, in July 1969. History has been kind to More but several biographers have painted a more complex picture of the man. His religious faith not only inspired his defiance to the king, but led him to zealously persecute Lutherans when Lord Chancellor. He sent six dissenters to the stake and even interrogated a number in his own home. There is another monument to More in Holborn (see page 202).

322

# Greenwich

# London's Monuments • Greenwich

1) New Zealand Memorial
2) Royal Naval College Busts
3) Sir Walter Raleigh
4) Joseph René Bellot
5) George II
6) Horatio Nelson
7) Vice-Admiral Sir Thomas Boulden Thompson
8) Royal Hospital Memorial
9) Admiral Sir Sidney Smith
10) Admiral James Saumarez
11) Captain Sir William Peel
12) Admiral Sir Edward Pellew, Lord Exmouth
13) Captain James Cook
14) Lord Horatio Nelson
15) William IV
16) General James Wolfe

# Greenwich

General James Wolfe sailed from Greenwich in 1759 for the Battle of Quebec that was to prove his last. His monument was unveiled at the highest point in Greenwich Park in 1930 and looks out upon a landscape that would astound the 18th-century warrior with the distant towers of Canary Wharf dominating the skyline. There are several monuments here which Wolfe would recognise; Captain James Cook sailed with him to the Caribbean, while George II was a great admirer of the young Wolfe's exploits.

It is the Hanoverian dynasty and the naval men who fought their battles that predominate in Greenwich. Admiral Nelson was the greatest of these and has three monuments, the finest being the bust behind the National Maritime Museum. William IV, the 'sailor king', was the best man at Nelson's wedding, but was prevented from taking command of a ship because of fears about his competence. His monument stands close to Nelson's in its own garden. Within the National Maritime Museum are three monuments to naval men who worked with Nelson – the Admirals Smith, Saumarez and Pellew – and one to the Victorian Captain Sir William Peel. At the front of the museum is a column in memory of Sir Thomas Thompson who was a protege of Nelson's, and an obelisk to the 20,000 seamen patients of Greenwich Naval Hospital.

At the entrance to what used to be the Royal Naval College are reliefs commemorating many great sailors and closer to the Thames are Victorian obelisks, one in memory of those who lost their lives in the last significant war against the Maori and the other commemorating Joseph Bellot for his courage during the 1851 expedition to find Franklin. Sir Walter Raleigh is the only Tudor among the many Hanoverians, but his statue is the most recent, having been moved here from Whitehall in 2002.

# 1. New Zealand Memorial (1863-4)

*Location: River front near Greenwich Pier, SE10*
*Sculptor: n/a*
*Material: Granite*

There were 13 wars during the 19th century which are collectively known as the New Zealand or Maori Wars. This obelisk commemorates those who lost their lives in one of the last battles of the conflict. The wars resulted from the gradual displacement of the native Maori tribes of New Zealand by white settlers. The 1840 Treaty of Waitangi protected the Maori lands but the settler occupation continued and in 1843 the first of the New Zealand Wars was fought. The Maori tribes were skilled warriors and during the Northern (1845-6), the Wellington–Hutt (1846) and Whanganui (1847-48) Wars they fought the settlers to a standstill. Having achieved very little by military means, an uneasy peace was kept for 12 years until the growing settler population led to the First Taranaki War (1860-1), another unsuccessful attempt to drive the Maori from the land which led to stalemate after 12 months of fighting.

Until this time the settlers had largely fought unaided, but from 1860 they were assisted by Royal Naval ships based in the Australian colonies. This monument commemorates those who lost their lives during the Battle of Gate Pa, in April 1864, which was part of the last major war fought in New Zealand, finally driving the Maori from their land. The crews from HMS Curacoa, Miranda, Esk and Harrier were heavily involved in the bloody campaign which involved hand to hand fighting. The victory enforced the New Zealand Settlements Act of 1863 which confiscated about 4 million acres from the Maori.

## 2. Royal Naval College Busts

*Location: Greenwich Visitor Centre,*
*Cutty Sark Gardens, SE10*
*(entrance to the Old Royal Naval College)*
*Date: 1874-75*

Above the entrance to the Royal Naval College at the Greenwich Visitor Centre are busts of great naval heroes.

## George Anson (1697-1762) – He defeated the French off Cape Finisterre in 1747 and was made a full admiral a year later. He attained the position of admiral of the fleet in 1761.

## Sir Francis Drake (1540-1596) – He voyaged to Africa where he sold slaves and spent much of his career fighting the Spanish fleet under the patronage of Elizabeth. In 1579 he was the first to sail the Pacific Ocean and was knighted in 1581. He is best known for his successful battle against the Spanish Armada in 1588.

## Captain James Cook (1728-79) – see pages 93.

## Admiral Charles Howard (1536-1624) – Lord Howard of Effingham was an admiral and courtier who, along with Drake, played a key role in the defeat of the Spanish Armada.

## Robert Blake (1598-1657) – He fought for the Parliamentarians during the Civil War and later against the Dutch and Spanish. Blake was the first English Admiral to keep a fleet at sea during the winter and developed several naval techniques.

## Vice-Admiral John Benbow (1653-1702) – Benbow had a reputation for his reckless command against pirates, the French and the Spanish. While serving in the West Indies in 1702 he suffered a mutiny while chasing four French vessels and was fatally injured. He became known as Brave Benbow for his heroic death.

## John Montagu, Fourth Earl of Sandwich (1718-1792)

– He was first lord of the Admiralty during the American Revolution and promoted Britain's naval exploration. An inveterate gambler who while at the gaming tables would eat meat between bread and so gave his name to the sandwich.

## Admiral Lord George Rodney (1719-1792) – Perhaps

the greatest of Britain's 18th-century admirals, he distinguished himself against the French and Spanish during the Seven Years War and the American War of Independence. In 1781 he became Vice-Admiral of Great Britain.

## Admiral Adam Duncan(1731-1804) – Duncan's defeat of

the Dutch at Camperdown in 1797 was one of Britain's great naval victories for which he was made a baronet. Duncan was a mentor to Nelson who kept a portrait of him in his cabin.

## Admiral Cuthbert Collingwood (1748-1810) – He

fought under Howe and Jervis during the first naval engagements of the French Revolutionary wars and was made vice-admiral in 1799. Collingwood was second-in-command at Trafalgar.

## Admiral Richard Howe (1726-1799) – Howe played a

major part in the Seven Years War and the American War of Independence against the French. Howe's relief of Gibraltar in 1782 gained him the post of Lord of the Admiralty. He successfully commanded

the first naval battle against revolutionary France in 1794.

## Horatio Nelson (1758-1805) – see page 19.

## Admiral John Jervis (1735-1823) – He commanded the

Mediterranean fleet in 1795, won a crushing victory against the Spanish off Cape St Vincent in 1797 and blockaded the French fleet at Brest in 1799. As first Lord of the Admiralty he did much to fight corruption in the navy.

## 3. Sir Walter Raleigh (1552-1618)

*Location: Outside Greenwich Visitor Centre, Cutty Sark Gardens, SE10*
*Sculptor: William Macmillan*
*Material: Bronze*
*Date: January 2002, unveiled in Whitehall 1959*

As a young man, Walter Raleigh embarked upon a naval expedition which was little more than piracy. Later, as a soldier, he crushed a Catholic rebellion in Ireland which earned him a knighthood and brought him into the court of Queen Elizabeth. He became one of her favourites and used his royal influence to shamelessly enrich himself. Raleigh, using royal patronage, embarked on an expedition to the New World between 1584-89. The adventure failed to colonise America but brought the potato and tobacco to Europe. It is said that when Raleigh first smoked, his servant doused him with ale, thinking he was on fire.

Raleigh's fall began when Elizabeth discovered his affair with one of her ladies-in-waiting. He was sent to the Tower and when released banished on another expedition. The Queen died in 1603 and Raleigh was even more out of favour with King James I. He was placed in the Tower where he began his book *History of the World*. After 12 years, Raleigh was sent on a further expedition to South America, but failed to return with the promised treasure and was executed in 1618. As was the custom in Tudor times his preserved head was given to his wife – a grisly token which she kept until her death nearly 30 years later.

This monument was erected over 350 years after Raleigh's execution. The delay may be explained by the complexity of Raleigh's character; he was both courageous and brutal, an embodiment of renaissance culture and a flagrant opportunist.

330

# 4. Joseph René Bellot (1826-1853)

*Location: River front near Greenwich Pier, SE10*
*Sculptor: Philip Hardwick*
*Material: Red Aberdeen granite*
*Date: 1855*

Joseph René Bellot is a name that has largely been erased from the history books. The obelisk that stands outside the Maritime Museums commemorates his role in the expedition in search of John Franklin (see page 101).  Franklin set forth in May 1845 to navigate the Northwest Passage, with over 180 men and two well stocked ships. He and his men disappeared and the search to find them captured the Victorian imagination, with 30 rescue expeditions undertaken between 1847 and 1880. Joseph René Bellot was second-in-command of The Prince Albert, which set sail from Aberdeen in May 1851 under the captaincy of William Kennedy. At one stage in their adventures, when attempting to enter Port Leopold, Kennedy was left stranded. Bellot established winter quarters at Batty Bay and then returned to find Kennedy who had fended for himself on the ice for five weeks. William Kennedy's account of their unsuccessful expedition to find Franklin gave a good account of Bellot's actions and helps to explain this monument in his honour. The stone used for the statue originates from Aberdeen, from where Kennedy and Bellot sailed in 1851. It was later discovered that Franklin and his men met a terrible fate when their ships became trapped in the ice and they were forced to abandon them, eventually starving to death. Bellot also has a crater on the moon in his name.

## 5. George II (1683-1760)
Location: Old Royal Naval College Gardens, SE10
Sculptor: J.M. Rysbrack
Material: Marble
Date: 1735

It is fitting that this much eroded statue is made from marble captured from a French ship in the Mediterranean as its subject was a military man whose greatest personal achievements surrounded his military exploits against the French. George was the last British monarch to lead his men into battle and spent much of his time talking of military matters and explaining in details his military achievements. His last battle was at Dettingen in 1743 which was the first battle for the young James Wolfe (see page 342), whose statue now looks down upon his king from Greenwich Park. George's wife, Caroline of Ansbach, is said to have been by far her husband's intellectual superior and to have had a very great influence upon his decision-making. The situation was recognised by politicians at the time who sought to win favour with the Queen in order to influence the King. After her death in 1737, George II proved an ineffectual political strategist – failing to manipulate parliament (as his son was later able to). It was on the battlefield that his reign had its greatest successes, with the defeat of the Jacobites at Culloden in 1746 and the triumphs of Clive in India and Wolfe in North America. The latter part of his reign marked the ascendancy of Pitt the Elder in parliament and it was to Pitt's leadership that these victories were credited. George II died in October 1760. There is also a statue to him in Golden Square (see page 35)

# 6. Horatio Nelson (1758-1805)

*Location: Outside The Trafalgar Tavern, Park Row, SE10*
*Sculptor: Lesley Pover*
*Material: Bronze*
*Date: 2005*

This monument to Nelson (see page 19) shows the great admiral looking out across the Thames and is remarkable for the ample dimensions attributed to the naval man's breeches, prompting one wit to remark 'so that's what they mean by Nelson's column'. The monument was commissioned by the Trafalgar Tavern alongside which it stands, and was unveiled by that other great Englishman, the interior designer Lawrence Llewellyn-Bowen.

# 7. Vice-Admiral Sir Thomas Boulden Thompson (1766-1828)

*Location: Old Royal Naval College, SE10*
*Material: Stone*
*Date:*

This stone column commemorates one of the great naval men of the Napoleonic Wars, who went to sea at the age of 12, was a lieutenant at 16 and took command of his first ship at 20. It was at the Battle of the Nile on 1st August 1798 that the 50-gun Leander, with Thompson at the helm, played a major part in the defeat of the French. The success of the campaign was marred by the later capture of the Leander and Thompson was court-martialed for the loss of his ship, but quickly acquitted and awarded a knighthood. In the spring of 1799 he was given command of the much larger ship, Bellona, and took part in the blockade of the French at Brest in 1801, later joining Nelson for his attack on the Danish fleet. Thompson did some harm to his reputation when he ran the Bellona aground within reach of the Danish guns, resulting in considerable casualties. It was the courage Thompson showed under fire and the loss of his own leg in battle that saved his reputation.

Thompson's career at sea was over but he did serve as a naval administrator and was made a rear-admiral in 1809. He worked as a treasurer for Greenwich Hospital for many years and also represented Rochester in parliament from 1807 to 1818. Thompson was married to the eldest daughter of the pioneer of Sunday Schools, Robert Raikes (see page 134). This stone column, in the former grounds of the hospital where Thompson worked for many years, gives an account of his deeds. The names of the two ships he commanded, the Leander and Bellona, are engraved on either side of the column.

## 8. Royal Hospital Memorial (1749-1869)

*Location: Old Royal Naval College, SE10*
*Sculptor: n/a*
*Material: Portland stone*
*Date: 1892*

The Greenwich Royal Hospital stood on this site from 1694 until 1869 to provide residential care for seamen wounded in battle. The grounds of the hospital also served as a burial ground for former inmates and over 20,000 Marines and Royal Navy men are thought to have been interred here, with several of the more prominent stones still to be seen just a little further back from the road and close to the National Maritime Museum. Many of the remains were moved from the grounds when the hospital became the Royal Naval College, and reinterred at East Greenwich Pleasaunce where a tablet was placed in their memory. Among the famous naval men to have seen out their days here was Vice-Admiral Hardy who was Nelson's second-in-command on board the Victory.

# 9. Admiral Sir Sidney Smith (1764-1840)

*Location: Upper foyer, National Maritime Museum, SE10*
*Sculptor: Thomas Kirk*
*Material: Marble*
*Date: 1845*

Sidney Smith joined the Navy at the age of 12 and saw action in the American War of Independence. In 1780, at Cape St Vincent, Smith demonstrated his bravery and continued to distinguish himself against the French at the Battles of Chesapeake and Saintes. Following the Versailles treaty of 1783, Smith served as a commander with the Swedish Navy in 1790 and was given a knighthood by the Swedish king for helping to defeat the Russians. Six British officers had died on the Russian side which made Smith an unpopular figure among his fellow officers.

When war recommenced with France, Smith was given his own ship and special orders and successfully lifted the Siege of Acre (Syria) in 1799 – helping to drive the French from Egypt. He returned to England in 1801 but his achievements were overshadowed by those of Nelson at Copenhagen. After Trafalgar, Smith served in a number of roles in the Mediterranean; beating the French at the Battle of Maida, accompanying Admiral Duckworth in negotiations with the Turks in February 1807 and organising the passage of the Portuguese fleet to Brazil to avoid capture by the French in 1808. He even lent his services to Wellington at Waterloo – making provision for the treatment of the wounded and negotiating the return of King Louis XVIII to Paris.

Smith spent the final years of his life in Paris to avoid his English creditors. Although under-valued by the Royal Navy, Napoleon accurately said of him, 'That man made me miss my destiny'.

## 10. Admiral James Saumarez,
## 1st Baron de Saumarez (1757-1836)

Location: Upper foyer, National Maritime Museum, SE10
Sculptor: Sir John Steell
Material: Marble ◆ Date: 1854

James Saumarez was born in 1757 in Guernsey to an established naval family. He began his career at the tender age of 13 and rapidly gained promotion through initiative and courage. He commanded his first ship in 1778 when his senior officers were injured and was promoted to commander in 1781 for his bravery during the Battle of Dogger Bank. His actions contributed significantly to Admiral Rodney's victory over the French at the Battle of Saintes in April 1782, and he went on to play a major part in the naval battles against revolutionary France; he was knighted for his capture of the French frigate La Reunion in 1793. In 1795, he took command of the 74-gun Orion and fought under Admiral Jervis at the Battle of Cape St Vincent and the Blockade of Cadiz in 1797. Saumarez was among those who helped secure Nelson's victory at the Battle of the Nile in 1798, where he was wounded.

Having taken command of the 80-gun Caesar, Saumarez was given responsibility for restraining the French fleet at Brest and was made Rear Admiral for his services in 1801. One of his greatest naval triumphs was the defeat of a much larger French and Spanish fleet in July 1801 at the Battle of Algeciras. As the threat from Napoleonic France began to lessen Saumarez provided valuable service in the naval conflict with Russia between 1809 and 1814 in the Baltic. The Treaty of Vienna marked the end of Saumarez's active career but he went on to serve in the Admiralty and was made a Vice-Admiral of Britain in 1821. Unlike many of his naval contemporaries Saumarez died peacefully in his bed in 1836 having been awarded a peerage a few years earlier.

# 11. Captain Sir William Peel (1824-1858)
*Location: Upper foyer, National Maritime Museum, SE10*
*Sculptor: William Theed*
*Material: Marble*
*Date: 1860*

The dashing Sir William Peel, was the third son of the Tory politician and Prime Minister, Sir Robert Peel (see page 67). William Peel joined the navy in 1838 and had attained the rank of captain by the age of 24. In 1849 he took leave of absence to travel in the Middle East and Africa and published an account of his travels *A Ride Through the Nubian Desert*. Peel resumed his naval career in 1852 and was soon posted to the Crimea where he established a reputation as a fearless and daring officer prepared to lead his men into battle. His advice to his soldiers to 'disregard fire in the battery, by always walking with head up and shoulders back and without due haste', was not sensible by today's military standards but earned him the respect of his troops. He was awarded a Victoria Cross for his disposal of a live shell at Sebastopol in October 1854 (the medal is still on display at the National Maritime Museum, close to where this monument now stands). Peel went on to play a major part in the Battle of Inkerman in November 1854, but it is not surprising that his courage and disinclination to duck resulted in severe injury in June 1855. He soon recovered and went on to serve in India, playing a part in the Relief of Lucknow where he was again badly wounded. He did not manage to return home but was struck down with smallpox at the age of only 33 while recovering from his injuries.

Throughout his time in the Crimea, Peel was ably assisted by his ADC, midshipman Edward St John Daniel, who rescued his captain on several occasions and who was also awarded the VC. Daniel was stripped of the medal in 1861 for what was described as 'taking indecent liberties' and later served in the New Zealand Wars (see page 285). He died of natural causes on Hokitika Island in 1868, just ten years after the captain he served so well.

## 12. Admiral Sir Edward Pellew, Lord Exmouth (1757-1833)

*Location: Upper foyer, National Maritime Museum, SE10*
*Sculptor: Patrick Mac Dowell* ◆ *Material: Marble*
*Date: 1846*

Edward Pellew joined the Royal Navy at only 13 and rose to prominence at a time when Britain was first fighting revolution in America and then confronting Napoleonic naval power. He first distinguished himself in the Battle of Valcour Island in 1776 and later fought with General John Burgoyne (see page 97) at Saratoga, where he was captured and repatriated. In 1793 Pellew was given command of the 36-gun Nymphe and quickly made his reputation by capturing a French frigate and the secret naval code on board. The French captain, while in his death throes, had attempted to swallow the code, but had taken the wrong paper. Pellew was knighted for his capture of the ship and its secrets and given command of the much larger 76-gun Indefatigable in 1795. It was at the command of this giant ship that Pellew inflicted even greater damage upon the French, sinking and capturing several of their ships.

One of Pellew's greatest acts of heroism was not in battle, but rescuing passengers from a grounded ship near Plymouth. Pellew was a very strong swimmer and swam to the stranded ship with a line which was used to rescue the passengers. His courage earned him a baronetcy. In 1802 he became an MP, but continued his career, commanding vessels in the East Indies between 1804-09. In 1816 Pellew led an Anglo-Dutch fleet against the Barbary state that was trading in slaves, and their bombardment of Algiers was to secure the release of over a thousand Christian slaves. A gold-plated trophy was given to Pellew by his officers to commemorate this action – it can be seen in one of the glass cases close to where this statue stands today. The Pellew Group of barren Australian islands are named after him.

## 13. Captain James Cook (1728-1779)

*Location: Rear of the National Maritime Museum, SE10*
*Sculptor: Anthony Stone*
*Material: Bronze*
*Date: 1994*

Captain James Cook served alongside James Wolfe in the Battle of Quebec in which Wolfe lost his life. Cook's monument now looks up towards the Royal Observatory where his colleague's monument stands. There is a more prominent monument to Captain Cook on the Mall (see page 93).

## 14. Lord Horatio Nelson (1758-1805)

*Location: Rear of the National Maritime Museum*
*Sculptor: Sir Francis Leggatt Chantrey*
*Material: Marble*
*Date: 1835*

This is one of the four busts Chantrey made for Greenwich Hospital. The other busts were for the admirals Duncan, Howe and Vincent. There are several monuments to Nelson in Greenwich but his most important monument is, of course, in Trafalgar Square (see page 19).

# 15. William IV (1765-1837)

*Location: King William Walk, Greenwich Park, SE10*
*Sculptor: Samuel Nixon*
*Material: Foggit Tor granite*
*Date: 1844 (in the City), moved here 1938*

William IV was known as the 'sailor King', because he spent much of his life in the navy. William saw limited active service during the American War of Independence and in the West Indies but spent much of his career on land, as Lord High Admiral, in whose costume he is commemorated. When William insisted on commanding the Channel Fleet in 1828, there was such protest that he resigned his position.

William IV's main achievement as king was not being like his brother, George IV (see page 14). His reign witnessed the passing of the Reform Bill (1832), the abolition of slavery in the colonies (1833) and reform of the Poor Laws (1835), but the changes were driven by politicians and popular political movements – the monarchy becoming a symbolic rather than actively political institution. William's only intervention into politics was his dismissal of Melbourne's Whig ministry in 1834. In the following elections, Melbourne was returned to power and this proved the last time a British monarch dismissed a government against the wishes of parliament. William sired ten illegitimate children by his long-term mistress before coming to the throne. As a King he proved less fertile, his two daughters by Queen Adelaide died in infancy. On his death in 1837 the crown passed to his niece Victoria. The rules of the House of Hanover would not permit a female monarch and so William's reign marked the end of the royal family's direct link with the German Principality.

# 16. General James Wolfe (1727-1759)

*Location: Greenwich Park, SE10 (next to The Royal Observatory)*
*Sculptor: Dr Tait Mackenzie (1867-1938)*
*Material: Bronze*
*Date: 1930*

The statue of James Wolfe stands at the highest point in Greenwich Park. Wolfe joined the army at only 16, and took part in his first battle at Dettingen against the French in 1743. The courageous young soldier soon made a name for himself and gained the favour of George II (see page 35) who was greatly impressed with accounts of Wolfe's exploits. Wolfe saw action against the Spanish and Bourbon armies and put an end to the Jacobite claim to the throne at Culloden in 1746.

James Wolfe embarked from Greenwich in 1759 to strengthen Britain's claims upon Canada against those of the French monarchy. On arrival, in order to surprise the French force, Wolfe led his army over the cliffs and a fierce battle commenced on the Plains of Abraham, where Wolfe took a bullet and died. The French were defeated and General Montcalm met his end the following day.

Wolfe's body was embalmed and returned to Greenwich. He is buried at nearby St Alfege's Church in the family vault. There is an impressive monument within Westminster Abbey which was erected 13 years after his death. This imposing monument was presented by the Canadian people in 1930 and was unveiled by the Marquis de Montcalm, a descendant of the vanquished French general. Wolfe's victory secured Canada for a great many hardy Scottish migrants of which the sculptor Dr Robert Tait Mackenzie could count himself a descendent. .

# Distant and Alone

There are many interesting monuments that
stand alone and usually have some particular
connection with their location. The isolation of
these commemorative statues is not indicative of
the obscurity of their subjects, for among those
reviewed here can be found William Gladstone,
Sigmund Freud and Karl Marx.

HAMPSTEAD HEATH

HAMPSTEAD

WILL...

...BURN

CAMDEN

REGENT'S PARK

MARYLEBONE

SHEPHERD'S BUSH

KENSINGTON PARK

HYDE PARK

SOHO

KENSINGTON

WESTMINS...

CHELSEA

River Thames

BATTERSEA

FULHAM

BAR...

River Thames

CLAPHAM

HOLLOWAY
LEYTON
ISLINGTON
HACKNEY
VICTORIA
BOW
CITY
STEPNEY
POPLAR
River Thames
SOUTHWARK
DEPTFORD
CAMBERWELL
BRIXTON
LEWISHAM

## 1. John Colet (1467-1519)
*Location: St Paul's School, Barnes, SW13* ◆ *Date:1898*
*Sculptor: Sir Hamo Thornycroft* ◆ *Material:Bronze*

John Colet was ordained deacon in 1497 and soon after made a priest. He inherited a substantial fortune, the great part of which he used for the endowment of St Paul's School, originally located in the City of London near the cathedral after which it is named. The monument is in the grounds of the school and is not open to the public.

## 2. Cardinal John Henry Newman (1801-1890)
*Location: Brompton Oratory, SW3* ◆ *Date: 1896*
*Sculptor: Léon-Joseph Chavalliaud* ◆ *Material: Marble*

The Cardinal's statue is a small feature of this High Renaissance Early Baroque church (consecrated in 1884) which was the first Catholic church to be built in London since the Reformation. Newman began his career as an Anglican churchman, but was always trying to move towards Rome and played a key role in the Oxford Movement which attempted to re-introduce many aspects of Catholic worship. Newman suffered a spiritual crisis which forced him to abandon his position in Oxford in 1843 and eventually join the Catholic Church in 1845. He was to serve the Catholic faith with renewed conviction, becoming a cardinal in 1889.

### 3. Henry Vassall-Fox, 3rd Baron Holland (1773-1840)
*Location: Holland Park* ◆ *Date: 1926*
*Sculptor: G.F. Watts & Edgar Boehm* ◆ *Material: Bronze*

On the north side of the park, Lord Holland's seated statue rises from the centre of a small pond. Educated at Eton and Oxford, Lord Holland became a major figure in Whig politics in the early 19th century. His uncle was the great Whig orator Charles James Fox (see page 239).

### 4. St Volodymyr the Great, (960-1015)
*Location: outside Holland Park Station, W11* ◆ *Date: 1988*
*Sculptor: Leonard Moll* ◆ *Material: Bronze*

Standing on a circular plinth the statue of St Volodymyr the Great was erected by the Orthodox Church to commemorate 1,000 years of Christianity in Russia. Volodymyr was originally a pagan prince who brought Christianity from Constantinople (Istanbul) in 988 and baptised the people of Kievan Rus' on the banks of the Dnieper River. More recently, this statue was the focal point for Ulkrainians demonstrating their support of Viktor Yushchenko, who 'lost' the presidential election in Ukraine amidst much controversy.

### 5. Charles Dickens (1812-1870)

*Location: Ferguson House, Marylebone High Street, W1*
*Sculptor: Eastcourt J. Clark* ◆ *Material: Sculptural Panel*

Dickens (see page 50) lived in a house that stood at the junction of Marylebone High Street and Marylebone Road for many years. Several of his novels were written here including *David Copperfield* and *A Christmas Carol*. On the wall of Ferguson House can be found this relief featuring the author in the company of characters from his novels.

### 6. Charles II (1630-1685)

*Location: Soho Square, W1* ◆ *Date: 1681*
*Sculptor: Caius Gabriel Cibber* ◆ *Material: Stone*

Carved by Caius Gabriel Cibber (also responsible for the bas reliefs on the Monument), this statue of Charles II once stood in the centre of the square. A decline in the condition of the garden in the mid-19th century saw its removal. The monument came into the hands of W.S. Gilbert the lyricist, whose widow returned it to the square in 1938.

### 7. General Francisco de Miranda (1750-1816)

*Location: Corner of Fitzroy St & Grafton Way, W1,*
*Material: Bronze*

Miranda was born in Spanish occupied Venezuela and after serving in the Spanish navy fought for Venezuelan independence. Miranda spent 14 years in exile in London and lived in this house for much of that time. After a failed coup attempt in his homeland he was captured by the Spanish and died while in prison in Cadiz.

## 8. Robert Stephenson (1803-59)
*Location: Euston Station, NW1 ◆ Date: 1871*
*Sculptor: Baron Marochetti ◆ Material: Bronze*

Robert Stephenson was one of the great 19th-century engineers. This monument stands in Euston Station, the terminus for the London to Birmingham railway for which Stephenson was the chief engineer. He also helped his father, George, complete the famous Rocket locomotive.

## 9. Sir Isaac Newton (1642-1727)
*Location: British Library ◆ Date: 1995*
*Sculptor: Eduardo Paolozzi ◆ Material: Bronze*

This monument to Newton takes as its inspiration William Blake's depiction of the mathematician planning the universe. There is another monument to Newton in Leicester Square (see page 27).

## 10. Anne Frank (1929-1945)
*Location: British Library ◆ Date: 1999*
*Sculptor: Doreen Kern ◆ Material: Bronze*

This bust was unveiled in the courtyard of the British Library to mark the 70th anniversary of Anne Frank's birth. Her vivid account of the Frank family's life in hiding during the Nazi occupation of Amsterdam was first published in 1947. She was killed in a German concentration camp just before the war's end.

### 11. Richard Cobden (1804-1865)
*Location: Camden High Street, NW1* ◆ *Date: 1868*
*Sculptor: W and T. Wills* ◆ *Material: Sicilian Marble*

Richard Cobden was a wealthy calico trader who formed the Anti-Corn-Law League (see Robert Peel page 67, Lord Bentinck page 261). Once the Corn Laws were reformed Cobden became a Liberal MP and a fierce opponent of Palmerston's aggressive foreign policy. Napoleon III was the largest contributor to this monument which is now very badly eroded.

### 12. Isambard Kingdom Brunel, (1806-1859)
*Location: Paddington Station* ◆ *Date: 1982*
*Sculptor: John Doubleday* ◆ *Material: Bronze*

Paddington station was designed by Brunel as the grand terminus of the Great Western Railway and was completed in 1854. This recent monument to Brunel can be found on platform 1 and a larger monument to the great engineer is on the Embankment (see page 127).

### 13. Mrs Sarah Siddons, (1755-1831)
*Location: Paddington Green* ◆ *Date: 1897*
*Sculptor: Léon-Joseph Chavalliaud* ◆ *Material: Marble*

Sarah Kemble was born into an acting family and began her acting career in the provinces. By the mid-1780s Sarah Siddons was an established actor and socialite, her portrait painted by both Gainsborough and Reynolds. Reynold's painting was the inspiration for this white marble sculpture which was unveiled by another great actor, Sir Henry Irving (see page 26).

## 14. Edward Onslow Ford, (1852-1901)

*Location: Abbey Road, NW8* ◆ *Date:1903*
*Sculptor: A.C. Lacchesi* ◆ *Material: Bronze*

Ford was one of the most successful sculptors of the Victorian era. His memorial was erected by friends and admirers and stands by the Abbey Road pedestrian crossing made famous by the Beatles. Ford was responsible for many fine monuments including his statue of Rowland Hill in the City of London (see page 351) and several fine busts in Westminster Abbey (see pages 82).

## 15. Sigmund Freud, (1856-1939)

*Location: Adelaide Road, NW3* ◆ *Date:1970*
*Sculptor: Oscar Nemon* ◆ *Material: Bronze*

Sigmund Freud was the father of psychoanalysis which attempts to explain the complex forces that underlie human personality. He brought into the public realm ideas of the subconscious, sexuality, ego and repression that were to profoundly shape the 20th century and a method of treating psychological problems through analysis that was to spawn a wide array of treatments. Freud spent much of his life as professor of neurology at Vienna University, but as a Jew he was forced to flee Nazi Austria in 1938. He spent his last years at 20 Maresfield Gardens which is close to this monument and is now home to the Freud Museum.

## 16. Sir Sydney Waterlow, (1822-1906)

*Location: Waterlow Park, N19* ◆ *Date: 1900*
*Sculptor: Frank Taubman* ◆ *Material: Bronze*

Sir Sydney Waterlow inherited the family printing company and later made a fortune in banking. He worked as a councillor, member of parliament and served as Lord Mayor of London. He gave his 30-acre estate to the London County Council in 1889 as a 'garden for the gardenless' and his statue stands in the park that bears his name.

## 17. Karl Heinrich Marx, (1818-1883)

*Location: Highgate Cemetery, NW6* ◆ *Date: 1956*
*Sculptor: Laurence Bradshaw* ◆ *Material: Bronze*

Karl Marx was a German philosopher who spent much of his life in exile in London, supported by his friend Friedrich Engels. Marx devised a way of understanding politics that identified antagonistic economic classes and regarded the conflict between these classes as being the engine for progress through revolution that would lead to a utopian communist state. Marx died in London long before his ideas were adopted during the Russian revolution and embodied in the Soviet state. This monument to Marx was unveiled at the height of the Cold War in 1956 and long before the fall of the Berlin Wall which marked the end of Communism as a powerful force in world history.

### 18. Sir Hugh Myddleton (1560-1631)
*Location: Islington Green, N1 ◆ Date: 1862*
*Sculptor: John Thomas ◆ Material: Marble*

In the early 17th century Myddleton built an underground water system which brought fresh water into London from Hertfordshire to supply the capital's growing population. The project took four years to complete and was one of the largest engineering achievements of its time. This now eroded monument was unveiled by William Gladstone in 1862.

### 19. John Wesley (1703-1791)
*Location: 49 City Road Chapel, N1 ◆ Date:1891*
*Sculptor: J.Adams Acton ◆ Material: Bronze*

This monument to the founder of Methodism stands in the City Road Chapel which was built under Wesley's instruction. There is another monument to Wesley in the grounds of St Paul's Cathedral (see page 221).

### 20. James Hulbert (d.1720)
*Location: Fishmonger's Hall, London Bridge, SE1 ◆*
*Date: 1978 ◆ Sculptor: Robert Easton ◆ Material: Marble*

James Hulbert was a successful fishmonger who founded the Fishmonger's Almshouses at St Peter's Hospital, Southwark. His investment in the South Sea Company was sold just before the stock crashed which greatly increased the value of his estate and enabled a much larger almshouse to be built.

### 21. Samuel Pepys (1633-1703)
*Location: Seething Lane Gardens, EC3  ◆  Date: 1983*
*Sculptor: Karin Jonzen  ◆  Material: Bronze*

Samuel Pepys was a naval administrator who would
have disappeared into the dustbin of history had he
not kept a diary which chronicled his life in 17th
century London. Pepys lived in Seething Lane and
it is in this garden that he recounts burying state papers and his parmesan cheese when the Great Fire of
London threatened.

### 22. Site of Scaffold – Trinity Square
*Location: Trinity Place, EC3*

Trinity Square has a memorial area which marks
where prisoners from the Tower of London were
executed between 1388 and 1747. The square also
contains a more recent memorial to merchant seamen who died in the two World Wars and close by is
a statue of Emperor Trajan...

### 23. Emperor Trajan (53-117)
*Location: Trinity Place, EC3  ◆  Date: 1980*
*Sculptor: not known  ◆  Material: Bronze*

Close by Trinity Square is the only statue of a Roman Londoner in the form of Emperor Trajan. The
monument was reclaimed from a scrapyard by the
vicar of All Hallows' Church and erected here in
1980.

### 24. Sir Robert Geffrye (1613-1704)
*Location: Geffrye Museum, E2* ◆ *Date: 1723*
*Sculptor: John van Nost* ◆ *Material: Lead*

Robert Geffrye was a successful ironmonger who left provision for the establishment of an almshouse in his will. The almshouse moved away from London and the building has since become the Geffrye Museum. This monument is a 1913 copy of the John van Nost original.

### 25. Edward VII (1841-1910)
*Location:Whitechapel Road* ◆ *Date: 1911*
*Sculptor: W.S. Frith* ◆ *Material: Stone and bronze*

Edward VII encouraged the acceptance of Jewish refugees into the country at the turn of the century and the integration of those Jews already established here. This elaborate column was erected in gratitude to the King by the Jewish community of east London. There is a much larger equestrian monument to Edward on Waterloo Place (see page 99).

### 26. Queen Alexandra (1809-1898)
*Location: Courtyard of London Hospital, E1* ◆ *Date: 1908*
*Sculptor: George Edward Wade* ◆ *Material: Bronze*

Queen Alexandra was the long suffering wife of Edward VII. She was also a patron of the hospital and introduced the Finsen Light cure for lupus into this country from her native Denmark. She has another monument on Marlborough Road (see page 113).

### 27. General William Booth (1829-1912)
*Location: Mile End Road, E1* ◆ *Date: 1927*
*Sculptor: George Edward Wade* ◆ *Material: Bronze*

William Booth was a methodist preacher who founded the Salvation Army in 1865. This bust stands on
the site of Booth's first open air service, following
the practice of John Wesley (see page 221). In 1979,
a second monument to Booth was unveiled close by,
based on a copy of the monument that stands on
Denmark Hill in South London (see page 362).

## 28. William Gladstone
*Location: Bow Church Yard, E3* ◆ *Date: 1882*
*Sculptor: Albert Bruce-Joy* ◆ *Material: Bronze*

This is one of the few monuments to be unveiled
while its subject was still alive. This tribute was the
gift of the local match manufacturer Theodore Bry-
ant. The hands on this monument have been painted
red in protest at the terrible conditions of the local match factories which killed and disabled many,
mostly female, factory workers.

## 29. Clement Attlee (1883-1967)
*Location: Limehouse Public Library* ◆ *Date: 1988*
*Sculptor: Frank Forster* ◆ *Material: Bronze*

Clement Attlee began as a social worker and became
a Labour politician. He served in Churchill's coalition government and became prime minister in
the first post-war government. Attlee's government
established the National Health Service, nationalised
many industries, carried through education reforms
and granted independence to India and Pakistan.

### 30. Michael von Clemm (1935-1997)
*Location: Cabot Square, E14 ◆ Date: 1998*
*Sculptor: Gerald Laing ◆ Material: Bronze*

Michael von Clemm was an American who came to England to study anthropology before becoming a successful investment banker. Clemm helped establish the Eurodollar Market and contributed to the transformation of Docklands in the 1980s. He also helped raise the money required to establish the famous Roux brothers' first restaurant.

### 31. Robert Milligan (1746-1808)
*Location: West India Quay, E14 ◆ Date: 1875*
*Sculptor: Richard Westmacott ◆ Material: Bronze*

Robert Milligan was deputy chairman of the West India Dock Company and instrumental in the opening of the West India Dock in 1802 which was the main arrival point for sugar from the West Indies. Milligan's monument has moved several times but since the mid-1980s has found its place on the dock which he did so much to establish.

### 32. Richard Green (1806-1863)
*Location: East India Dock Road, E14 ◆ Date: 1866*
*Sculptor: E.W.Wyon ◆ Material: Bronze*

Richard Green was a ship owner and philanthropist who showed concern for the welfare of seamen. Green's efforts were exceptional given the widespread harsh practices of other ship owners (see Samuel Plimsoll on page 144). Unlike those of his rivals, Green's funeral attracted large crowds.

### 33. Virginia Settlers Memorial
*Location: East India Dock Road, E14* ◆ *Date: 1951*
*Sculptor: Wendy Taylor* ◆ *Material: Stone*

This tablet was a gift from the Virginian people and commemorates the three ships that left from Blackwall in 1606 to establish the colony of Jamestown. The monument to Captain John Smith has a more detailed account of the voyage and initial settlement (see page 217).

### 34. Brass Crosby (1725-1793)
*Location: Harmsworth Park, SE1* ◆ *Date: 1771*
*Material: Stone Obelisk*

Brass Crosby was a magistrate sent to the Tower for refusing to convict a printer for publishing the proceedings of parliament. The law prohibiting the publication of parliamentary proceedings was eventually repealed following a long campaign by John Wilkes (see page 181).

### 35. Thomas Guy (1644-1724)
*Location: Guy's Hospital, SE1* ◆ *Date: 1733*
*Sculptor: Peter Scheemakers* ◆ *Material: Brass*

Thomas Guy was a bookseller and businessman who made a good deal of his fortune printing and selling English Bibles and a further fortune from South Sea stock. He was well known as a philanthropist and built three wards at St Thomas's before founding the hospital which bears his name in 1721.

### 36. William R. Morris, Viscount Nuffield (1877-1963)
*Location: Guy's Hospital , SE1 ◆ Date: 1944*
*Sculptor: Maurice Prosper Lambert ◆ Material: Bronze*

William Morris began his career repairing bicycles in Oxford before adapting his skills to the manufacture of cars. Morris made a fortune from the car company which carried his name and was a major benefactor to Guy's Hospital, where his monument now stands.

### 37. Alfred the Great (849-899)
*Location: Trinity Church Square , SE1 ◆ Date: c.1395*
*Sculptor: Anonymous ◆ Material: Stone*

The origins of this statue are unclear but it is believed to be a likeness of the Anglo-Saxon king Alfred the Great. It was moved here from the old Palace of Westminster in 1822, but has some claim to being the oldest outdoor monument in London.

### 38. Colonel Samuel Bourne Bevington (1832-1907)
*Location: Tooley Street , SE1 ◆ Date: 1910*
*Sculptor: Sydney Marsh ◆ Material: Bronze*

Samuel Bevington was a local businessman and philanthropist who employed and gave help to many in Bermondsey and was the area's first mayor. This monument was erected soon after his death and shows Bevington in his mayoral finery.

### 39. Ernest Bevin (1881-1951)

*Location: Tooley Street, SE1* ◆ *Date: 1955*
*Sculptor: E. Whitney Smith* ◆ *Material: Bronze*

Ernest Bevin had very little education but became
a trade unionist and Labour politician who founded
the Transport and General Workers Union. Bevin
was Minister for Labour in the wartime coalition
government. He was made Foreign Secretary in
Clement Attlee's government but died before the
defeat of Labour in the 1951 election.

### 40. Circle Dray Horse

*Location: Queen Elizabeth Street, SE1* ◆ *Date: 1987*
*Sculptor: Shirley Pace* ◆ *Material: Bronze*

This monument commemorates the Courage Dray
Horse Stable which stood on this site – the horses
being used to transport the heavy casks of beer from
the brewery. The area is now occupied by smart flats
and visitors are more likely to see a Porsche than a
dray horse on the narrow streets.

### 41. Robert Aske (1619-1689)

*Location; Pepy's Road, SE14* ◆ *Date: 1836*
*Sculptor: W. Croggan* ◆ *Material: Coade Stone*

Robert Aske was a successful merchant and philanthropist who established several almshouses and helped establish the Haberdashers'
Aske's School, outside which his monument stands. His statue is one
of the few to be made from Coade stone (see Coade Stone Lion on
page 162).

### 42. Joseph Paxton (1803-1865)
*Location: Crystal Palace* ◆ *Date: 1869*
*Sculptor: W.F. Woodington* ◆ *Material: Marble*

Paxton was an architect and the Duke of Devonshire's head gardener whose design of a colossal glass building was chosen to house the Great Exhibition of 1851. Paxton supervised the construction of his Crystal Palace in Hyde Park and its move to Sydenham after the exhibition closed. He went on to serve as MP for Coventry.

### 43. Guy the Gorilla (1946-1978)
*Location: Crystal Palace* ◆ *Date: 1962*
*Sculptor: David Wynne* ◆ *Material: Bronze*

This statue commemorates the most popular attraction at London Zoo for 30 years until his death in 1978. Another statue by the sculptor William Timym, now stands in the Zoo itself as a tribute to this gentle giant.

### 44. Edward VII (1841-1910)
*Location: Tooting Broadway* ◆ *Date: 1911*
*Sculptor: L.F. Roselieb* ◆ *Material: Bronze*

The first decade of the 20th century was also that of Edward VII's reign, unknowingly marking the demise of an older way of life which would change irrevocably with the First World War. The largest monument to Edward VII can be found at Waterloo Place (see page 99).

### 45. Sir Henry Tate ( 1819-1899)
*Location: Brixton Library, Effra Road, SW2 ◆ Date: 1905*
*Sculptor: Sir Thomas Brook ◆ Material: Bronze*

Henry Tate made a considerable fortune from the re-fining of sugar and became one of the great Victorian philanthropists, funding. He funded the foundation of the Tate Gallery on Millbank, Liverpool University library and the public library outside which this bust stands.

### 46. William (1829-1912) & Catherine Booth (1829-1890)
*Location: Denmark Hill, SE5 ◆ Date: 1929*
*Sculptor: G.E.Wade ◆ Material: Bronze*

The monuments to William Booth and his wife Catherine stand outside the training offices of the Salvation Army which they founded in 1861. There are several monuments to William Booth in Whitechapel (see page 356).

### 46. Dr Robert Bentley Todd (1809-1860)
*Location: King's College, Denmark Hill, SE5 ◆ Date: 1862*
*Sculptor: Matthew Noble ◆ Material: Marble*

This statue commemorates the Irish doctor who helped to found King's College Hospital. The monument was unveiled at the hospital's original location just off the Strand, but it moved to Denmark Hill with the hospital in 1913. Todd wrote many medical papers and was an expert in the study of paralysis.

### 46. Haile Selassie (1892-1975)
*Location: Cannizaro Park, SW19* ◆ *Date: 1955*
*Sculptor: Hilda Seligman* ◆ *Material: Stone*

Haile Selassie was the Emperor of Ethiopa driven from his land by Mussolini's Fascist army in 1935 and spent a period of exile in Wimbledon. His host, Hilda Seligman, made this statue of the 'Lion of Judah' during his stay. The bust was placed in the park after her death in 1955, by which time Selassie had been returned to the throne by the Allies.

### 49. William Huskisson (1770-1830)
*Location: Pimlico Gardens, SW1* ◆ *Date: 1836*
*Sculptor: John Gibson* ◆ *Material: Stone*

William Huskisson was a Tory politician and head of the Board of Trade. He has the dubious distinction of being the first person to be killed by a train when he was struck by Stephenson's Rocket during the opening of the Liverpool to Manchester Railway. The monument stood on several sites before finding a home in Pimlico Gardens.

### 50. Sir John Everett Millais (1829-1896)
*Location: John Islip Street, SW1* ◆ *Date: 1904*
*Sculptor: Sir Thomas Brock* ◆ *Material: Bronze*

A founder of the Pre-Raphaelite Brotherhood, Millais went on to establish himself as a conventional and sentimental portrait painter. His saccharine-sweet portrait of a Victorian boy, 'Bubbles', became famous as the image of Pear's soap. He was knighted in 1895 and became President of the Royal Academy a year later.

# General Index

# Subject index

## Seven Years War (1756-1763)

## Terrorism

## Theatre, Film, Arts & Architecture

# Order our other Metro Titles

The following titles are also available from Metro Publications. Please send your order along with a cheque made payable to Metro Publications to the address below. Postage and packaging free.

Alternatively call our customer order line on 020 8533 7777 (Visa/Mastercard/Switch), Open Mon-Fri 9am-6pm

**Metro Publications**
PO Box 6336, London N1 6PY
info@metropublications.com
www.metropublications.com

**London Market Guide**
Andrew Kershman
£6.99  ISBN 1-902910-14-1

**Bargain Hunters' London**
Andrew Kershman
£6.99  ISBN 1-902910-15-X

**Food Lovers' London**
Jenny Linford
£8.99  ISBN 1-902910-22-2

**Veggie & Organic London**
Russell Rose
£6.99  ISBN 1-902910-21-4

**Book Lovers' London**
Lesley Reader
£8.99  ISBN 1-902910-26-5

**Museums & Galleries**
of London
Abigail Willis
£8.99  ISBN 1-902910-20-6

**London Architecture**
Marianne Butler
£8.99  ISBN 1-902910-18-4

**London's Parks and Gardens**
Nana Ocran
£6.99  ISBN 1-902910-19-2

**London's City Churches**
Stephen Millar
£6.99  ISBN 1-902910-24-9

**London's Cemeteries**
Darren Beach
£6.99  ISBN 1-902910-23-0

**London's Monuments**
Andrew Kershman
£7.99  ISBN 1-902910-25-7